A Stranger in My Own Land

A Stranger in
My Own Land

*Sofía Casanova, a Spanish Writer
in the European Fin de Siècle*

Kirsty Hooper

Vanderbilt University Press
Nashville

© 2008 by Vanderbilt University Press
Nashville, Tennessee 37235
All rights reserved

12 11 10 09 08 1 2 3 4 5

This book is printed on acid-free paper
made from 30% post-consumer recycled paper.
Manufactured in the United States of America

Publication of this book has been supported by a
generous subsidy from the Program for Cultural
Cooperation between Spain's Ministry of Culture
and United States Universities.

Library of Congress Cataloging-in-Publication Data

Hooper, Kirsty.
A stranger in my own land : Sofía Casanova,
a Spanish writer in the European fin de siècle
/ Kirsty Hooper.
p. cm.
Includes bibliographical references and index.
ISBN 978-0-8265-1613-8 (cloth : alk. paper)
ISBN 978-0-8265-1614-5 (pbk. : alk. paper)
1. Casanova, Sofía, 1861–1958—Criticism
and interpretation.   I. Title.
PQ6605.A826Z65 2008
861'.62—dc22
2008023782

In memory of Dr. G. Clive Jones,

who started it all

Acknowledgments

I thank the many people and organizations that have helped me in various ways during the writing of this book: The Arts and Humanities Research Board, the Newby Trust, Oxford University (through the Labouchere and de Osma Funds), the government of Poland, the Xunta de Galicia, Hertford College Oxford (including the Starun Fund), the Queen's College Oxford (including the Laming Fund), Merton College Oxford, and the University of Liverpool all provided financial and material support. Gerald Stone, my master's supervisor, introduced me to Polish studies and started me down the long road in search of Casanova. John Rutherford, my doctoral supervisor, not only helped me reach the end of that road but also introduced me to Galicia and Galician studies—I could not have asked for a more inspiring guide. Catherine Davies and Jacqueline Rattray constructively and encouragingly examined the doctoral thesis on which this book is based. For their love and their confidence, I thank my husband, Steven Barge, and my parents, Angela and Keith Hooper, who listened to, read, and lived with this project for nearly a decade. Friends and colleagues in Oxford, Liverpool, and elsewhere who contributed moral and intellectual support include Nina Taylor-Terlecki, Manolo Puga Moruxa, Núria Martí i Girbau, Nuria Capdevila Argüelles, Lourdes Lorenzo García, Claire Williams, Kathy Bacon, and Anja Louis. I am grateful to Ofelia Alayeto, Casanova's first biographer, for her generosity; to the Vanderbilt University Press reviewers for their constructive readings of the manuscript; and to Betsy Phillips at Vanderbilt University Press for bringing the project to life.

Sections of Chapter 1 first appeared as "Las Autoras de unas Novelitas? Spanish Women Writers, 1890–1916," in *Making Waves Anniversary Volume: Women in Spanish, Portuguese and Latin American Studies,* edited by Ann Davies, Par Kumaraswami, and Claire Williams ([Newcastle: Cambridge

Scholars Publishing, 2008], 43–59). A very early version of Chapter 2 first appeared as "Fin de Siècle Anxieties and Future(s) Perfect: Sofía Casanova's *El doctor Wolski* (1894)" (*Bulletin of Hispanic Studies* 79.2 [2002]: 175–87); sections of Chapter 3 first appeared in "Reading Spain's African Vocation: The Figure of the Moorish Priest in Three Novels of the *Fin de Siglo* (1891–1907)" (*Revista de Estudios Hispánicos* 40.1 [2006]: 175–99); and sections of Chapter 5 first appeared in "Girl, Interrupted: The Distinctive History of Galician Women's Narrative" (*Romance Studies* 21.2 [2003]: 101–14). I am grateful to the editors at *Bulletin of Hispanic Studies*, Cambridge Scholars Publishing, *Revista de Estudios Hispánicos,* and *Romance Studies* for their kind permission to incorporate revised versions of this material.

A Stranger in My Own Land

CHAPTER I

"Like Atlantis Swallowed Up by the Sea"

The Vanishing of Spain's
Early Twentieth-Century Women Writers

¿Qué sabe y conoce Europa de nuestras mujeres? . . . ¿A qué confines
de la intelectualidad extranjera han llegado las creaciones de nuestras
artistas o los estudios de nuestras sabias? . . . Me duele confesarlo, pero
no vale callar: la mujer española *está borrada* de la *cosmogonía intelectual*
de Europa, cual Atlántida que devoró el mar, flotador epitafio de solo dos
nombres: Isabel la Católica y Teresa de Jesús. (Casanova 1910, *La mujer
española en el extranjero*, 5, emphasis Casanova's)[1]

[What does Europe know of our women? . . . What horizons of foreign
intellectual life have the creations of our female artists or the studies of
our female scholars reached? . . . It pains me to confess it, but there is no
sense in remaining silent: Spanish women *are erased* from the *intellectual
cosmogony* of Europe, like Atlantis swallowed up by the sea, their floating
epitaph just two names: Isabella the Catholic Queen and St. Teresa of
Ávila.][2]

[En Polonia], pues, no fue conocida por Sofía Casanova, ni por mujer
de letras. . . . Únicamente era la señora de Lutosławski. . . . Esto duró
dieciséis años, en el decurso de los que no cogió la pluma sino para
escribir cartas, considerando—por aquel entonces—que todas las glorias
que la proporcionara la fama conquistada en España, por su labor
intelectual, no pesaban, en definitiva, en la balanza de su existencia
nueva, lo que significaba el cumplimiento de los deberes del hogar.
(Pitollet 1958, 135)

[(In Poland), then, she was not known as Sofía Casanova or as a woman
of letters. . . . She was simply Mrs. Lutosławski. . . . This went on for
sixteen years, during which she picked up her pen only to write letters,
believing—at the time—that all the glory of the fame she had earned in
Spain, for her intellectual work, could not compete, in the end, with her new
life, which meant carrying out her domestic duties.]

On the evening of Saturday, April 9, 1910, the Galician-Spanish expatriate poet, novelist, and journalist Sofía Casanova lectured to a packed auditorium at the Ateneo de Madrid. Her subject, which twenty years of living and
traveling throughout Europe made her uniquely qualified to address, was *la
mujer española en el extranjero* [the Spanish woman abroad], and her talk was
illustrated with evidence from interviews that she had conducted with such
European politicians, intellectuals, and celebrities as Sir Henry Morton Stan-
ley, Marie Curie, and Leo Tolstoy.[3]

For those who read the lecture today, it is immediately apparent that, despite the title, the image of Spain and its women viewed from overseas is only
part of Casanova's theme. By deliberately playing on her public profile as one
of Spain's best-known and best-connected expatriates, with access to the salons of the most famous names in Europe, she mitigates the fact that much of
the hour-long lecture is, in fact, a passionate defense of Spanish women's contribution to the emerging modern nation. Her dramatic conclusion is that it
is not foreign intellectuals but men—Spanish men—who are responsible for
downplaying the participation of Spanish women in Spain's past and present.
In consequence, she argues, it is the duty of Spanish men to ensure that this
contribution is not lost in the future:

> Es de vosotros, señores, de quienes depende la suerte nuestra. Es de vosotros,
> los hacedores en público de leyes que deshacéis en privado, a quienes toca
> encauzar el espléndido manantial de la actividad femenina, que hoy se pierde
> . . . en las murmuraciones de la holganza, o la devoción sin caridad de los
> conventos. (Casanova 1910, *La mujer española en el extranjero*, 35)

> [It is you, gentlemen, on whom our fortune depends. It is you, the makers
> in public of laws that you unmake in private, who must undam the splendid
> torrent of feminine activity, which today is disappearing . . . into idle gossip,
> or the devotion without charity of the convent.]

This radical demand is framed by a celebration of the myriad Spanish women
who have contributed in various ways to Spain's history, as Casanova outlines

a glorious female intellectual tradition that stretches from the Renaissance into the future—in which, she argues, she and her contemporaries must be allowed to play their part.

The lecture received a rapturous reception, albeit not, perhaps, for the reasons Casanova might have hoped. Although the thrust of Casanova's lecture was strikingly different from the xenophobic, jingoistic view of Spanish culture and history promoted by her better-known male contemporaries, contemporary reviewers used it as proof of the persisting influence of the *leyenda negra* [black legend] of backward Inquisitorial Spain throughout Europe.[4] On the whole, the commentators neither responded to Casanova's debate on an intellectual level nor acknowledged that her criticism was directed much closer to home. Their silence was an omen. In January 1958, forty-eight years after that triumphant night at the Ateneo, the news of Casanova's death in the Polish city of Poznań at the age of ninety-seven reached her friends and relations at home. Almost instantly, the fears she had expressed in *La mujer española en el extranjero* were vividly realized with respect to her own place in Spanish history.

Back in 1910, in that auditorium in Madrid, Casanova had argued that Spanish women were erased from European intellectual history, "like Atlantis swallowed up by the sea." This dramatic image, meant to inspire change, proved to be an uncannily accurate prediction of Casanova's own fate. The tide began to encroach immediately after her death, when a flurry of obituaries, principally by Galician writers and journalists, appeared in Spain's local, regional, and national press. For many years, these brief and often impressionistic evocations of a long and productive life were the only source of information available to scholars who sought to learn more about Casanova's life and work. It is largely thanks to these obituaries that, despite Casanova's formidable and heterogeneous oeuvre, she is no longer remembered as a writer and intellectual but as an exotic figure on the fringes of Spanish culture and— even worse—an idealized symbol of nationalist womanhood. In just one of several such write-ups that he produced for the Spanish and Galician press, Casanova's family friend José Luis Bugallal y Marchesi, the self-appointed guardian of her reputation, describes her as "la santa que murió de saudade" (1958a, 18) [the saint who died of homesickness]. In a subsequent article, he wrote of her love for both "España, para quien Sofía Casanova—méritos literarios aparte—era una mártir, y Galicia, que la veneraba como a reliquia" (1958b, 139) [Spain, for whom Sofía Casanova—literary merits apart—was a martyr, and Galicia, which venerated her as a holy relic]. Six months earlier, the Galician author and scholar Victoriano García Martí had claimed that her life was "llena de luchas en países extranjeros, pero siempre [conservaba] las raíces raciales de su patria y de su tierra" (1957, 12) [full of struggles in foreign lands, yet she always (retained) the racial roots of her homeland and her native soil].

More striking than any of the Galician obituaries, however, is the obituary written by Camille Pitollet, a French Hispanist close to the Franco regime (see the second quotation at the head of this chapter), which claims that during the first sixteen years of her marriage (which took place in 1887), Casanova abandoned her budding literary career and stayed at home to devote herself to husband and children. This outrageous misrepresentation is typical of the strategies employed by Francoist sympathizers to neutralize the impact of successful women—and Casanova was, without a doubt, a successful woman. Far from retreating into domestic bliss in the decade after her marriage, she had, in fact, expanded her professional horizons: She had collaborated assiduously in the Galician, Spanish, and Polish press, had published several critically acclaimed books, and had traveled widely throughout Europe meeting with intellectuals from a variety of countries—all of which she describes in the four essays contained in the travelogue *Sobre el Volga helado* [Across the Frozen Volga], first published in 1899. This effort was, however, to no avail. By the end of the 1950s, Casanova—a woman who had traveled throughout Europe; who had moved in the highest political circles; who had witnessed the Russian Revolution, the rise of Franco, and the Nazi invasion of Poland; who had been a writer of internationally popular fiction; and who had served for twenty years as the Eastern European correspondent for one of Spain's most prestigious daily newspapers—was all but forgotten. Thanks to the obituaries that rebranded her as a saint, a martyr, and a holy relic, she was remembered in the second half of the twentieth century—where she was remembered at all—not as a pioneering, cosmopolitan intellectual and an accomplished professional writer but as a passive, sentimentalized icon of Francoist femininity.

Back to Basics: A Brief Biography of Sofía Casanova

The disappearance of anything but a patchy and sanitized account of Casanova's own life and work from the official record vindicates the fears she so lucidly expressed at the Ateneo in 1910. Casanova's invocation of a forgotten history to legitimize her claims in the present is a strategy shared by more recent feminist historians for whom, as Joan Scott has written, "if women's subordination—past and present—was secured at least in part by their invisibility, then emancipation might be advanced by making them visible in narratives of social struggle and political achievement" (1997, 2). As Scott goes on to argue, however, the metaphor of visibility is problematic, as it can imply that "the feminist historian's task [is] simply the recovery of previously ignored facts" (3). Nevertheless, the recovery of facts is an essential starting point for the study of not only women but all marginalized groups and cultures. As Casanova herself recognized, it is only once the visibility of forgotten writers is restored through the recovery of names, dates, places, and texts that "the questions of why these facts had been ignored and how they were now to be understood [can be] raised" (Scott 1997, 3). In this spirit, then, it seems appropriate to begin with a brief outline of Casanova's life and work.[5]

Sofía Guadalupe Pérez de Eguía Casanova was born in A Coruña in Spanish Galicia in 1861. After her father disappeared while *en route* to Cuba when she was very young, Sofía and her two younger brothers were raised by their mother and maternal grandparents, in whose honor she took the name Casanova.[6] Casanova began publishing poetry in Galician newspapers and journals as an adolescent, and when the family moved to Madrid in the early 1870s, she became part of the circle of poets that included Ramón de Campoamor, José de Echegaray, and Gaspar Núñez de Arce. By the time she married the Polish philosopher Wincenty Lutosławski in 1887, Casanova was widely celebrated in Spain as one of the most exciting young poets of either gender. In his introduction to her first collection of verse, *Poesías*, Ricardo Blanco Asenjo noted that "a Sofía no se la debe considerar poetisa" (1885, xv) [Sofía should not be considered simply a poetess]. Upon her marriage, however, she left Spain for Eastern Europe, accompanying her husband during his various temporary academic positions and research visits to Warsaw, Dorpat (now Tallinn, Estonia), London, Kazan (Russia), and Moscow. Throughout this period, during which she gave birth to three daughters, Casanova not only continued to write poems, many of which were collected in *Fugaces* (1898), but also began to experiment with prose. Her first novel, *El doctor Wolski*, set among the Polish community of Kazan, was published in 1894. In the introduction to the novel, Casanova notes that she wrote it at the request of friends in Spain who were interested in learning about "los hábitos y costumbres de dos curiosos pueblos del Norte" (n.p.) [the habits and customs of two curious peoples of the North]. Following the death of their third daughter, Jadwiga, in 1895, the Lutosławskis returned to Casanova's native Galicia, where she gave birth to her fourth and last child, Halina. Casanova continued to write short stories and articles about life in Poland and Russia, some of which were published in Spanish and Galician periodicals, such as *Revista Gallega*, *Galicia Moderna*, *España Artística*, and *Revista Contemporánea*, and one of which—a sketch of life in a Galician village—was published in the Polish journal *Słowo*. In 1899 four articles entitled "Cien leguas sobre el Volga helado" [One Hundred Leagues across the Frozen Volga], which chronicled Casanova's 1893 journey from Drozdowo (her husband's family estate near Warsaw) to Kazan, appeared in Madrid's *Revista Contemporánea.* The articles were so popular that in 1903 and again in 1919 they were reissued in book form as *Sobre el Volga helado.*

When the Lutosławskis returned to Poland in 1899, they moved to the southern city of Kraków. The city—which was part of Austrian Poland and therefore subject to fewer restrictions on Polish language and culture than the partitions occupied by Russia and Prussia—had a thriving and dynamic literary community, in which Casanova was enthusiastically involved. In 1907, however, having separated from Lutosławski, Casanova returned to Madrid, taking an apartment close to the one shared by her mother and her brother Vicente. Until her return to Poland in 1914 (at the first sign of the outbreak of war), she collaborated with many newspapers and periodicals of differing political and cultural hues. Among these were not only the relatively traditional *El Liberal* but also *La Nueva Era, Galicia* (Buenos Aires), *El Imparcial, La Tribuna,* and on one occasion even *Prometeo,* which César Antonio Molina considers the most important precursor of the *vanguardista* journals of the 1920s (1990, 44). She also published four novels: *Lo eterno* [The Eternal] (1907), *Más que amor* [More Than Love] (1908), *Princesa del amor hermoso* [Princess of Beautiful Love] (1909), and *El crimen de Beira-mar* [The Crime of Beira-mar] (1914); a collection of short stories (some of which had originally been published as early as the 1890s) called *El pecado* [The Sin] (1911); and a play, *La madeja* [The Bobbin] (1913), which was produced by Benito Pérez Galdós.[7] In 1913, she published a collection of many of her articles from this Madrid interlude, under the title *Exóticas* [Exotic Tales], before she returned to Warsaw at the outbreak of World War I. Casanova would never thereafter live permanently in Spain.

Back in Poland, Casanova's life changed immeasurably. The war meant that her communications with Spain were often interrupted for weeks at a time, while day-to-day life in Warsaw was overshadowed by the constant threat of invasion from Russia to the East and Germany to the West. In 1915 Casanova was offered a position as Eastern European correspondent for the Madrid daily newspaper *ABC,* a job she would hold until the newspaper's (temporary) demise in 1936. Through the pages of *ABC,* Casanova chronicled events in Poland and Eastern Europe, interpreting them for her Spanish readers as she publicized Poland's predicament and raised awareness and sympathy in a country whose neutral status fostered little interest in events on the other side of Europe. Casanova was one of a number of star columnists at *ABC,* which, since its foundation in 1903, had peddled "an audacious, reformist sort of journalism" (Gómez Aparicio 1974, 177, my translation), investing in new technology and foreign correspondents and removing the conventional page limit in order to accommodate its contributors. The newspaper's sympathies were monarchist and patriotic, as were Casanova's; unusually, however, "en una época en que la gran mayoría de los periódicos tenían una concreta filiación partidista, [*ABC*] izó, en política, la bandera de la independencia, para servir al interés de España y al del público" (Gómez Aparicio 1974, 179) [in an era when the vast majority of newspapers had a particular party affiliation, (*ABC*) raised the flag of political independence, to serve the interests of Spain and the public]. In time, other newspapers would follow *ABC*'s lead, but *ABC* retained its reputation as innovative and independent. Casanova's articles for *ABC* during World War I were posted from all over Poland, and after her family's evacuation during the invasion of Warsaw in 1915, they were posted from from Minsk, Moscow, and St. Petersburg. She remained in St. Petersburg for two years, experiencing the horrors of the Russian Revolution at first hand, and despite the virtually insurmountable practical difficulties that she faced, she never ceased to record her observations and impressions for her Spanish readers. Her wartime articles were collected and published in *De la guerra: Crónicas de Polonia y Rusia* [On War: Chronicles from Poland and Russia] (1916), *De la revolución rusa en 1917* [On the Russian Revolution in 1917] (1917), and *La revolución bolchevista (diario de un testigo)* [The Bolshevik Revolution (an Eyewitness Diary)] (1920).

In 1919 Casanova returned to Spain in poor health as a result of her wartime experiences and almost blind as a result of an accident with a cart on a St. Petersburg street. Received as a heroine in Madrid and Galicia, she traveled the country giving lectures and attending receptions; during this time she took the opportunity to observe Spain, especially her beloved Galicia, and to chronicle for *ABC* the changes she perceived since her departure in 1914. Throughout the 1920s Casanova continued to write regularly for *ABC,* living permanently in Warsaw but paying an extensive visit to Spain every two to three years. She covered the Russo-Polish war of 1919–1921 and the subsequent Lithuanian and Silesian plebiscites, the Polish transition to independence, and the economic and ministerial crises that lasted throughout the 1920s, all of which were set against the backdrop of her increasing concern over the rise of Bolshevik Russia. During her trips to Spain, she reported on the changes she perceived in Spanish life and the similarities to and differences from life in Eastern Europe and offered her recommendations for economic and cultural development.

During the 1920s she also published a number of short novels; a children's book, *Viajes y aventuras de una muñeca española en Rusia* [Travels and Adventures of a Spanish Doll in Russia] (1920); a history of the decline of Tsarist Russia, *En la corte de los zares (del principio y del fin de un imperio)* [At the Court of the Tsars (of the Beginning and End of an Empire)] (1924); and a number of articles on cultural topics for *Blanco y Negro* (a weekly publication from the same stable as *ABC*) and for Galician periodicals such as *La Voz de Galicia* and *El Eco de Santiago*. Some of her articles from *ABC* and *Blanco y Negro* were collected in *De Rusia: Amores y confidencias* [From Russia: Romance and Secrets] (1927), the fourth and last volume of her *Obras completas* [Complete Works]. She continued to write for *ABC* on a regular basis until 1936 (two isolated articles appeared thereafter in 1939 and 1944), but her collaboration with other periodicals all but ceased after 1930. Casanova's last two original works of fiction were the novels *Como en la vida* [As in Life] (1931) and *Las catacumbas de Rusia roja* [The Catacombs of Red Russia] (1933); her last original publication was *Polvo de escombros* [Dust from the Rubble], a day-by-day account of the Nazi invasion of Warsaw in 1939, published in *El martirio de Polonia* without her knowledge or consent in 1945. After World War II she remained with her family behind the Iron Curtain, able to communicate with Spain only sporadically. In 1958 she died in Poznań, Poland.

Contesting the Myth: Women Intellectuals at the *Fin de Siglo*

My chief concern in this book is the disparity between the evidence of active participation in *fin de siglo* social, cultural, and political debates by women such as Casanova and their absence from the historical record. It is scandalous that despite the great advances in Hispanic literary scholarship in general and feminist scholarship in particular, since the 1980s, the myth of the absence of women from *fin de siglo* culture remains largely uncontested. In fact, Casanova and her peers are so markedly missing from accounts of both the Galician *fin de século* and the Spanish *fin de siglo* that if we look at published sources, the history of women's writing in Galicia seems to jump forty years from Rosalía de Castro's *Follas Novas* in 1880 to Francisca Herrera Garrido's *Néveda* in 1920—and, even so, Herrera often merits little more than a footnote (Hooper 2003). With regard to Spain, Maryellen Bieder writes that "while a great many more women published fiction than those few whose names we remember today, no *one* author occupies a secure niche in the canon" (1992, 313–14), and she quotes Alda Blanco's "bold prediction" that "un estudio de esta generación de escritoras revelaría que existió en España, en las primeras décadas del siglo, un movimiento literario femenino equivalente al que surgió en Estados Unidos y en Inglaterra" (Blanco 1989, 23 n. 22) [a study of this generation of women writers would reveal the existence in Spain, in the first decades of the century, of a female literary movement equivalent to the one emerging in the United States and in England]. A year later, Roberta Johnson observed that "the '98 Generation stands out as a desert for women writers of any kind, and the reasons for their disappearance from the Castilian literary scene for a period of some thirty years have yet to be sorted out" (1993, 12).

My intention in this volume is, in part, to "recover" Casanova and her works as a case study to demonstrate the participation of women writers in the forging of "modern" Spain. In so doing, I develop Bieder's then-radical proposition that "the recovery of such a vibrant literary movement would make untenable the exclusion of the twentieth-century woman writer from the current codification of Spanish letters" (1992, 314). At the same time, I offer a new perspective on what Denise Riley has called "the misleading familiarity of 'history'" (1988, 5), thus contributing to the current move to reconceive the way that we teach and research the transition to modernity in Spain.

From the official record, it appears that women writers disappeared from the Spanish and Galician literary scene at the beginning of the twentieth century. The nineteenth century is well covered—at least from the bibliographical point of view—by María del Carmen Simón Palmer's monumental *Escritoras españolas del s. XIX* (1991), and recent interest in Western modernism has brought a certain amount of recognition for women who began their careers in the 1920s and 1930s. Many of the women within my realm of interest, however—although they published too late or too little to be included by Simón Palmer—were already middle aged (or dead) by the 1920s and therefore of limited interest to students of literary modernism. Moreover, few of these women published the kinds of works, or in the kinds of venues, that have traditionally attracted scholarly attention. In this light, therefore, it is essential that, following Kathleen McNerney and Cristina Enríquez de Salamanca, we take into account the following:

> A standard . . . based solely on the publication of books would [show] a complete lack of understanding of the problems these women faced when trying to publish their work. . . . It is impossible to determine if someone is a "writer" by counting the number of her works. Other criteria are involved in judging literary achievement—value judgments, social effects, literary influence, and so on—which means that this label eludes easy definition (1994, 11).

According to my own research, more than 250 women were active in Spanish cultural and intellectual circles in the two decades around the turn of the twentieth century, and at least 15 women were actively writing in Galician. Extending McNerney and Enríquez's recognition of "gray areas . . . within the genres" (6), I include in this figure not only imaginative writers but also the authors of religious and autobiographical texts, journalists, translators, and educators, all of whom contributed in various ways to the cultural life of *fin de siglo* Spain. These women did not exist in a vacuum, either from society or from one another. There is evidence, if we know where to look, that although, as Bieder (1995) has shown, some women—Emilia Pardo Bazán for example—consciously held themselves apart from the idea of a "women's literature," others "view[ed] themselves as part of a community and a continuum" (Walker 1995, 21). For example, both Casanova's 1910 Ateneo lecture and Carmen de Burgos's 1906 address to the Press Association of Rome, *La mujer en España* [Women in Spain], argue strongly that there existed in turn-of-the-century Spain a dynamic and wide-ranging female artistic community. As shown by both Burgos's and Casanova's inclusion of writers who were already dead by the 1900s, the present-day community was founded on an equally vibrant heritage. In *La mujer en España*, Burgos states that "la facultad artística abunda en las mujeres de España" (1906, 34) [artistic ability is abundant in Spain's women] and goes on to name not only writers but also singers, such as María García (known by her stage name, María Malibrán [circa 1809–1836]) and Adelina Patti (1848–1919); actors, such as Matilde Díez (1818–1883), Teodora Lamadrid (fl. 1860–1875), María [Álvarez] Tubau [de Palencia] (1854–1914), and María Guerrero (1867–1928); painters, such as Rafaela Sánchez Aroca, Clara Salazar, and María Luisa [de] la Riva [y Callol de] Muñoz (1859–1926); and a writer and composer, María del Pilar Contreras de Rodríguez (1861–1930). Among the writers that she names are Carmen Blanco y Trigueros (fl. 1878–1918), Sofía Casanova, "the illustrious old lady" Carolina Coronado (1823–1911), Rosa Eguílaz [y Renart de Parada] (born 1864), Magdalena [de Santiago] Fuentes (1873–1922), Concepción Gimeno [de Flaquer] (1850–1919), Emilia Pardo Bazán (1851–1921), and Blanca de los Ríos [y Nostench de Lámperez] (1862–1956) (34–37). Casanova agrees with Burgos about Gimeno, Pardo Bazán, and De los Ríos and adds Concepción Arenal (1820–1893) and Patrocinio de Biedma [y la Moneda] (1858–1927) to the group that she describes as "sangre y verbo de la literatura española" (Casanova 1910, *La mujer española en el extranjero,* 35) [blood and word of Spanish literature]. She makes separate mention of those who are active in poetry, drama, and journalism, including Rosario de Acuña (1851–1923), Consuelo Álvarez [Poll] (known as Violeta [fl. 1900–1930]), Carmen de Burgos, Rosalía de Castro

(1837–1885), Filomeno Dato Muruais (1856–1926), Gloria de la Prada [Navarro] (known as Mimí [1886–1951]), Salomé Núñez y Topete (fl. 1878–1926), and Melchora [Herrero y Ayora de] Vidal (fl. 1890–1927) (35).[8] These women, she notes,

> tendrán continuadoras; y así como hoy sus nombres van, fronteras adelante, a posarse cual rayo de luz precursor de plenitud meridiana en los escasos elegidos de la intelectualidad extranjera, así irán los de otras doctoras que . . . perseveren en la dura labor de hacer por España lo que más necesita. (36)

> [will have followers; and just as today their names travel across frontiers to pause, like a sunbeam announcing the brilliance of noon, on the chosen few foreign intellectuals, so will those of other learned women who . . . persevere in the struggle to do for Spain what it needs the most].

Despite Casanova's optimistic prediction, the vast majority of these women do not feature in modern accounts, and little is known about them. Even those such as Carmen de Burgos and Concha Espina, whose lives and works are reasonably well documented, have received only limited critical attention. The absence of all but a handful of these women from the official record of Spanish and Galician literature shows that the national model of literary history that we have known since the nineteenth century does not adequately represent the full range of cultural expression. This is important, because women's perceived silence during this crucial period in the formation of modern Iberian identities continues to have significant repercussions, not least in the remarkable and regrettable lack of female novelists in Galicia today (Hooper 2003).

What, then, are the answers to these seemingly intractable issues? Is it enough simply to try to reconstruct the fragmented history of women's writing in Galicia, filling in the gaps between Rosalía de Castro and Francisca Herrera or between Francisca Herrera and María Xosé Queizán forty-five years later and inserting the result into the master narrative? Should we, as the Spanish critic Ámparo Hurtado does, look for a female Generation of 1898? That is, to extend the famous metaphor of Audre Lorde (1983), should we use the master's tools (in this case, the categories, periods, labels of literary history) to dismantle the master's house, or should we go out and find our own tools and build our own house? Unquestionably, this discussion has implications far beyond the limited fields I have taken as my object in this study; indeed, the debate over whether the master's tools can ever, in fact, dismantle the master's house is relevant to all of us who study marginal identities and cultures. In the case of turn-of-the-century Iberian women's writing, the question of women's absence from the official histories is compounded by the lack of information about their lives and the lack of access to their works, many of which have never been reprinted and are confined to one or two academic libraries. In consequence, as Lou Charnon-Deutsch has observed, a great deal of groundwork remains to be laid, since "the process of reassessing a feminine tradition begins with a search, discovery, reediting and reevaluation of what has been excluded from the predominantly male canon" (2003, 122). Although this work is essential, the implications of simply transferring the strategies and apparatus of the hegemonic culture (the "master's tools") to these newly discovered texts are serious. To this end, I argue for a two-pronged approach to the study of such works, always bearing in mind, as feminist scholars have been arguing for decades, that "the writing of women into history necessarily involves redefining and enlarging traditional notions of historical significance" (Gordon et al. 1976, 89). That is, with the ammunition provided by comprehensive and, even more important, accurate bio-bibliographical and textual details, we can begin to reevaluate the grand narratives of history and literature themselves and then, as Bieder has argued, "not really redesign—regender—the literary canon, but explode it" (1992, 321).

Gender and the Modern Nation: Writing Women at the *Fin de Siglo*

The project proposed by Bieder (and many others) is based on the conviction that the canon is not natural and essential but has been constructed and legitimized by and for a particular group. In this light, its terms and categories become objects (rather than instruments) of analysis, allowing us to consider the canon's multiple absences and exclusions as resulting from particular discursive strategies. If we analyze the discursive strategies at play in *fin de siglo* Spain, we can begin to explain how and why the exclusion of women such as Casanova and her contemporaries occurred. Susan Kirkpatrick (1995) argues—with reference to novels such as Leopoldo Alas's *Su único hijo* (1891) and Benito Pérez Galdós's *Tristana* (1892)—that the *fin de siglo* was pervaded by a sense of crisis based on the fear of a link between the erosion of gender distinction and the breakdown of fundamental systems of social organization and meaning. In order to contain the problem, "feminized" culture had to be stripped of its authority and reconfigured in negative terms. Thus, "denigrating images of femininity—as perverse, pathological, weak-minded and dangerous—become the operative elements in much of the . . . *fin de siglo* rhetoric deploying the tropes of gender" (Kirkpatrick 1995, 97). As Kirkpatrick has observed, it is ironic that the binary division between the canonical literary groups known as the Generation of 1898 and *modernistas*, although it served to eliminate women's contributions to *fin de siglo* culture, was itself founded on a gendered distinction between the "virile" Generation of 1898 and the "effeminate" *modernistas* (2003, 10). The rhetorical structures of gender and nation increasingly coincided, so that to be masculine was to be *castizo* [genuinely Spanish], patriotic, and realist (like the Generation of 1898), whereas to be feminine was to be degenerate, idealistic, and worst of all (like the *modernistas*) tainted by foreignness.

Plenty of evidence of this kind of imagery exists in *fin de siglo* writings, demonstrating that the very existence of women writers was a source of great disquiet to their male contemporaries. Thinkers such as Miguel de Unamuno (see his article "A una aspirante a escritora" [To an Aspiring Lady Writer], first published in 1907) sought to reinforce the boundaries between the masculine and feminine, or the public and private spheres that the woman writer was viewed as breaching. Responding to an inquiry from a fictional young lady who wants advice on becoming a writer, Unamuno is distinctly discouraging:

> Me parece dificilísima y muy delicada la posición de una mujer que entre nosotros quiere dedicarse a la carrera de las letras. Me parece dificilísima su posición en todo país y en todo tiempo, pero mucho más en nuestro país, y tal vez en nuestro tiempo. (1959–1964, 479)

> [The position of a lady who wants to devote herself to a literary career in this country seems to me really quite difficult and very delicate. Her position in any country and at any time seems to me really quite difficult, but far more so in our country and, perhaps, in our time.]

This is the case, he says, because literary language belongs to men—"es un producto de una civilización predominantemente masculina" (479) [it is the product of a predominantly masculine civilization]—and therefore "el escribir una mujer para el público en lengua literaria masculina es algo así como ponerse los pantalones" (480) [for a woman to write for the public in masculine literary language is rather like her putting on a pair of trousers]. That is, it is a huge and almost unthinkable social transgression and one that would certainly compromise the respectability of any woman who dared to try it.

One solution to the "problem" of the woman writer encroaching on the public sphere was simply to ignore her seemingly inappropriate interventions in favor of more appropriate actions. This occurs increasingly throughout Casanova's career, and overwhelmingly after the Spanish Civil War, as her (exclusively male) biographers and reviewers focus on her exotic life, her personality, and her social work rather than on her literary and intellectual production. In a review of her third and final collection of poetry, *El cancionero de la dicha* (1911), Eduardo Gómez de Baquero describes Casanova's work as predominantly feminine, contrasting her favorably with "las mujeres que cultivan una literatura desgarrada, de tonos crudos y violentos" [women who cultivate a scandalous literature, with crude and violent overtones], whom he sees as "fuera de su papel, como un cura anticlericalista o un soldado antimilitarista" (1911, 3) [out of place, like an anticlerical priest or an antimilitarist soldier]. In his introduction to *La revolución bolchevista* (first published in 1920), "RC" (José Ruíz Castillo Basala) sees two sides to Casanova's character, which reflect the dichotomized feminine ideal of the time—she is "heroica, fuerte, española" [heroic, strong, Spanish] but at the same time "sensible, delicada, mujer y poeta" (1989, 83) [sensitive, delicate, woman and poet]. The editorial blurb on the cover of the 1947 edition of *Como en la vida*, the last of her works to be published during her lifetime, abandons any hint of this dichotomy. It focuses instead on her social work—"ha puesto siempre su pluma al servicio de causas humanitarias" [she has always placed her pen at the service of humanitarian causes]—and the alleged expression of her gentle, womanly character through her writing: "De cuanto escribe emana una tierna delicadeza femenina." [A tender feminine delicacy emanates from whatever she writes.]

Whereas some attempted to neutralize rebellious women writers by rewriting their lives to fit dominant notions of femininity and Spanishness, others took a different approach—they turned them into objects of ridicule. In his memoirs, Rafael Cansinos-Asséns—a Jewish acquaintance with whom Casanova had a heated correspondence when he accused her of anti-Semitism—recalled his first meeting with her at one of Carmen de Burgos's literary salons, probably some time between 1909 and 1913. In Cansinos-Asséns's account Casanova comes across as a foolish, excitable woman with a ridiculous tendency toward patriotic babble: "Yo estoy por España y por los españoles . . . , ¡oh españolitos de mi alma! . . . [y] también por el polvo y las moscas . . . , ¡moscas españolas!" (1982, 214). [I'm all for Spain and for the Spanish . . . oh, my dear darling Spaniards! . . . and for the dust and the flies too . . . Spanish flies!] He links what he sees as her overdeveloped sense of patriotism with the Catholic fanaticism of the Inquisition and reports a comment allegedly made by someone else who was present: "Es como el marqués de Bradomín; fea, católica y sentimental" (215). [She's like the (fictional) Marqués of Bradomín; ugly, Catholic, and sentimental.]

The novelist Juan Valera's description of Casanova's attendance at one of his *tertulias* in 1901 is equally unflattering. Valera remembers what occurred when he and the others present asked Casanova to recite some of her verses:

> Ella los recitó con mucho manoteo, haciendo mil muecas y con una musiquilla tan rara y tan lúgubre que fue milagro que no soltasen el trapo a reír todos cuantos componían el auditorio. (1956, 272)

> [She recited them with much hand waving, making a thousand faces and in such a strange and lugubrious singsong voice that it was a miracle that everyone in the audience didn't burst out laughing.]

Valera acknowledges Casanova's literary activity, however, describing her as "una gran literata, gallega como Doña Emilia" [a great lady novelist, Galician like Doña Emilia (Pardo Bazán)] and "un pasmoso fenómeno, digno de contemplación y estudio" (272) [a fearsome phenomenon, worthy of contemplation and study]. One cannot help but wonder—and it is impossible to know—whether he is being entirely serious and whether (in the light of his anecdote) it is her character rather than her work that he deems worthy of study. His use of the term *literata* is certainly unsympathetic. For male writers, as Bieder has argued, "a *poetisa* or *literata* is always an inferior imitation of an unattainable male model" (1995, 101).

In contrast to Valera, Cansinos-Asséns is explicitly dismissive of Casanova's work, describing her as "la autora de unas novelitas de las que sólo conozco los títulos" (1982, 212) [the lady author of some silly novels of which I know nothing more than the titles]. He makes no mention of her poetry or her journalism but goes into great detail about her life and particularly her marriage: "Constituye una novela" (212). [It constitutes a novel in itself.] Valera too is intrigued by Casanova's husband, referring to him as "un sabio polaco que de puro sabio se ha vuelto loco" (1956, 272) [a Polish scholar who has gone mad from pure scholarship] and commenting that his name is so difficult that he dare not try to write it down. Clearly, even relatively early in her career, the exoticism of Casanova's circumstances was becoming more attractive to casual observers than the quality of her works, but this is by no means the only reason for Valera's and Cansinos-Asséns's focus on her personality. Joyce Tolliver observes a similar phenomenon in accounts of Casanova's compatriot and contemporary Pardo Bazán: "Many of her detractors," Tolliver writes, "attend far more to her person than they do to her work; and the annoyance expressed in many of the criticisms of her comportment is due to little more than the perception that [she] does not 'know her place' " (1998, 21).

The difficulty for those of us who study minority writers—among whom, in this case, we must include *fin de siglo* women—is that the place that was allocated to them and that for many years they were expected to accept without question inevitably sets them outside existing models of cultural and literary history. This is partly because, as we have seen, these models are predicated on exclusivity and on boundaries drawn around the national literature. The difficulty of challenging these boundaries is intensified because the criteria for inclusion and exclusion are often distinctly unclear and based on vague notions of "quality." The continued influence of such criteria is evident in the question that all of us who study minority writers have faced at some point: But are they any good? (Blanco 1993). The danger of this question, of course, is that it assumes a consensus about what, precisely, is meant by "good"—a consensus that, since the canon wars and the institutionalization of formerly marginalized writings, has become increasingly less possible or, indeed, desirable. Furthermore, it highlights the continued need to relativize the notion of "quality" and deconstruct its supporting rhetoric.

In the case of *fin de siglo* women, as we have seen, such investigation shows that decisions about their inclusion or exclusion were based on social and biographical rather than textual and intellectual factors. The effects of these decisions have been intensified by the peculiar development of Spanish literary studies during the twentieth century. Although it is now a critical commonplace to question the divide between the Generation of 1898 and the *modernistas*[9] and although more and more scholars are beginning to question the continued critical focus on writers traditionally associated with those groups, rather fewer are prepared to challenge the main stumbling block: the dominance of the generational system itself. The reluctance of many Hispanists to move away from what has been, after all, a defining factor in Spanish literary studies reflects the tension between the centripetal pull of the national literature and the increasingly centrifugal dynamic of interdisciplinary cultural studies, in which Hispanism has until recently played a relatively limited part. This reluctance—as Mary Lee Bretz has convincingly argued—"reveals a discomfort with plurality and an insistent homogenization of the cultural and intellectual currents of a given moment" (2001, 68). Although I agree with Michael Ugarte that "the very formation of any literary tradition or history assumes the presence of a historical continuum, a dialogue between and among specific historical moments . . . and the term generation can be a useful tool . . . in the understanding of the dialogue," I also share his belief that "in the long run, the shortcomings [of generational categories] outweigh the insights" (1994, 262). This view is particularly pertinent to minority writings. In the case of *fin de siglo* women's writing, for example, some scholars (such as

Hurtado in her 1998 "Biografía de una gencración") have taken the pragmatic option, adapting the dominant, generational model (whose efficacy has, of course, already been proved) to the needs of the minority. Although this can be a useful strategy in the short term at least, picking up the master's tools without considering the implications of this decision means risking unthinkingly continuing his work. The principal danger of this is, of course, that our house will thus end up looking all too similar to his.

But Is It Any Good? Reclaiming Sentimentality for the Modern Reader

For minority groups, the dilemma of what to do with long-standing models is a real one. The only solution is to relativize both apparently universal notions of quality and their associated scholarly apparatus. As Rita Felski (1995) has argued with regard to European modernism, this means that we must start by rethinking the categories themselves.[10] The critical focus on canonical modernist standards based on aesthetic innovation continues to authorize as the norm the aesthetically experimental (if often ideologically conservative) works of Casanova's male contemporaries—both the Generation of 1898 and the *modernistas*—as it marginalizes "sentimental" women's fiction.[11] In consequence, the works of Casanova and her peers—which display comparatively few of the features normally associated with literary modernism—have been dismissed as parochial, sentimental, and of marginal interest to "modern" Spain. This has been the case at least since Padre Francisco Blanco García's 1890s dismissal of "la larga y no gloriosa serie de escritoras más o menos consagradas a la imitación y al cultivo de un género [la novela romántica] que tanto se adapta a las fogosidades y los arrebatos del sentimentalismo femenino" (1891, 388) [the long and not very glorious succession of lady writers more or less dedicated to imitation and to the cultivation of a genre (the romantic novel) that adapts so well to the fervors and ecstasies of female sentimentality].

The apparent obsession with sentimentality that underpins Blanco García's dismissal of women's writing is as deceptive in Spain as elsewhere. The reality that *fin de siglo* women frequently base their works on domestic or sentimental models and take the private sphere as their starting position has led to the swift dismissal of their works—even by feminist critics—as melodramatic, conventional, and idealized (judgments of Casanova's work that have all been made since the 1990s and that are discussed further in later chapters). My contention is, however, that many of these women—and Casanova is a prime example—deliberately use the conventions of sentimental fiction as a smoke screen for their examination of social and political concerns, recognizing the value of literature, and narrative in particular, as an arena for describing and contesting the social realities of interest to them.[12]

A central concern of the present study is to examine the relationship between what Roberta Johnson calls the "form" and the "message" of Spanish modernism (2003, 5)—that is, to look at the ways in which Casanova and her contemporaries used the conventions of sentimental fiction to convey their radical message. One of my goals is thus to extend Johnson's theory to demonstrate not only that aesthetic and social experimentation are not necessarily mutually exclusive but that it is, indeed, only when we read female-authored texts against modernist aesthetic standards that they appear to be aesthetically conservative. In consequence, it is imperative that we learn how to read these texts on their own terms and to recognize the formal experimentation that they carry out as they play with the conventions and vocabularies of a whole variety of literary genres, including the sentimental. A key means by which *fin de siglo* women sought to manipulate the conventions of the sentimental genre in order to reflect their social and political concerns was to imagine plots that did not lead their heroines to the hitherto inevitable marriage—a strategy that Rachel Blau DuPlessis has called "writing beyond the ending" (1985). In fact, Casanova and her female contemporaries increasingly reject marriage as an ending for their narratives, demonstrating the relevance of DuPlessis's contention for Spanish women too: "It is the project of twentieth-century writers to solve the contradictions between love and quest and to replace the alternate endings in marriage and death that are their cultural legacy from nineteenth-century life and letters by offering a different set of choices" (4).

DuPlessis focuses primarily on English- and French-language sources. The choices other than absorption into a heterosexual couple or death that she cites, however, are evident too in Spanish women's writing. We can find examples of "reparenting, woman-to-woman and brother-to-sister bonds, and forms of the communal protagonist" (1985, 5) in the works discussed in the chapters that follow. Of the female protagonists of Casanova's early works, Mara (*El doctor Wolski*) flees Russia and her fiancé for Lithuania, where she founds a female commune; María Cruz (*Más que amor*) rejects marriage and Spain in favor of an independent life in Poland; Laura (*Princesa del amor hermoso*) refuses to marry either of her suitors, the aging Don Juan or the young Galician poet; and the story of Rosa María (*El crimen de Beira-mar*) begins after her marriage, while her husband is away working in America. Only Consuelo's story (*Lo eterno*) ends with the conventional wedding (or at least the promise of one). Significantly, however (as I argue in Chapter 3), marriage in this novel symbolizes not bourgeois repression but freedom and the passage into modernity. By the beginning of the next decade, the course of events was starting to change. Carmen de Burgos's short novel *La flor de la playa* (1920), for instance, is frequently cited as an example of what Johnson has called "a rather utopian idea for early twentieth-century Spain" (1999, 248). It describes a young unmarried couple who go on holiday together to Portugal to give married life a try, only to go their separate ways on their return to Madrid, when they realize that marriage is not for them. The fact that this experiment takes place in Portugal and that the return to Spain is accompanied by the restoration of moral order—especially when compared with Casanova's heroines who remain outside the dominant national space—suggests that Casanova may have been farther ahead of her time than we have tended to assume.

Casanova's exploration of the social realities outlined in *La mujer española en el extranjero*, in the context of the plots she constructs for her heroes and more pertinently her heroines, is in perpetual tension with the need for women writers to maintain a veneer of respectability—that is, to minimize, as far as possible, the inevitable hostility to their presence in the public sphere of Spanish letters. In their analysis of the different strategies that women writers have employed to authorize their participation in the public debates from which they were so often excluded, feminist narrative theorists provide a framework for examining the consequences of this tension in female-authored texts. Critics such as Susan Lanser (1992) and Robyn Warhol (1989) proceed on the understanding that because narrative voice embodies the social, economic, and literary conditions under which it has been produced, narrative discourse can be considered a cultural production, and as a result the sex of the author or narrator can play a key role in the formation of narrative meaning. Arguing that every act of authorship can be read as representing an implicit appeal for discursive authority, Lanser identifies a narrative category of "extrarepresentational" acts that offers a means by which women writers, who are often barred from overtly participating in public discourse, might gain such authority. These acts may include "reflections, judgments, generalizations about the world 'beyond' the fiction, direct addresses to the narratee, comments on the narrative process, [or] allusions to other writers and texts" (1992, 16–17).

The effect of this strategy is to mitigate the normative identification of female-authored fiction with the private, personal voice, enabling female authors to transcend the fictive world and—albeit indirectly—assert their narrative authority over the public sphere. Sometimes this proved successful, as in Concepción Gimeno's novella *Una Eva moderna* (1909), which—although

ostensibly a sentimental romance—uses dialogue between the male protagonist (a Spanish politician) and his female counterpart (an educated but domestic woman) to discuss changes in the Spanish legal code. Similarly, in
Casanova's novel *Más que amor*, Carlos (also a politician) and María discuss
potential changes in Spanish law with respect to religious orders. This strategy
was, however, also fraught with danger: Casanova's use of Carlos to voice her
belief in Poland's future political independence, for example, backfired when
the Russian authorities, after being apprised of it, fined Casanova and closed
down the newspaper that had published the novel (see Chapter 4 herein). The
absence of a similar reaction in Spain may be a consequence of the fact that
the majority of the novel's action takes place in the liminal space of epistolary
contact rather than in a recognizably Spanish setting; the profoundly gendered and spatialized nature of Spanish society meant that within Spain such
experimentation was all but inconceivable.

Reading Sofía Casanova: Outline of the Study

How, then, should we approach the works of Casanova and her contemporaries? It is tempting to think that because the discursive maps of *fin de siglo*
Spain were drawn up largely along gendered lines, women occupied an unproblematically passive or marginal role in the construction of the national
imaginary. This is, however, very far from the case. One of the most important moves in recent feminist scholarship has been the call to acknowledge
that women have been participants—often active participants—in various
imperialist projects and in the forging of modern nations and modern societies and that to ignore what Charnon-Deutsch calls "the hidden scenes of
collaboration" (2003, 124–25) in their works is to collude in the "forgetting"
that feminist scholarship endeavors to counter. Furthermore, to read women
simply as victims of essentializing patriarchy, I have learned, is to disregard
the evidence of their own texts; the realization that women participated in
nationalist and imperial projects, not least through the almost continual eli-
sion of differences of class, race, and ethnicity in their otherwise radically
revisionary imagined landscapes, has very much shaped my understanding of
Casanova and her works.

Since I began working with Casanova's texts as a graduate student in the
late 1990s, I have found myself shifting from a utopian vision of the author as
documenter of female and Galician oppression to a more complex analysis of
her work as a site for multiple, often contradictory, representations of power
relationships. The area in which this is probably most marked is Casanova's

treatment of differences of race and ethnicity—especially in her first two novels, *El doctor Wolski* and *Lo eterno,* and in the travelogue *Sobre el Volga helado,* three texts that explore the consequences of Spain's renewed imperial project in the second half of the long nineteenth century. Juxtaposing our readings of the narratives of feminine victimization that dominate Spanish women's writing through the nineteenth and into the twentieth century with the way these women write about the working classes and the subjects of Spain's former colonies (Charnon-Deutsch 2003, 125) often produces completely unexpected and unsettling readings of texts that I had previously read as straightforward and unproblematic.

My focus in this book, then, is the connections between representations of difference (largely, but not exclusively, of gender) and the emergence of the modern nation in the novels and novellas that Casanova produced during the first part of her career. I look at each of the six major narrative works that she published between 1894 and 1914 in turn, examining her settings and strategies in order to locate her works and their protagonists within contemporary debates about the place of women and other minorities in the modern nation. Underlying all is Casanova's desire—despite the fear that she so poignantly expressed in *Lo eterno* that she would always remain "extranjera en mi patria" (1907, 5–6) [a stranger in my own land]—to mark out for herself, her foremothers, her sisters, and her daughters a place in Spain's past, present, and future. The chapters that follow look at individual texts that foreground questions of women's place in society and the nation. Taking the texts in chronological order allows us to trace not only Casanova's increasing dissatisfaction with the processes by which national and gender stereotypes and grand narratives of nation, history, and literature were created but also her growing conviction that change was impossible within the dominant spaces of the modern Spanish nation.

I begin my analysis, in Chapters 2 and 3, by examining two novels that explore contrasting responses to fin de siècle fears about the breakdown of boundaries of gender, race, and class. Both *El doctor Wolski* (1894) and *Lo eterno* (1907) culminate with the protagonists' rejection of their respective home nations in favor of alternative, peripheral spaces. In Chapter 4, I consider *Más que amor* (1908), in which Casanova exploits the potential of the epistolary format to dramatize the search of the female artist for a space beyond the borders of either nation or narration. Chapters 5 and 6 investigate the shift to briefer narrative forms (the *novela corta* and short story) and Galician settings that accompanied Casanova's return to Spain after more than two decades abroad. In *Princesa del amor hermoso* (1909), *El pecado* (1911), and *El crimen de Beira-mar* (1914), she turns her attention to the process by which cultural models of masculinity, femininity, Spanishness, and Galicianness are constructed and explores the peripheries as a potential locus for imagining social change.

I close with some observations about how a consideration of these six texts might (1) influence the reception of Casanova and her works and (2) offer a new perspective to complement the growing body of revisionist scholarship in Iberian studies that seeks to break down the boundaries and divisions, both externally imposed and internally reinforced, that continue to keep Spain at the margins of interdisciplinary studies. Works by women such as Casanova offer fascinating and often unexpected alternatives to the monolithically masculine Castile-focused version of Spanish culture that still informs many studies of the *fin de siglo* today. They demonstrate that these writers were far more than simply "la[s] autora[s] de unas novelitas" [the lady author(s) of some silly novels]—and they knew it. They were also aware, however—as Casanova put it—that "cual Atlántida que devoró el mar" [like Atlantis swallowed up by the sea], they and their works ran the risk of being submerged by what we might now, following Riley, call "the misleading familiarity of 'history.'" Our task, then, is to challenge the familiar narrative with alternative ways of seeing, reading, and understanding the *fin de siglo,* a goal that can be achieved only through serious and searching analysis of the writings of the women who contributed so critically to this crucial period in the formation of modern Iberian identities.

CHAPTER 2

Poland–Russia–Lithuania

El doctor Wolski: Páginas de Polonia y Rusia (1894)

Sofía Casanova's marriage to Wincenty Lutosławski in 1887 introduced her to a world that was significantly broader, both geographically and intellectually, than she could ever have imagined from her Madrid salon. She now had the opportunity not only to travel extensively throughout Europe but also to meet and associate with some of Europe's most brilliant writers, philosophers, and politicians—intellectuals who took her, and her intellectual aspirations, seriously (a rare circumstance for a middle-class, provincial Spanish woman). As she continued to write and publish the poetry that had established her reputation at home, her newfound freedom from the scrutiny of Spanish literary critics and social expectations allowed her to explore the serious social and political issues to which she was now exposed. This new social and intellectual environment, which inspired a sudden change of literary direction, resulted in Casanova's first novel—indeed, her first published narrative work—*El doctor Wolski* (1894).[1] Like Casanova's other works, *Wolski* has, in recent times, received only sparse critical attention, most of it restricted to brief (and often inaccurate) plot summaries in histories of Spanish women's literature (Galerstein and McNerney 1986; Pérez 1988) or passing mentions in biographical studies of the author (Alayeto 1992; Osorio 1997; Martínez 1999).

The consensus among recent scholars has been that the novel is primarily autobiographical and primarily of interest for the light it can shed on Casanova's relationship with her husband. Illustrating the tendency to equate women's writing with the personal, Ofelia Alayeto reads the eugenicist doctor Enrique Wolski as a biographical portrait of Lutosławski:

> Lutosławski's belief in eugenics was documented in his memoirs, family recollections, and his wife's account of "hygienic" ideas in *El doctor Wolski*.

He believed that one could improve the human race by researching
the health of the two families involved in a marriage, and by matching
individuals of acceptable histories. (1992, 28)

María Victoria López Cordón agrees, quoting the long description of Enrique
in chapter 1 of the novel (Casanova 1894, *El doctor Wolski*, 25–26) to support
her claim that the novel "refleja bastante bien algunos aspectos idealizados
de la personalidad de Lutosławski" (López Cordón 1989, 16) [is quite a good
reflection of some idealized aspects of Lutosławski's personality]. Although
Rosario Martínez is of the same mind about the autobiographical nature of
the novel, her interpretation of the character of Enrique differs from that of
López Cordón. Martínez states bluntly:

> El protagonista de esta novela . . . es un claro trasunto de Wincenty
> Lutosławski y la propia obra constituye . . . una abierta crítica a
> determinadas metas y actitudes intelectuales suyas. (1999, 93)

> [The protagonist of this novel . . . is a clear portrait of Wincenty Lutosławski
> and the work itself is . . . an explicit critique of certain of his objectives and
> intellectual attitudes.]

Alayeto takes the autobiographical thesis even further, identifying Casanova
with the character of Mara:

> Sometimes [Casanova] felt inadequate to the challenge of sharing such
> an unusual life. In [her] novel *El doctor Wolski*, Mara (the brilliant young
> physician's fiancée) echoes her thoughts: "Enrique es un hombre superior.
> Su vida tiene una noble misión que cumplir. ¿Podré ayudarle? ¿No me
> encontraré inferior a él?"[2] (1992, 21 [quoting Casanova 1894, *El doctor Wolski*,
> 58–59])

She wonders whether perhaps "the two unforgivable feminine imperfections
that shatter Enrique's idealistic plans (Mara's consumption and Gelcha's ste-
rility) were, in Casanova's mind, associated with her own 'failure' to bear her
husband a male child" (Alayeto 1992, 34). Although this critical focus on autobiographical readings of *Wolski* is understandable, it is also risky in that it
perpetuates the propensity for presenting women's works simply as a reflection
of personal experience, thus limiting their significance to that of a roman à
clef. There is no doubt that Casanova drew extensively on her own experiences

in her writing, but she did so in a selective and—as I argue in this chapter—strategic manner.

Wolski is the only one of Casanova's novels—and one of very few Spanish novels of the period in general—that not only is set entirely outside Spain but also lacks a single Spanish protagonist.³ The choice of geographical setting has been read as autobiographical, and there is certainly an element of this. More significantly, however, Poland's peculiar situation as a nation without a political territory of its own allows Casanova to make significant theoretical points about the process of nation construction in general and the role of cultural media in this process in particular. Furthermore, the displacement of the novel's action to (from a Spanish perspective) "exotic" Poland provides a smoke screen for Casanova's participation in many of the great debates that preoccupied European thinkers at the fin de siècle—from the growing authority of science and technology to the relevance of Romantic paradigms in a post-positivist society and from the debates surrounding women's education to the fears of racial and cultural degeneration.

The smoke screen is intensified and also undermined by the novel's prologue, which was signed in London in March 1894 and dedicated to Casanova's mentor, the poet Ramón de Campoamor. By describing herself as "la autora" in the prologue, Casanova claims a position of public authorship that stands in sharp contrast to the more usual private voice of female fiction. Even so, this daring claim of moral and intellectual authority is mitigated by Casanova's recourse to the modesty topos so characteristic of female authors. She swiftly turns the reader's attention away from the act of authorship and toward the novel's doubly distanced position with regard to Spain—by virtue of her own position as an expatriate and the novel's exotic setting:

> Tracé estas humildísimas líneas pensando en mi patria, y sin poder dominar el impulso de escribir en español, ya que no podía hablarlo, viviendo en una sociedad tan distante de la mía, y que nada tiene en común con ella. (1894, *El doctor Wolski*, 1)

> [I sketched out these most modest of lines thinking of my homeland and unable to curb the impulse to write in Spanish, since I could not speak it, living as I do in a society that's so far from my own, and that has nothing in common with it.]

According to the prologue, *Wolski* was published by mere chance, after Casanova read some sketches to friends "que las juzgan interesantes, porque ven algo del carácter y de la manera de vivir de dos curiosos pueblos del norte" (2) [who find them interesting, for they see in them something of the character and way of life of two curious northern peoples]. In other words, Casanova presents her novel not as an imaginative, intellectually engaged work of fiction but as a more modest semijournalistic or *costumbrista* piece, which—as we will see—is very far from the case.

The tension expressed in the prologue to *Wolski*, between the desire for recognition of authorship and the need to maintain "feminine" respectability, is an important feature of *fin de siglo* Spanish women's writing. Susan Lanser observes a similar phenomenon in English and French women's writing at the turn of the previous century, which she identifies as the result of the tension between "women's sense of literary entitlement by the 1790s" and "the political conservatism of the 1790s [that] sharply increased the rigidification of sexual spheres and the valorization of female domesticity" (1992, 64–65). A century after Jane Austen, Fanny Burney, and Mesdames de Genlis and de Staël, writers such as Sofía Casanova, Carmen de Burgos, Blanca de los Ríos, and Emilia Pardo Bazán found themselves struggling with similar constraints. The resulting tensions are addressed—whether directly or indirectly—in many of the female-authored prologues that began to appear around the turn of the twentieth century. At the start of her first novel, *Los inadaptados* (first published in 1909), Burgos employs a strategy similar to that of Casanova, claiming, "Jamás fue de mi agrado detener al lector con observaciones ni prólogos, innecesarios la mayor parte de las veces, antes de penetrar en las páginas de un libro" (1990, 15). [It has never been my pleasure to detain the reader with observations or prologues, so often unnecessary, before penetrating the pages of a book.] Like Casanova, Burgos offers an interpretation of her novel not as original literature—"no quiero que se la crea producto de mi fantasía" [I don't want it to be thought a product of my imagination]—but as faithful reporting of "esa vida primitiva y hermosa que pretendo presentar a los lectores" (16) [the primitive, beautiful life I am trying to depict for my readers]. Even Pardo Bazán (a rather special case in her confident assertion of narrative authority), who rarely wrote prologues to her work, included one in her 1905 novel *La quimera*. In her prologue, Pardo Bazán, like Burgos, notes that she has not previously sought to influence the reader through any "unfeminine" display of authority:

Había prescindido en mis novelas de todo prefacio, advertencia, aclaración o prólogo, entregándolas mondas y lirondas al lector, que allá las interpretase a su antojo, puesto que tanta molestia quisiera tomarse. (2003, 5)

[I had foregone any preface, warning, clarification or prologue to my novels, handing them over whole and unscathed for the reader to interpret at leisure, if he or she wanted to go to so much trouble.]

In its confident tone and in Pardo Bazán's proud acknowledgment of the extratextual relevance of her work, her prologue provides a striking contrast—indeed, almost a challenge—to the prologues of Casanova and Burgos: Pardo Bazán asks, "Si bajo la ficción novelesca palpita algún problema superior a los efímeros eventos que tejen el relato . . . ¿por qué ocultarlo?" (9). [If beneath the novelesque fiction there beats some problem superior to the ephemeral events woven in the story . . . why conceal it?]

For whatever reason, Casanova—unlike Pardo Bazán—did indeed feel the need to conceal, or at least downplay, her novel's treatment of issues of public debate. The balance and complexity of *Wolski*, however, clearly contradict her claims of journalistic mimesis. The novel begins as Enrique Wolski, a member of the exiled Polish community in central Russia, graduates in medicine from the University of Kazan. After his graduation he spends two years abroad developing his theory that judicious breeding to eliminate hereditary illness can be used to improve the human race. When he returns, he finds that his fiancée, Mara (who, it is important to note, is also Polish—not Russian, as Carolyn Galerstein and Kathleen McNerney [1986] and Janet Pérez [1988] claim), is suffering from tuberculosis. Because her disease is inherited, it rules her out as a suitable mate. Mara breaks off their engagement to save Wolski from having to compromise his ideals, after which he goes abroad again and hears nothing more from her. Four years later, he meets Gelcha, a healthy but simple girl from a good Polish family, and after he investigates her family history and finds no evidence of inherited illness, he marries her. A year later, she gives birth to a son, who dies within days, and the same week, Wolski's model hospital burns to the ground. His project has failed both on a personal and a professional level, in what has been interpreted as "the ironic hand of fate [destroying] all his ideals" (Galerstein and McNerney 1986, 70). In a final twist, the novel reveals that Mara (whom both the reader and Wolski have presumed to be dead) is alive and working as a schoolmistress in Lithuania, happily surrounded by children. Thematically, the novel can be broadly divided in two: Chapters 1–13 concern the development of Enrique's theories, and chapters 14–21 reveal what happens when he puts them into practice.

Accompanying the principal theme of Wolski and his relationships with Mara and Gelcha is a subplot that involves his friendship with the Russian student Iwan Iwanowicz. Galerstein and McNerney and (repeating them almost word for word) Pérez see this as the most important element of the novel, claiming that "Casanova's first novel traces the friendship between the idealistic, Russian-educated Polish doctor and his skeptical, hedonistic Russian friend" (Galerstein and McNerney 1986, 70; see also Pérez 1988, 19–20). My interpretation of the subplot is somewhat different; the passages that involve Enrique and Iwan do nothing to move the action forward, but their dialogues about the relative merits of will and determinism, and the role of science in the progress of humanity, give Casanova the opportunity to outline the intellectual debates that underpin Wolski's story. By putting the debates into the mouths of her male characters, Casanova neatly avoids the risks inherent in the overt expression of authorship. Nevertheless, in the bigger picture the relationship between Wolski and Iwan is subordinate to the relationship between Wolski and Mara. This is evident in the novel's climax, which sees Iwan's project fail as definitively as Enrique's. While Enrique is abroad for the second time, Iwan is sent to Siberia as punishment for his involvement with the revolutionary underground press. He returns after Enrique's marriage and, although he is in poor health, he resumes his work at the press. There he is arrested, and there he commits suicide rather than return to Siberia. The last two chapters thus add a postscript to the main climax of Enrique's story, drawing first Iwan's and then Mara's story to a close.

The full significance of the novel's geographical setting and, in particular, Mara's eventual relocation to Lithuania cannot be understood without reference to contemporary Polish nationalist discourse, with which Casanova was becoming increasingly familiar through both her husband's connections and her own social circle. She made her first journey to Poland after her marriage in 1887. After an extended honeymoon, during which the newlyweds visited Lutosławski's acquaintances in Portugal, Paris, and London, the couple returned to the Lutosławski family estate at Drozdowo, situated to the northeast of Warsaw in Russian Poland. For the next few years, they moved regularly as Lutosławski took various temporary academic positions. Their first daughter, María, was born in Dorpat (now Tallinn), Estonia, in 1888, and their second daughter, Izabela, was born in Moscow in 1889. They spent the academic year of 1889–1890 in London. Then they moved to Kazan, a Russian city eight hundred kilometers east of Moscow on the Volga (now in Tatarstan), where their third daughter, Jadwiga, was born. They remained in Kazan from 1890 to 1892, during which time Casanova began *Wolski* (which is set almost exclusively in that city). At the end of the 1891–1892 academic year, the family returned to Drozdowo for their vacation, and in January 1893 Casanova and Lutosławski left their daughters in Poland and made the journey back to Kazan alone.[4] This time, they remained in Kazan for only one semester. Casanova completed *Wolski*, and it was published in Madrid in 1894, by which time the family was once again in London.

The Lutosławski family, fervently Catholic and equally patriotic, was part of Poland's minor landowning nobility. The Lutosławskis were known for their social work and for their links with the Polish nationalist movement. Alayeto (1987, 25–26) connects the family with the liberal, positivist tendency, although in later years the Lutosławski daughters would be strong supporters of the right-wing National Democracy Party. Alayeto also suggests that, through her relationship with her husband's family, Casanova herself quickly became sympathetic to the Polish national cause (24). Lutosławski, for his part, was of a different mind. He adhered to the Romantic belief in Poland as "Christ among nations" and awaited the coming of the Messiah described in Adam Mickiewicz's great nationalist poem *Dziady* [Forefathers' Eve] in 1832.[5] One of Lutosławski's reasons for marrying Casanova was Mickiewicz's statement in part 3 of *Dziady* that the Messiah would be born of a foreign mother, since Lutosławski believed that he himself was destined to be the father.[6] According to Alayeto, Lutosławski's family and friends did not share his views, and although he was generally regarded as academically brilliant, he was also considered rather strange (1987, 29). Andrzej Walicki summarizes Lutosławski's early attitude toward Poland in his study of the controversies over Polish self-definition:

> The metaphysical philosopher Wincenty Lutosławski, world-famous as an expert on Plato, worked out a system of evolutionary spiritualist monadology, based upon the romantic idea of progressive reincarnation (which he found in the writings of the Polish messianic poets Adam Mickiewicz and Juliusz Słowacki). The Polish nation was presented in this system as a community of the most developed and hence most perfect spirits, leading humankind towards its final destiny: universal regeneration and salvation on earth, the prefiguration of which could be seen in the ancient Polish-Lithuanian Commonwealth. (1994, 45)

Walicki rejects Lutosławski's views as representing "only an elitist fashion, relevant, to some extent, for the understanding of the alienated modernist intellectuals but of no real significance for the processes of nation-building and national modernization in Poland" (46). Although Casanova never engaged with the more outlandish mystical beliefs that Lutosławski shared with other "modernist intellectuals" of his generation (principally the writers and artists of *Młoda Polska* [Young Poland]), basic elements of his neo-Romantic conception of Poland—notably the association of universal regeneration with Polish independence and the symbolic importance of the commonwealth—underpin her depiction of Poland in *Wolski*.

This depiction centers on the paradox that despite the central role of Poland and the struggle for Polish independence within the novel and despite the fact that the novel is subtitled "*Páginas de Polonia y Rusia*" [Pages from Poland and Russia], none of the action takes place in Poland. Although Poland is constantly in their thoughts, none of the three main representatives of the younger generation who are at the center of the novel—Enrique, Mara, and Gelcha—has ever lived in Poland. Enrique writes to Mara while he is abroad, telling her to keep her spirits up by thinking about the "delicioso estío [que] pasaremos en nuestra Polonia que tú y yo dejamos en la infancia" (Casanova, 1894, *El doctor Wolski*, 69) [delicious summer we will spend in our beloved Poland, which you and I left as babies], and although Gelcha was born in Siberia and has never been farther west than Kazan, she declares that she wants to die in Poland (170–71). When Mara finds out about her illness, she cries out, "Yo no veré nunca mi patria. . . . [S]í . . . la veré, porque en ella quiero morir" (125–26). [I will never see my homeland. . . . Yes . . . I will see it, because it is where I want to die.] Poland's lack of physical presence in the novel reflects its lack of physical presence in reality. Since 1772 the nation had been partitioned between Russia, Prussia, and Austria. Faced with the impossibility of regaining independence in the immediate future, the Poles devised other strategies for maintaining the existence of the nation. As Brian Porter has explained, "By reconceptualizing the nation as a spirit or an ideal, these Poles could sustain their national identity without depending on the immediate reestablishment of the state" (2000, 16). Their principal strategy involved the use of Polish culture, or what Porter dubs "the politics of Mickiewicz" (100).

Poland's lack of political existence allows Casanova to explore key implications of nation construction without the risk of encroaching on the public sphere of politics and the state. This is especially true from the perspective of her Spanish readers, for whom (as she remarks in the prologue) Poland was a distant and exotic concept and the novel was little more than an evocation of local color. From a Polish perspective, however, Casanova's work has far more importance in its proposition of nationalist ideals that, owing to the comprehensive repressive powers exercised by the Russian censors, could be expressed only with great difficulty within Poland itself. As John Bates writes in *Censorship: A World Encyclopedia*, the provisions of censorship

> were intended to destroy the Poles' sense of national identity, and the memory of ever having had an independent state. Censors rigorously

eliminated the terms "Polish" and "Poland" from journalistic and literary works, replacing them by "domestic" ("krajowy") or "our"; during periods of intensive repression, the term "fatherland" proved impermissible. Terms designating national dress and traditions disappeared from print; Russian censors habitually degraded Polish kings to the status of "prince." (2001, 1887)

Casanova's defense of Polish nationhood, both in her published work and in her personal life, attracted the attention of Polish politicians and intellectuals, who (unlike their Spanish counterparts) welcomed her as an active, productive asset to the Polish national cause. In a serious and perceptive review of *Wolski* published in the prestigious fortnightly journal *Świat*, the eminent Polish Romance scholar Edward Porębowicz (1862–1937) recognized with awe the wide-ranging intellectual framework of Casanova's writing:

> Rodaczka Cyda piesząca romans na tle słowiańskiego wschodu, a co więcej, w dostroju do najświeższych prądów literackich, z głębokością filozofa, gruntownością uczonego i namiętnością satyryka-socyologa . . . nie ma dość wyrazów na uczczenie takiego daru. (1894, 498–99)

> [A compatriot of El Cid writing a novel set in the Slavonic east and, what is more, in the style of the most brilliant literary currents, with a philosopher's depth, the thoroughness of a scholar and the passion of a satirist-sociologist . . . there are not enough words to describe such a talent.]

Porębowicz, like many of his fellow intellectuals, hailed Casanova as an honorary Pole who had adopted Poland as her "druga ojczyzna" [second homeland] and thus as a welcome participant in the debates about Poland's future. The contrasting reception of Casanova by those who engaged in Polish and Spanish intellectual debates about the nations and their respective futures highlights the marked difference between Polish and Spanish concepts of the nation and its borders. As we have seen, the "modern" Spanish nation was discursively gendered in masculine terms, and women—linked in this discourse with either "tradition" or "the foreign"—were thus, by implication, located outside its temporal and spatial boundaries. The result, as Casanova argued in her 1910 lecture and on many other occasions, was that women were only rarely allowed any active input into the nation's present or future development. The Polish national project, in contrast—as she shows in *Wolski*—was an inclusive enterprise, in which both men and women could play an active role. The dynamic contribution of Polish women to the intellectual, social, and even political life of the nation is a favorite topic of Casanova's—one that she would return to repeatedly in her nonfictional writing.

Wolski, then, provides an arena for Casanova to describe and participate in the Polish national project. One of her favorite strategies for achieving this goal is her ideologically loaded use of Polish cultural icons such as the works of Adam Mickiewicz and the historical paintings of Jan Matejko. As we have seen, literature and art were fundamental to Polish self-definition during the period of the partitions; Polish cultural icons have an unparalleled importance in the world of the novel, as they did in real life. Enrique's surgery, although otherwise plain and simple, is adorned with examples of Polish art, whose significance Casanova neatly explains for her Spanish readers through unobtrusive textual footnotes:

> En sencillos estantes veíanse los libros; en las paredes dos soberbios grabados, copia del célebre pintor de la historia Matejko, y en dos lienzos lindamente encuadrados brillaba la luz en dos *escenas de Oriente*, firmadas por el maravilloso colorista Siemiradzki. (1894, *El doctor Wolski*, 213, emphasis Casanova's)

> [The books were on simple shelves; on the walls were two superb engravings, copies of the well-known painter of historical scenes Matejko,[7] and illuminated on two beautifully framed canvases were two *Oriental scenes*, signed by the marvelous watercolorist Siemiradzki.][8]

The cultural media that Casanova employs extend to music and iconography. Mara distracts herself by playing Chopin mazurkas on the piano, and her room, like Enrique's, is full of significant images:

> En uno de los muros, suspendidos a la inglesa, podían admirarse cuatro copias de los más famosos maestros polacos; algunos retratos de familia, y encerrada en primoroso marco, una imagen de la Virgen de Ostrobrama, que es veneradísima en toda Polonia. (1894, *El doctor Wolski*, 54–55)

> [On one of the walls, hung English-style, for all to admire were four copies of the most famous Polish masters; some family portraits, and in a delicate frame, an image of the Virgin of Ostrobrama, who is highly venerated throughout Poland.][9]

Mara's veneration of the Virgin of Ostrobrama is the novel's only explicit reference to the Catholic Church; in comparison, pride of place in Enrique's medical chambers is given to a bust of Mickiewicz, who has his own shrine and is treated almost as a god:

> Sobre artística columna, en el hueco de dos ventanas, destacábase un busto del cantor de Polonia, del inmortal Mickiewicz, y al pie de la columna, en labrado escabel de ébano, había tiestecillos con vegonias [*sic*] y yedras, una de las cuales . . . subía apoyándose en dorados clavitos de intento allí colocados, y a la altura de la estatua curvábase y descendía como para coronar la frente del poeta. (213–14)

> [On an artistic column, in an alcove between two windows, stood a bust of the bard of Poland, the immortal Mickiewicz, and at the foot of the column, on a hand-finished ebony stool, were little pots of begonias and tendrils of ivy, one of which . . . twined up around golden nails put there expressly for the purpose and when it reached the statue, curved around and descended as if to crown the poet's brow.]

Enrique's father, Juan, shares his son's near-religious adoration of Mickiewicz. When his old friend Pominski announces that he and his daughter Gelcha (Enrique's future wife), who are visiting, must leave the village of Orloff, Juan persuades them to stay, by promising, "Por la noche leeremos un rato a nuestro inmortal Mickiewicz . . . un magnífico ejemplar de la edición prohibida por la censura" (194). [In the evening we will read a little of our immortal Mickiewicz . . . a magnificent copy of the edition banned by the censors.] For Juan, as for all Polish nationalists, the poet symbolizes the Polish struggle against Russian cultural repression: His works, which were completely banned from the time of the publication of *Dziady* in 1832 until the 1850s, were subject to censorship until well into the twentieth century.

Another strategy that Casanova and her characters use to construct their imagined Poland is the creation of a collectively authorized historical narrative that seeks to galvanize the collective national memory. Again and again, for example, they refer to emblematic events of Poland's past, such as the insurrections of 1830–1831 and 1863. Early in the novel, Mara's companion Doña María reminds Enrique of her active part in the insurrection of 1863: "Perdí a mis hijos en la revolución, y en Lituania no han olvidado aún mi patriotismo" (Casanova 1894, *El doctor Wolski*, 17). [I lost my children in the revolution, and in Lithuania they have not yet forgotten my patriotism.] Enrique's parents and Pominski also remember their participation in "el 63," which led to their exile in Siberia. This passage enables us to place the novel in a historical context. Pominski accuses Juan Wolski of "los mismos ardores que nos condujeron hace treinta y un años al otro lado del Ural" (139) [the same passions that drove us thirty-one years ago to the other side of the Urals], where they remained for fifteen years. The novel was published in 1894, thirty-one years after the 1863 insurrection, and the memories of the older generation extend the narrative back thirty-two more years, from 1863 to the previous failed insurrection of 1830–1831. Enrique tells Doña María, "Yo trabajaré y haré de mis hijos los hombres que quizás salvarán a nuestra Polonia" (16). [I will work and make my sons into the men who will perhaps save our beloved Poland.] She replies pessimistically, "Hace sesenta años que oigo esa frasecita y los redentores no llegan" (16). [I've been hearing that for sixty years and the redeemers never come.] According to the scheme, this early part of the novel would take place in 1891, exactly sixty years after the first failed insurrection. Pominski draws a parallel between his generation—the insurrectionaries of 1863—and his parents' generation—the insurrectionaries of 1830–1831:

> ¿Te acuerdas cómo nuestros padres al mismo tiempo que condenaban nuestra resolución de sublevarnos, nos daban instrucciones para la lucha y nos proporcionaban el armamento? . . . Nosotros, hoy, seguiríamos su ejemplo, porque no somos capaces de dominar el patriotismo, aunque nos conduzca a la esclavitud o a la muerte. (138–39)

> [Do you remember how our parents, even as they condemned our determination to rise up, gave us instructions for the battle and provided us with arms? . . . We, today, would follow their example, for we are incapable of curbing our patriotism, even if it drives us to slavery or death.]

The thirty years between the two insurrections and the additional thirty years between the second insurrection and the events described in the novel suggest a cyclic pattern in which Enrique's story represents the next manifestation of the struggle for independence:

> Adivinábase al mirar al doctor Wolski, que de haber nacido en el siglo XVII como Sobieski,[10] hubiera luchado por una idea generosa; contemporáneo de Kościuszko,[11] como él hubiera combatido en extranjero suelo por la libertad que no lograra para el suyo. (Casanova 1894, *El doctor Wolski*, 26)

> [It was evident from looking at Doctor Wolski that had he been born in the seventeenth century like Sobieski, he would have fought for a generous ideal; a contemporary of Kościuszko, he too would have fought on foreign soil for the freedom he had not achieved for his own land.]

Enrique is explicitly presented in the novel as the heir to the Polish national-ist struggle; the legacy of this struggle is problematic, however, for although both Jan Sobieski and Tadeusz Kościuszko were heroes of the Polish Roman-tic movement, they had signally failed to maintain (in the case of Sobieski) or restore (in the case of Kościuszko) Poland's independence. Enrique is nonethe-less certain that he will succeed where Polish heroes before him have failed. Comparing himself to another fundamental figure of Polish Romanticism, the Promethean hero exemplified by Mickiewicz's Konrad, he declares that he will not suffer the apparently inevitable fate of such heroes: "Yo sé, la razón me demuestra, que la voluntad puede robar su fuego a los dioses sin temor al castigo imaginado por la fantasía griega" (41–42). [I know, reason shows me, that will can rob the gods of their fire without fear of the punishment imagined by the Greek fantasy.] This Promethean struggle is to be carried out on behalf of both his nation and his generation. Although, like the national-ists of his parents' generation, he conflates the Polish nationalist project with the regeneration of humanity, he rejects their inclusive Romantic ideals in fa-vor of policing national boundaries and controlling or excluding groups that threaten to undermine his particular concept of progress. He is driven by con-temporary fears about the breakdown of society; the "fire" that he hopes to steal is the scientific knowledge that he believes will enable him to take con-trol of this breakdown and thus save Poland and humanity from their fate.

In their reader on the fin de siècle, Sally Ledger and Roger Luckhurst re-mark that "one of the most marked features of the fin de siècle is the authority given to science" (2000, 21), and the question of this authority is at the center of *Wolski*. The driving force behind Enrique's struggle to regenerate Poland and win the nation's independence is his realization that humanity is strug-gling to fulfill its potential. He rationalizes:

> Degeneramos porque nos faltan los dos elementos, base de las sociedades trabajadoras y fuertes: la higiene que preserva y fortifica el cuerpo, y en el orden moral un fin elevado y generoso. (Casanova 1894, *El doctor Wolski*, 49)

> [We are suffering degeneration because we lack the two basic elements of strong, hardworking societies: the hygiene that preserves and fortifies the body, and an elevated and generous moral objective.]

His answer is "estirpar el mal para que la propagación de la especie se perfec-cione" (165) [to root out the sickness so the propagation of the species can be perfected], a Darwinian solution clearly influenced by the new science of eugenics:

Todos los hombres de buena voluntad, deben emplear su energía combatiendo ese terrible enemigo de la herencia morbosa, impidiendo *en absoluto* las uniones entre personas enfermas y entre parientes. . . . Hay que atajar el mal en su origen, haciendo entender a todas las clases sociales, *que es el mayor de los crímenes dar la vida en condiciones perjudiciales al nuevo ser.* (67, emphasis Casanova's)

[All men with strength of will must use their energy to fight the terrible enemy of inherited sickliness, preventing *absolutely* unions between the unhealthy and between relatives. . . . We must attack the sickness at its root, making every social class understand *that it is the greatest of crimes to create life in conditions that are prejudicial to the new being.*]

Enrique's use of the term *degenerar* situates him and his project firmly within contemporary intellectual debates in both Poland and Spain. The twin concepts of degeneration and regeneration pervaded European thought in the last decades of the nineteenth century, as people tried to come to terms with uncertainties—inspired by the approaching turn of the century—about the future of civilization and the human race. Commenting on the origins of degeneration theory, William Greenslade observes that, "founded on the Darwinian revolution in biology and harnessed to psychological medicine, the idea of degeneration spread to social science, to literature and art. In its scientific and rational practices it offered to diagnose the agencies of the irrational component threatening the orderly progress of the society" (1994, 16). In other words, for those who were looking for someone or something to blame for the perceived disintegration of society, ideas of degeneration offered a solution. Since the possibility of changes to the status quo most concerned those who stood at the center of the threatened establishment—white, middle-class men—blame tended to fall on people who differed from their perception of the norm: nonwhite, lower-class, nonmale (or nonstereotypically male) members of society. Thus, fears of degeneration focused on four central axes: race, class, gender, and nation. In *Sexual Anarchy*, a study of gender and culture at the fin de siècle, Elaine Showalter explains why:

In periods of cultural insecurity, where there are fears of regression and degeneration, the longing for strict border controls around the definition of gender, as well as race, class, and nationality, becomes especially intense. If the different races can be kept in their places, if the various classes can be held in their proper districts in the city, and if men and women can be fixed in their separate spheres, many hope, apocalypse can be prevented and we can preserve a comforting sense of identity and permanence in the face of that relentless specter of millennial change. (1991, 4)

Situated in a time and place characterized by acute cultural insecurity, Wolski provides Casanova with the ideal means to examine the implications of these "strict border controls"—in particular, for those who are considered a threat to the nation and its future. The descriptive framework within which he is placed reflects his insecurity. He occupies an ambiguous position in both space and time, as part of a generation torn between past and future, Romantic and post-positivist beliefs, tradition and modernity. His aggression is translated, within this framework, into the language of war, making Kazan the battleground for his struggle against the menace of racial, social, and national degeneration.

Wolski lives in a world governed by the principles of "racialised Darwinism, which placed the spatial diffusion of different peoples along a single temporal axis, moving from the 'primitive' to the 'civilised'" (Ledger and Luckhurst 2000, xvii). He sees his mission in Kazan as a civilizing one, describing it in terms that echo the rhetoric of Spain's neocolonialist project, which had intensified throughout the 1880s and 1890s and which Casanova would criticize directly in her next novel. In one particularly telling example, he justifies his civilizing mission to his Russian friend María Fiodorowna:

Aseguro a usted que no hay conquistador pacífico, deseoso de captarse la simpatía y la confianza de los indígenas del país conquistado, que emplee más medios que los que voy a emplear con esas gentes. (Casanova 1894, *El doctor Wolski*, 251)

[I assure you there is no peaceful conqueror, eager to win the hearts and minds of the natives of the conquered land, who employs more measures than the ones I shall employ with those people.]

"Those people" are, of course, the non-European inhabitants of Kazan, a frontier society, a city in which (as the narrator tells us) "la civilización entra lentísimamente, como medrosa de librar batalla con los mahometanos que la habitan y con las legiones de rusos semibárbaros allí nacidos" (1) [civilization enters tentatively, as if fearful of waging war with the Muslims who live there and with the legions of semibarbarous native-born Russians]. This vision of Kazan corresponds to Enrique's vision of the world. His attitude toward the Tartars, the indigenous Russians, the "Chuwashis,"[12] and the "Chirimyses"[13] who form his potential constituency is, as Iwan points out, patronizing, to say the least. Iwan repeatedly challenges Enrique's arguments and his self-definition as a conquering hero of the "uncivilized": "¿Y con qué derechos quieres violentar a esas pobres criaturas que viven como pueden? . . . ¿Con qué derecho quieres imponer la salud a quien no la desea?" (228). [And what right do you have to violate those poor creatures who are doing their best to survive? . . . What right do you have to impose good health on anybody who doesn't want it?] Enrique offers no response; still, like many of his peers, he remains convinced that the only way to protect the dominant race from becoming "tainted" is to force the "bárbaros"—whether they like it or not—to adapt.

Enrique fears the contaminating influence of not only the ethnic minorities within his constituency but also the ethnically Russian urban poor. In this view, again, he echoes contemporary debate. Many *fin de siglo* thinkers agreed that the explosion in urban dwelling, which resulted in the subsequent growth of an urban working class, was a primary factor in degeneration. Throughout the 1870s and 1880s, Spanish novelists such as Benito Pérez Galdós (see, for example, *La desheredada* [1881]) and Emilia Pardo Bazán (see especially *La Tribuna* [1883]), following in the footsteps of Charles Dickens and Honoré de Balzac, had brought the plight of Spain's urban poor before the public eye. By the same token, Casanova's detailed descriptions of Kazan portray the poverty-stricken Bulak district through Enrique's eyes, in an unforgiving account of the destitution and degradation that he encounters when he accompanies the Russian *starowiary*[14] Sergui Serguieyewich to the home of a sick child:

> Sergui y Wolski entraron, descendieron a tientas dos escalones, y halláronse en una habitación semi a oscuras, en la cual era la atmósfera fétida e irrespirable. Allí distinguíase confusamente a la luz escasa que penetraba por la claraboya del techo, un banco, una criatura echada por tierra en un montón de paja, y sobre la *pietchka* (especie de fogón empotrado en la pared) la cabeza de otra criaturita moviéndose entre andrajos. (1894, *El doctor Wolski*, 275)

> [Sergui and Wolski went in, groped their way down the stairs, and found themselves in a gloomy room, where the air was fetid and unbreathable. They could just about make out, in the scanty light coming through the skylight, a bench, a creature laid out on a pile of straw, and on the *pietchka* (a sort of stove pushed up against the wall) the head of another little creature moving around in some rags.]

As Greenslade writes, "The post-Darwinian city was imagined not merely as a city of moral darkness and of outcasts. Here were tracts of new degenerate energies, menageries of sub-races of men and women" (1994, 38). Enrique shares in this nightmarish "imagining" of the contemporary urban landscape, where vice and disease rage hand in hand:

> Los hombres, cegados por la vanidad y el egoísmo, se agrupan, se apelmazan, se asfixian en los grandes centros. . . . El aire esparce los gérmenes morbosos, y las escrófulas, las herpes y las úlceras malignas. . . . [S]e contagian a otras gentes en la plaza, en las tiendas, en el bulak de Kazán, en el cual viven hacinadas muchas familias miserables. Por los mil medios de propagación que cada enfermedad tiene, ha llegado a nuestro país el *coltun* [*sic*], la *plica pletórica*,[15] esa repugnante enfermedad del cuero cabelludo que los tártaros nos trajeron, y que hoy, casi extinguida entre esa raza, aún existe en muchas aldeas de Polonia. (Casanova 1894, *El doctor Wolski*, 168–69)

> [The men, blinded by vanity and egoism, huddle and cling together, suffocating, in the great centers. . . . The air spreads the deadly germs, and the scrofulas, herpes, and malignant ulcers. . . . They infect others in the town square, in the shops, in Kazan's Bulak district, where many miserable families are squeezed in together. Thanks to the thousands of ways each sickness spreads, the *kołtun* or *plica pletórica* has reached our country; that repugnant scalp infection the Tartars brought us, which, today almost eradicated among that race, still exists in many Polish villages.]

Enrique lays much of the blame at the door of women—both working- and middle-class—whom he sees only in terms of their role in the propagation of the species:

> El sabía por experiencia que entre las jóvenes de los grandes centros de población, apenas una por ciento se halla en condiciones favorables de ser madre. (183)

> [He knew from experience that of the young women in the great population centers, barely one in a hundred was healthy enough to become a mother.]

As he advises María Fiodorowna:

> Emplee usted toda su energía, hasta la amenaza y el castigo con esas madres que, holgazanas y viciosas, prefieren a dejar sus hijos en las casas benéficas,

traficar con ellos moviendo a compasión al transeúnte, llevando en brazos
al pobrecito ser, que, lleno el cuerpo de llagas, deja tras sí un rastro de
infección, y está condenado a morir precozmente o a vivir hecho un idiota.
(244–45)

[You must use all your energy, even threats and punishment with those
mothers, indolent and depraved, who, rather than leave their children in
charity homes, prefer to take them begging to inspire compassion in the
passer-by, carrying the poor little thing, who, with a body full of sores, leaves
a trail of infection, condemned to an early death or to life as an imbecile.]

Enrique's relationships with the women he loves are both shaped and destroyed by his beliefs. On the evening when he falls in love with Gelcha,
we are able to follow his thoughts as he observes her in vivid physical detail,
from "el ancho seno, que un justillo sostenía sin oprimir, y que la respiración
agitaba mansamente" [the ample bosom, supported but not compressed by its
bodice, which rose and fell softly with each breath] to "las caderas amplias
bajo el talle, y la firme delineación de la pierna, que el traje permitía divinar"
(181) [the hips spreading out beneath the waist, and the firm outline of the
legs, just visible through her dress]. Then the tone changes, and he sees her
not through the eyes of a lover but through the eyes of a physician, contrasting her health and strength with the many invalids he meets in the course of
his work:

Como médico . . . fijaba su atención el cuerpo de aquella joven, sano,
palpitante de energía vital, centro de una vida perfectamente equilibrada,
que era, para sus ojos, fatigados de descubrir miserias y miserias, espectáculo
nuevo, apetecido y grato. (181–82)

[As a doctor . . . he looked closely at the young woman's body, healthy,
throbbing with vital energy, the center of a perfectly balanced life that was,
for his eyes, tired of the endless misery, a novel sight, desired and welcome.]

Finally, in one of Casanova's most naturalistic passages, Enrique sees Gelcha
through the eyes of a physiologist:

Le interesaba aquella organización . . . y complacíase examinando con el
pensamiento, a través de los tejidos y los músculos—que para la mirada del
hombre de ciencia eran trasparentes en aquel instante—los órganos motores
de la vida, activos y potentes; y seguía con la imaginación el complicadísimo

curso de la sangre, la cual, como madre cariñosa que tiene muchos hijos que alimentar, con igual solicitud envía sus calientes oleadas al cerebro, sagrario de las ideas, que a los pies, esclavos cargados con nuestro cuerpo. (182)

[He was interested in the organization . . . and took pleasure in mentally examining, under the fabric and the muscles—which were at that moment transparent beneath the scientist's gaze—the motor organs of life, active and powerful; and he traced in his imagination the highly complicated course of the blood, which, like a loving mother with many children to feed, sends its warm waves just as lovingly to the brain, sanctuary of ideas, as to the feet, slaves burdened with our bodies.]

Gelcha is no more than a vehicle for Enrique's experiments, a brood mare to supply him with the children he craves. He marries her and, metaphorically, squashes the life out of her. Our first impression of Gelcha is of the sound of her voice: She is lively, healthy, active, and robust. By imposing his beliefs on her, forcing her to live according to his "hygienic" rules—banning the theater, books, newspapers, noise, and activity—Enrique almost certainly contributes to her inability to bear a healthy child. After they are married, we see Gelcha only once before she fades out of the novel. Enrique clearly perceives a need to define and limit gender boundaries, and he acts on that need; in contrast with the way he handles race or class, however, he never explicitly voices his anxieties about women and their role.

Enrique's aggressive control of boundaries of race, class, gender, and nation on behalf of "modernity" and the future is partly a response to the sense of cultural insecurity that Elaine Showalter (1991) sees as characteristic of fin de siècle generations. It is also the result of his desire to emulate (and to outdo) the warriors and revolutionaries who people the Polish national mythology. Ultimately, however, like Sobieski, Kościuszko, Prometheus, and Konrad, he is left utterly defeated:

De su porte arrogante apenas quedaban vestigios en aquel cuerpo, que ahora encorvábase al andar, como si los músculos que le sostuvieran se hubiesen roto. La frente helada y sudorosa denunciaba flaqueza; aterradas salían de las órbitas las pupilas, y el mirar desconsolado y rebelde de Wolski en tal instante, traían a la imaginación la trágica figura de Prometeo encadenado a la roca. (Casanova 1894, *El doctor Wolski,* 301)

[Barely any traces of his arrogant bearing remained on that body, which now walked with a stoop, as if the muscles supporting it had snapped. The cold, sweat-beaded forehead indicated weakness; the eyes stood out from their sockets, and at that moment, with Wolski's disconsolate, rebellious gaze, it all brought to mind the tragic figure of Prometheus chained to the rock.]

In a final ironic twist, Enrique's hospital is destroyed by the literal manifestation of the fire he figuratively sought to steal. Our last sight of him combines images from the two myths he tried and failed to redefine, as he runs toward the flames "cual esforzado capitán . . . herido de muerte" (307) [like a courageous captain . . . mortally wounded]. By placing Enrique alongside these inherently masculine figures from the classical and military traditions, Casanova underlines the androcentric and imperialistic values of the worldview he represents. The dramatic failure of his project, on both a personal and a professional level, signals her dissatisfaction with a national project that sought to exclude all but a tiny minority from participation.

Enrique's reaction to the temporally and spatially, literally and figuratively ambiguous position in which he finds himself is aggressive, as he attempts to redefine and fix the threateningly permeable boundaries of race, class, gender, and nation in an effort to defend his vision of progress. Mara is of the same generation as Enrique and occupies the same geographical space; unlike him, however, she is a woman, and therefore she is not only excluded from but also perceived as a threat to the values he represents. Like Enrique, Mara faces the task of reconfiguring the past in order to forge the future, and throughout the first half of the novel, like Enrique—but for different reasons—she struggles against the weight of convention and the limitations this imposes on her. She is one of a long line of literary heroines in Spain and elsewhere who have to compromise their thirst for knowledge and education or suffer the consequences. She wants to study and become Enrique's equal; like her namesake in Rosalía de Castro's 1867 novel *Flavio* or Ana Ozores in Leopoldo Alas's *La Regenta* (1884–1885), however, she encounters resistance everywhere she turns. Mara's guardian, Doña María, who represents the older generation, tells Enrique that "en toda su vida [Mara] no ha hecho otra cosa que estudiar y con aprovechamiento" (Casanova 1894, *El doctor Wolski,* 21) [all her life (Mara) has done nothing but study, and with great success]. She disapproves of this behavior and later tells Mara, "Viéndote durante dos años engolfada en tus estudios, temí que perdieras tu *feminilidad* [sic]" (71, emphasis Casanova's). [Seeing you absorbed in your studies for two years, I feared you would lose your *femininity*.] Members of the younger generation too, or at least the male half, equally disapprove of the idea of women's participation in education. At the beginning of the novel, as Enrique's friends wait for him to emerge from his doctoral viva, one comments:

Para mí, en el caso de nuestro amigo, no sería lo peor ni la presencia del Claustro en pleno, ni las preguntas de los estúpidos, ni las miradas de los cientos de estudiantes que llenan la sala, sino la asistencia de tantas mujeres. ¿Qué vienen a hacer las mujeres a estos actos universitarios? (4–5)

[For me, in our friend's place, the worst thing would not be the presence of the full governing body, or the questions from the idiots, or the gazes of the hundreds of students filling the room, but the presence of so many women. What can women be doing at these university events?]

Enrique himself is not so dismissive. He encourages Mara to come to the viva, although afterward he admits that his motive is not exactly selfless: "¡Me hubiera gustado tenerte cerca de mí, poder mirarte!" (13). [I'd have liked to have you close by, to be able to look at you!] When he chastises her for not showing up, she explains:

He ido a la Universidad, he atravesado aquel laberinto de aulas y corredores, y cuando llegué a la puerta de la sala, atestada de gente, te oí, me detuve y se me ocurrió una tontería. Figúrate que pensé que mi presencia podría distraerte, y no me atreví a entrar. Desde la puerta he oído toda la discusión. (12–13)

[I went to the university, made my way through that labyrinth of lecture halls and corridors, and when I got to the door of the room, crammed full of people, I heard you, I stopped, and I had this foolish thought. Imagine this, but I thought my presence might distract you, and I didn't dare go in. I listened to the whole discussion from the door.]

The difficulty of Mara's journey to the room where Enrique is receiving the Holy Grail of education, his doctorate, clearly symbolizes the difficulties she faces in her own education, where receiving a doctorate is naturally out of the question. Enrique interprets her decision to wait outside as evidence of her timidity, which he seems to find attractive, but it also shows her awareness of his desire to silence and objectify her as an image. By waiting outside, she removes herself from his gaze, and from the disapproving gaze of his friends, which allows her to listen to the proceedings and engage in them intellectually on her own terms.

The gulf between the real Mara and the image that Enrique and others have of her is one more example of the ambiguity of her position, as she negotiates the conflict between her desire for education and independence and the demands of social acceptance. Her sometimes difficult relationship with Doña María is a constant reminder of this conflict. Doña María fulfills the role of protector of "the nation" that Nira Yuval-Davis identifies as empowering older women "to rule on what is 'appropriate' behaviour and appearance and what is not and to exert control over other women who might be constructed as deviants" (1997, 37). Yuval-Davis's observation that "as very often this is the main source of social power allowed to women, they might become fully engaged in it" (37) explains Doña María's anxiety when she reminds Mara, "Tú serás el ángel tutelar de ese hogarcito tan higiénico, tan confortable y tan polaco como Enrique lo sueña" (Casanova 1894, *El doctor Wolski*, 59). [You will be the guardian angel of that dear little home, as hygienic, comfortable, and Polish as Enrique dreams it.] As Mara struggles to complete her studies while Enrique is away, Doña María pressures her to fulfill the duties of the stereotypical angel of the hearth. She can condone Mara's longing for education as long as it is the result of "ese deseo que tu cariño te da de no ser en instrucción inferior al marido para poder seguirle y ayudarle" (72) [the desire, born of your love, not to be less well educated than your husband so you can follow him and help him]. Similarly, she is not against women's education in principle, but she believes that it should be restricted to the aesthetic sphere:

A los sabios no les disgustan las mujeres *mujeres*; es decir, con sus inclinaciones delicadas, risueñas, superficiales alguna vez, que no quitan nada a la seriedad, base del carácter, pero que lo equilibran. (72, emphasis Casanova's)

[Learned men are not put off by *womanly* women; I mean, with their delicate, smiling, sometimes superficial inclinations, which take nothing away from the fundamental seriousness of character, but balance it.]

Refusing to accept Doña María's limitations, Mara continues to study and tells her guardian that "el estudio es el mejor auxiliar de los gustos de la mujer" (71) [study is the greatest helpmate of womanly tastes]. Meanwhile, she pacifies her guardian by carrying out the domestic duties she is assigned, leading Doña María to remark with relief:

Ya sé que tu buen sentido y tus aficiones artísticas te hubieran preservado siempre de caer en la tentación de hacerte *sabia* a la manera que lo suelen ser las mujeres olvidadas de su sexo. (72, emphasis Casanova's)

[I see now that your good sense and artistic inclinations would always have kept you from giving in to the temptation of becoming *learned* in the manner of those women who forget their sex.]

Mara is very good at playing the part that is required of her, but under stressful circumstances, her facade cracks. When she becomes ill, she refuses to accept that fact and accuses Doña María of stifling her and contributing to her illness:

> Alguna culpa tiene usted en todo esto, porque con sus cuidados y sus mimos, parece que soy de cristal. Me arropa usted como dama ociosa a gatito friolero. (96)

> [Some of the blame in all this is yours, because with all your fussing and flapping, it's as if I'm made of glass. You wrap me up like a lady of leisure does a pet kitten.]

In a later passage, filtered through Enrique's point of view, as it were, Casanova makes the link between the constraints placed on female bodies and minds and the physical weakness that was central to the concept of "femininity":

> [Enrique] veía pasar por su memoria un sinnúmero de adolescentes flácidas, anémicas, sin vigor, prensadas en los corsés, que son una barrera puesta al desarrollo en la pubertad y el grillete del sistema venoso. . . . Y viendo desfilar por su memoria la legión de adolescentes cuya miseria fisiológica aumenta una educación absurda y un género de vida irrazonable y perturbador, el médico comparaba con aquellos cuerpecillos linfáticos y débiles, el cuerpo robusto de [Gelcha]. (183)

> [(Enrique) saw in his mind's eye an endless number of weak, anemic, lifeless young women, squeezed into corsets, which are a barrier to normal development in puberty and the shackles of a poisonous system. . . . And seeing in his mind the parade of a legion of young women whose physiological misery augments an absurd education and an irrational and disturbing way of life, the doctor compared those lymphatic, weak little bodies with the robust body of (Gelcha).]

This passage illustrates the hopelessness—for the women who are subjected to the "miseria fisiológica," the "educación absurda," and the "género de vida irrazonable y perturbador" that constitute middle-class respectability—of living in a world governed by men like Enrique. The consequence, Mara's and Gelcha's experiences suggest, is inevitably sickness and an inability to function in either of the roles made available to them—as wives or as mothers.

There is, however, an alternative to Wolski's exclusive, masculine, imperial world. The final chapter of the novel, in which Casanova describes Mara's life in Lithuania, can be read as a manifesto for Casanova's alternative vision of the nation. The fact that Mara, having extricated herself from Enrique's demands, has survived considerably longer than anticipated, makes her decision to leave Enrique in essence an act of self-preservation. As we have seen, Enrique's treatment of Mara's replacement, Gelcha—who is healthy, strong, and apparently an ideal mother—is probably the principal cause of their newborn's ill health and Gelcha's subsequent infertility. Mara was well aware of the limitations imposed by Enrique's vision of their future, which positioned her as a silent producer of children.

Mara's life in Lithuania stands in sharp contrast to her life in Poland. In Lithuania, women are the driving force of society. Mara and Doña María have overcome their differences to work together to run a school for poor children. Mara teaches the children, feeds them, and—with her customary parting words, "si Dios quiere" (Casanova 1894, *El doctor Wolski,* 318) [God willing]—reminds them that human life is in God's hands. Although Lithuania appears idyllic, Mara and Doña María are aware that it is not perfect. Male violence can still intrude, as in the case of "la mujer de Wenceslao" [Wenceslao's wife]. Doña María reports:

> Ha venido hoy llorando como una Magdalena. Figúrate que su marido ha vuelto a pegarla, la arrojó de la choza y ha vendido los aperos de labranza y todo el ajuar. Hoy no tenía la pobre un bocado de pan para su hijo. (319)

> [She turned up today crying like a Magdalen. Just imagine, her husband has starting beating her again, he threw her out of their hut, and he has sold the farm tools and all the crockery. Today the poor thing didn't even have a mouthful of bread for her son.]

Mara's response is immediate: "¡Infeliz! . . . [Q]ue venga y vivirá con nosotros" (319). [Poor thing! . . . She must come here and live with us.] Female solidarity is the only solution in a world where the balance of power in male-female relationships is still tipped decisively in favor of men, and it must be maintained without regard to class or race. As Mara tells Enrique on the day of his viva, "El dolor no tiene nacionalidad" (16). [Suffering has no nationality.] Similarly, where Enrique sees the impoverished children of the Kazan Bulak as subjects to be conquered, Mara empowers the poor Lithuanian children by giving them access to the education that she had to struggle so hard to gain.

That this idyllic community is located in the former Polish territory of Lithuania and not in the metropolitan center of Warsaw is acutely significant for both the feminist and nationalist elements of Casanova's case. The two states had been joined by the Union of Lublin in 1569. Although the union became void under partition, Lithuania—as the birthplace of the great bard Mickiewicz—was vital to the nineteenth-century conception of Poland. As Tomas Venclova has observed, throughout the nineteenth century, there existed a "myth of Lithuania as 'the shadow' of Poland, the counterculture which presented a foil for the West—in a word, the archetypal 'other' for the Polish Crown—[which] enabled Mickiewicz to create an anticanonical paradigm which supplanted the cultural soliloquy of the Polish Enlightenment" (1998, n.p.).[16] The opposition between Lithuania and Warsaw was predicated as the opposition between spirit and reason as well as between tradition and modernity. According to Venclova:

> There was an old tradition of juxtaposing "sylvan" Lithuania to
> "agricultural" Poland, and also of opposing Lithuanian backwardness to
> Polish civilization; at the same time, Lithuanian gentry more often than
> not interpreted their lack of refinement as a sign of antiquity and nobleness,
> looking at the "people of the Crown" (*koroniarze*) with ill-concealed disdain.
> (n.p.)

When Casanova was writing *Wolski* in the early 1890s, the Romantic idea that "el corazón de Polonia está allí [en Lituania] como está en Varsovia su cerebro" (316) [the heart of Poland is in Lithuania, just as its brain is in Warsaw] was still current. Polish writers such as Eliza Orzeszkowa (in *Nad Niemnem* [On the Banks of the Niemen], 1887), and the Nobel laureate Henryk Sienkiewicz (in his *Trilogia*, 1884–1888) evoked an idealized Lithuania that symbolized the Polish nationalists' enduring faith in the commonwealth and its values.

Significantly, the Wolski family, their friends the Pominskis, and Mara's family are all originally from Lithuania, and at times the terms *Poland* and *Lithuania* are used interchangeably. Gelcha declares, "Yo . . . quiero morir en *Lituania*" (Casanova 1894, *El doctor Wolski*, 170, emphasis mine). [I want to die in *Lithuania*.] Enrique responds, "¿Usted no ha estado nunca en *Polonia*?" (170, emphasis mine). [Have you never been to *Poland*?] Casanova's interchangeable use of *Poland* and *Lithuania* recalls that of Mickiewicz: As Venclova observes, "In the well-known poem *The Review of the Army*, in *Pan*

Tadeusz and many other works, Mickiewicz . . . used the word 'Litwin' ('Lith-uanian') as a perfect substitute for 'Polak' ('Pole')" (1998, n.p.). In Casanova's description of Enrique, her contention that he is not "empequeñecido con los refinamientos de la moda varsoviana" (1894, *El doctor Wolski,* 25) [diminished by the refinements of Warsaw fashion] evokes the Romantic emphasis on tra-ditional national values (symbolized by insular, untainted Lithuania) over the ephemeral fashions of Warsaw, which are exposed to all sorts of dangerous foreign influence. It also shows that, at least on the surface, Enrique has not entirely rejected the values that Lithuania represents.

The seemingly straightforward restoration of moral order at the end of the novel follows nineteenth-century convention; Wolski, the Promethean tragic hero, is punished for his arrogance, whereas Mara's forbearance and apparent renunciation of her "unfeminine" ambitions are rewarded with survival and a return to her longed-for homeland. For a reader invested in the critical stance that Casanova has adopted up to this point, however, the sudden switch in tone to one that suggests complicity in the dominant view of women's place in the world is hard to swallow. I have found Rita Felski's explanation of the role of nostalgia in modern constructions of gender (particularly the femi-nine) very useful in untangling the threads of the novel's conclusion. Mara's ending can certainly be read as a perfect illustration of the Romantic view of women as "a redemptive refuge from the constraints of a modern civilisation identified with a growing materialism, the worship of scientific reason, and an alienating urban environment" (Felski 1995, 38). After undergoing a profound psychological crisis on discovering her illness, Mara turns to God. The imag-ery used to describe her from this point on is unequivocally Christian. Mara is compared variously to a martyr, an angel, and a saint; her decision to leave Enrique can be read as an example of selfless sacrifice, as it enables Enrique to be true to his ideals. The final paragraph of the novel appears all too explicitly to support this interpretation:

> En la diáfana serenidad de la tarde vibró pausado y melancólico el *Angelus*; Mara cruzó las manos sobre el pecho, y a través de los frondosos árboles, los rayos del sol que se apagaba descendían sobre su cabeza, colocando un nimbo de luz en sus sienes. (Casanova 1894, *El doctor Wolski,* 320)

> [In the diaphanous serenity of the evening, the *Angelus* resounded slowly and melancholically; Mara folded her hands on her breast, and through the abundant trees, the rays of the setting sun descended over her head, placing a halo of light on her temples.]

According to this reading, Casanova's description of Lithuania as an idealized, pure, traditional space reflects the "explicit temporal inflection" that Felski identifies as underpinning "this sentimental elevation of the feminine" (1995, 39). In particular, Casanova's evocation of "los ecos de las selvas seculares" (1894, *El doctor Wolski*, 315) [the echoes of the centuries-old forests] can be explained with Felski's observation that woman came to be identified with "the lost cyclical rhythms of a preindustrial organic society" (1995, 39). We might argue, however (following Roberta Johnson), that Mara's actions—setting up a commune for battered wives, making education universally available—are indeed modern: socially modern. Although Casanova does not insist on the role of organized religion, the early allusion to Mara venerating the Virgin of Ostrobrama provides a Catholic framework for Mara's actions. Far from the backward-looking, repressive Catholicism of Inquisitorial Spain, however, Mara's is the new, social Catholicism, which promoted a woman-centered ethos based on philanthropy and caring.

In this reading, Lithuania's importance lies in its simultaneous distance from and centrality to the metropolitan (and thus largely masculine) center of Poland and, as such, in its function as what the feminist geographer Gillian Rose (1993) terms a "paradoxical space." According to Rose, the concept of paradoxical space allows resistance to the hegemonic concept of space, structured around polarities (between mind and body, real and metaphorical, public and private spaces) and exclusions. We have already seen how such polarities and exclusions shape Wolski's view of the world. Paradoxical space, by contrast, allows the (female) subject both to acknowledge the way her life is shaped by the limitations of hegemonic space and to resist these limitations—to function as "both prisoner and exile" (Rose 1993, 15). The chief benefit of paradoxical space (which helps to explain the differing readings of Lithuania at the end of *Wolski*) is that "it allows the subject of feminism to occupy both the centre and the margin, the inside and the outside" (ibid., 155). In other words, Casanova is deliberately employing imagery that can be evoked in support of either reactionary or utopian arguments. As Felski points out, "The assumption that an authentic female culture would reverse the instrumental and dehumanising aspects of urban industrial society has been a recurring motif within both feminist and nonfeminist thought" (1995, 38). As a result, a reader invested in Wolski's androcentric, neo-Romantic world vision can understand the final chapter as reinforcing woman's distance from the modern, returning Mara (and, through her, the Polish nation) to her rightful place. In contrast, a reader for whom modernity must include both men and women can see Mara's move to Lithuania as an escape from the constraints of Wolski's world and as the creation of a new "paradoxical space" that draws on the best of the old world and the new. Casanova's vision of the nation in the final chapter of *Wolski* juxtaposes tradition—symbolized by the "recuerdos de otra edad" (1894, *El doctor Wolski,* 315) [memories of another age] that pervade the Lithuanian setting—with modernity, evident in Mara's reconfiguring of social roles to place women as a dynamic force at the center of society. Where Enrique's vision was based on exclusion and subjugation, Mara's is founded on inclusion and empowerment.

El doctor Wolski offers us a new perspective on the *fin de siglo* not only as a rare example of a Spanish novel set outside Spain but also as a consciously feminist intervention in pan-European conversations about fin de siècle fears of the breakdown of society. Casanova adopts the vocabulary of these conversations, examining universal questions through the specific prism of the Polish situation, which, although real to her, distances the narration from her Spanish readers. Through her use of the exotic (to Spaniards, at any rate) Polish setting, Casanova maintains the fiction presented in the prologue that this is simply an anodyne *costumbrista* narration. In consequence, the impact of her authorship is minimized, and the serious theoretical points she makes about the process of nation construction can pass beneath the radar.

The efficacy of Casanova's fiction of authorship hangs on our interpretation of the final chapter of the novel, which turns on the many available readings of Lithuania. When the fiction is maintained, Wolski's failure—and Mara's success—can be read as reflecting a belief that faith, rather than science, should be the ultimate source of guidance for humankind. Poland will be free if the Poles keep faith in God; humankind will be regenerated when scientists regain their faith; tradition, located in the emotive space of a bucolic Lithuania, will prevail. Casanova's many cues, however, can lead one to read the novel as a critique of the androcentric nature of the values that Enrique represents—his egotism, his godlessness, his desire to subjugate and exclude. In this reading, the final chapter of the novel can be viewed as a manifesto for Casanova's utopian vision of a future that is based on reconfiguration rather than rejection of the past and that is supported by faith, inclusion, and empowerment. The conclusion of *El doctor Wolski* is problematic, in part deliberately so, and Rose's concept of paradoxical space provides some means by which to unravel the maneuver that Casanova performs in the final chapter. Nevertheless, it is difficult to read the novel today without being aware that, despite its claims to inclusion, the alternative to Enrique's world that Casanova offers—based as it is on the middle-class, ethnically Polish women of whom Mara is the principal representative—is, in its way, equally limited.

CHAPTER 3

Andalusia–Madrid–Africa

Lo eterno (1907)

Despite (or perhaps because of) the success of *El doctor Wolski*, it would be thirteen years before Sofía Casanova published her second novel, *Lo eterno* (1907).[1] The need to avoid overt controversy—in life as well as literature—was particularly pertinent to Casanova at the time of *Lo eterno*'s publication, as she struggled to reestablish herself in Madrid after an absence of nearly two decades. In the years between the publication of *Wolski* and the publication of *Lo eterno*, she had continued to write in a variety of genres and had published not only a number of short stories and articles (in periodicals as diverse as *Revista Gallega*, *Galicia Moderna*, *Revista Contemporánea*, and *España Artística*) but also the travelogue *Sobre el Volga helado*, which appeared in book form in 1903. In addition, she had published some forty individual poems in Galician, Spanish, and Latin-American periodicals and the poetry anthology *Fugaces* (1898). During the previous decade, her personal life had been particularly traumatic, with the death of her five-year-old daughter, Jadwiga, in September 1895. The Lutosławskis returned to Galicia for Christmas in 1895, to allow Casanova to recuperate with her family. They remained there until April 1898, after their fourth daughter, Halina, was born. During this time, Casanova took the opportunity to renew contact with the world of Galician culture. She attended meetings of the *Cova Céltica* group of Galician intellectuals, published in Galician journals, and rekindled her friendships with eminent Galician writers and politicians, such as Manuel Murguía and Manuel Lugrís Freire. In November 1899 the family returned to Kraków, where Wincenty Lutosławski had a post at the university. Thanks to the relative freedom afforded by the government in the Austrian partition of Poland, turn-of-the-century Kraków was the hub of Polish art and culture, and Casanova became friends with many of Poland's most prominent writers and artists, including members of the avant-garde *Młoda Polska* [Young Poland] movement. By the time the Lutosławskis relocated their family to Warsaw in early 1907, however, their marriage was all but over.

Lo eterno, which was published while Casanova spent the summer of 1907 in Madrid, marks the start of her determined reentry into the world of Spanish letters. The following year, she would return for what she intended to be a permanent stay in Madrid, taking her own house and leaving only at the outbreak of war in 1914. Ofelia Alayeto claims that "during this period [1907–1914] she produced two different types of work. Her journalism focused on Eastern Europe. But her creative poetry and fiction were deeply personal expressions, and resonated with the nationalism that had emerged with Spanish literature as a reaction to the crises and bitter realisations of 1898" (1992, 56). This claim is something of a misrepresentation. Although it is true that Casanova's fiction in this period is engaged with questions of Spain and Spanishness to a greater extent than either her earlier or her later work, that engagement consists of problematization—not celebration—of the dominant national discourse. Where *Wolski* provides a cautious, deliberately distanced examination of national identities, *Lo eterno* is far bolder and looks much closer to home. Set in Casanova's native Spain, it replaces *Wolski's* critique of the positivist response to fears about the *fin de siglo* breakdown of national, racial, and sexual boundaries with an exploration of the dogmatic Catholic response to those fears. Where Enrique Wolski is secure in his privileged position as an educated, white male, *Lo eterno*'s Juan struggles to define himself against familiar models of priesthood and masculinity; where Wolski's overriding concern is with racial purity, Juan is himself a racial hybrid (an Andalusian Moor). The contemporary anxieties embodied in the church's fears about the perceived threat of Juan's racial heritage coupled with the author's very real concerns about getting published produce a double-layered narrative in which the reader must navigate between orthodox and subversive readings of Juan and his story.

Modern readers, however, do not seem to have discerned the complex nature of the narrative. The limited critical attention that the novel has received falls in line with Casanova's own (largely unfounded) reputation as a right-wing conservative, whereas its apparent adherence to the norms of romantic fiction has led critics to view it as a straight romance. A brief summary of the novel's plot seems to bear this out: It is the story of a reluctant priest (the Andalusian Juan) who falls in love with the poor but virtuous Consuelo, suffers a dramatic crisis of identity, first tries to prevent but then eventually facilitates Consuelo's marriage to the man she loves, and ultimately leaves Spain to work as a missionary in Africa. Carolyn Galerstein and Kathleen McNerney claim that despite Casanova's attempt at subtlety, the novel is basically conventional: "Although the temptation and salvation scenes are melodramatic, Casanova attempts a psychological study before invoking the martyrdom typical of the genre" (1986, 70). Janet Pérez, who is of the same opinion, observes that the novel "is tainted by melodrama and more than the required dose of plot complications . . . [and that] the conflict is resolved via the stereotypical device of martyrdom" (1988, 20). Alayeto is equally skeptical: "*Eterno* is a curious blend of novela rosa 'romance novel' and psychological study. In its parallel love stories involving Father Juan and Consuelo, it is full of clichés and heads towards the inevitable happy ending" (1992, 59). Writing in 2001 and referring to the 1920 edition, Rita Caterina Imboden offers this summary: "Describe a un joven cura que se enamora de su prima y que finalmente abdica de sus pasiones y se convierte en misionero en África, donde lo veneran como a un santo" (74 n. 83). [It describes a young priest who falls in love with his cousin and eventually renounces his passion and becomes a missionary in Africa, where he is venerated as a saint.] Leaving aside the fact that Consuelo is not Juan's cousin (although she is Lola's, for whom she also acts as governess), this reading not only makes no advance from the Galerstein and McNerney reading fifteen years earlier but also seems less nuanced. Not one of the scholars who has written on the novel has commented on Juan's ambiguous racial identity or the implications of his final move to Africa.

A summary of *Lo eterno*'s plot demonstrates why so many readers have been taken in by the apparently straightforward moral message. The novel begins with an interview between Juan (the young Andalusian priest) and his uncle, the bishop. The bishop is dismayed because, against the church's teachings, Juan has given a suicide victim a Christian burial (chapter 1 of the novel). To try to tame Juan, the bishop sends him to Madrid to serve as chaplain to the aristocratic Villabrizo family (chapter 2 of the novel). Over the next six months, Juan falls in love with Consuelo, a poor cousin to the family who is working as a governess for Lola, the daughter of the condes de Villabrizo (chapter 3 of the novel). Consuelo is keeping what she believes to be a terrible secret: She has been seduced and abandoned by her cousin, the son of the family she is living with. Juan secretly watches as she writes a letter to her cousin, informing him that he has made it impossible for her to marry her suitor Ramiro Álvarez, a professional man who is a friend of the family (chapter 4 of the novel). Juan's sudden realization of his love for and jealousy over Consuelo sends him into a spiritual and psychological crisis, and he resolves to leave the Villabrizo family the next day (chapter 5 of the novel). The next morning, however, he finds himself drawn back to the palace, where Consuelo—who has no idea of his feelings for her—asks him to hear her confession. She wants him to act as an intermediary to help her tell Álvarez that although she loves him, she cannot marry him (chapter 6 of the novel). After spending a night torn between the demands of his religious vows and his desire for Consuelo, Juan decides that if he cannot have Consuelo, no one will (chapter 7 of the novel). Instead of conveying Consuelo's message to Álvarez, Juan tells him that Consuelo does not want to marry him because she does not love him. As he walks back to the palace, he realizes what he has done and collapses from the shock (chapter 8 of the novel). After a week on the verge of death, during which he struggles with his conscience, Juan decides to confess the truth and bring Álvarez and Consuelo together (chapter 9 of the novel). The final chapter, in the form of a letter from a nameless priest to Juan's uncle the bishop, recounts Juan's missionary work in Africa, where he founds leper hospitals and ten years later dies rescuing a drowning man from a shipwreck (chapter 10 of the novel).

This summary shows the novel to be structured around a series of the well-worn plot devices that are key to sentimental fiction: the "expert ascriptions of sentimentality [that] mark moments where the discursive processes that construct emotion become visible" (Howard 1999, 69). Juan's character—the increasingly monstrous man behind the cassock—recalls what Rachel Blau DuPlessis calls "the doubled men of Gothic fiction" (1985, 45), whereas Consuelo's self-imposed suffering brings to mind "the masochistic powerlessness of the generic female" whose persecution is a central motif in the melodramatic, suspenseful Gothic genre (44). The episode with the letter, which leads to Juan's first crisis, is a classic example of suspense designed to keep the reader turning the pages, as the author deliberately withholds information about Consuelo's "secret" to maintain the mystery and pique our interest. At this point we have not yet been told where Consuelo's affections lie (we find out at the same time as Juan, during her confession in chapter 6), so the unknown recipient of Consuelo's letter and the mysterious "farsa vergonzosa" (Casanova 1907, *Lo eterno*, 48) [shameful farce] to which she alludes intensify the tension. Although Lola believes that Consuelo is in love with Álvarez, Consuelo denies it, and the reader—like Juan—is left to wonder whether the priest might be the object of her affection. Our expectations are shaped by the literary commonplace of the forbidden love between a priest and a woman, sometimes successful (consider Juan Valera's *Pepita Jiménez* [1874]) but more often not (consider Abelard and Heloise or Fermín and Ana in Leopoldo Alas's *La Regenta* [1884–1885]). After this rollercoaster of emotion, the novel's denouement—as Juan's disclosure enables Consuelo's marriage to the man she truly loves—satisfies the reader's expectations. Moral order is restored as Juan returns to the side of good and Consuelo achieves the Holy Grail of the romantic heroine.

It is certainly true that a first reading of the parallel stories of Juan's and Consuelo's struggles against the authority of the church—in Juan's case because he is a reluctant priest, and in Consuelo's case simply because she is a Spanish woman—seems to show a conventional restoration of moral order. Furthermore, in this reading the novel appears to celebrate the role of the church as Spain's gatekeeper and arbiter of moral order and ultimately its part in the neoimperial project of the first decade of the twentieth century: Juan seems to become an agent of colonial (and patriarchal) power, whereas his Andalusian Moorish blood is simply a justification for the imperial project. As satisfying as this reading may be to a reader who is emotionally invested in the idea of the restoration of moral order and the "script of heterosexual romance" (DuPlessis 1985, 2), however, to accept it at face value is to do Casanova a great disservice; although she clearly wants this reading to be available, a variety of cues suggest a radically different alternative. Critics such as Tania Modleski (1982) and Janice Radway (1984) have shown that the popular romance is characterized by its remarkable ability to transform in response to prevailing moral and social trends; consequently, it does not seem incongruous that *Lo eterno* should address issues of public interest. Certainly, *Lo eterno* is, from the start, a much angrier and more overtly critical novel than *Wolski*. This is evident in the prologue to the first edition (1907), in which Casanova responds to the anonymous editor of an unnamed weekly publication, who had rejected the manuscript of the novel, calling it "scandalous" and asking Casanova whether she had forgotten how to write for people "south of the Pyrenees."[2] Indignantly—and not without a hint of alarm—she responds:

¿Será posible que mi expatriación me haya dado convicciones éticas y puntos de vista artísticos que difieren absolutamente de los de aquí?

　¿Seré ya tan *extranjera en mi patria* que no perciba la pulsación de su vida psicológica, y que este drama de un alma—a la cual reverencio por su fuerza traspasada de sombra y su innata orientación al bien—*escandalice* a las gentes? (1907, *Lo eterno,* 5–6, emphasis Casanova's)

[Is it possible that my absence has given me ethical convictions and artistic points of view that differ entirely from those here in Spain?

　Am I now such a *stranger in my own land* that I cannot perceive the pulsation of its psychological life, and that this drama of a soul—which I revere for its strength in escaping the shadows and its innate orientation to good—*scandalizes* people?]

Casanova's anger reflects her dissatisfaction (so frequently expressed during this part of her career) with the limited and limiting narratives of nation that dominated *fin de siglo* literature. Although she always keeps a pragmatic eye toward the need to pay lip service, at least, to respectability, in *Lo eterno,* as in her other works, she deliberately pushes the boundaries of acceptability. Consequently, it is possible to trace an alternative reading of the novel that belies Casanova's claim in the prologue that this is simply a rather anodyne moral fable. In fact, as we will see, Casanova uses her characters to enter into important public debates about the future of the modern nation.

Looking at the significance of Juan's racial hybridity and his last years as a missionary in Africa in the context in which they were written is the key to revealing Casanova's engagement with these debates. Casanova was not the only author to have brought together questions of church, race, and colonialism during this period: Although their views were very different from Casanova's, Emilia Pardo Bazán (*Una cristiana* [first published in 1890]) and Benito Pérez Galdós (*Nazarín* [1895]) had also written of Moorish or Moroccan-identified priests (Hooper 2006b).[3] The recurrence of this apparently paradoxical figure clearly reveals one of *fin de siglo* Spain's most pressing concerns. Since the mid-nineteenth century, Spain's desire to be seen as a world player in the colonial game despite the rapid decline of the Spanish Empire had inspired a renewed interest in its African neighbor. For a turn-of-the-century reader, *Africa* as used in *Lo eterno* most likely meant North Africa, or specifically Morocco, which (dating from the loss of the American colonies in 1898) was, from both a military and a commercial point of view, the most significant of Spain's overseas interests. The loss of the Cuban markets meant Spanish industries needed new buyers, and, particularly in Catalunya, there was a great deal of enthusiasm for commercial expansion into Morocco (Balfour 2002, 141). The 1904 agreement with France that gave Spain responsibility for security in part of Morocco fanned the Spanish desire for international recognition in the wake of the defeat of 1898, bringing the Moroccan question back into the public eye. As Sebastian Balfour argues:

Spain's new role in Morocco re-awakened imperialist aspirations amongst the military which had lain dormant since the Disaster. . . . For any officer steeped in military traditions, North Africa was imbued with a mythical resonance. Popular myth had turned the messy and occasionally disastrous skirmishes with Moroccan tribes of the nineteenth century into heroic campaigns. (1997, 184)

During the first decade of the twentieth century, Balfour explains, Morocco took on a new significance in Spanish culture. Whereas "the traditional perspective had seen North Africa in terms of an unfinished religious crusade against the infidel," it was now also viewed as providing "a new role for the military as the trail-blazers of modern civilisation against barbarism" (185). The colonial relationship with Africa was inevitably shaped by the ongoing conflict between Spain's Islamic past and Catholic present. Although traditionalist ideologues such as Marcelino Menéndez y Pelayo and later Ramón Menéndez Pidal sought to reduce the Islamic period of Spain's history to a parenthesis in a teleological Catholic narrative (Tofiño 2003, 142), they also saw the value of a shared history as a tool in the colonizing struggle. The clash of *castizo* (racially pure) and multicultural narratives of Spanish history and identity was thus central to arguments that justified Spain's colonial expansion. Justification for the colonizing mission itself was found in the deathbed request of Isabel la Católica to her heirs, in which she asked them to continue the conquest of Africa with the help of the church (Pedraz Marcos 2000, 31). Perhaps inevitably, this request led to the 1880s foundation of the Sociedad de Africanistas and to the 1883 departure of the Congregation of the Sons of the Immaculate Heart of the Blessed Virgin Mary (Claretians) to set up a mission in the Gulf of Guinea (Pedraz Marcos 2000; Tofiño 2003). The effect was to inscribe the church as a colonial agent, as ideologues began to discuss "Spain's African vocation"—a phrase that, as Gustau Nerín shows, was central to the Francoist discourse of the 1940s (1997, 11). It is precisely this concept, and specifically its gendered implications, that Casanova places under scrutiny in *Lo eterno*.

The focus for this scrutiny is the novel's main protagonist, Padre Juan. Juan is a true racial hybrid, whose face "denotaba el tipo, tan frecuente aún en España, del moro andaluz que se formó de las almas de dos razas enemigas, cuando el amor creaba venturosas alianzas entre los cristianos y los sarracenos" (Casanova 1907, *Lo eterno*, 11) [denoted the figure, still so common in Spain, of the Andalusian Moor formed from the souls of two enemy races, when love created chance alliances between Christians and Saracens]. Given the central role of the church in the Spanish social fabric, the use of a priest as protagonist is not, in itself, particularly surprising; men of the cloth are common figures in modern Spanish literature. A number of recent studies, such as those by Ricardo Krauel and Maryellen Bieder, have drawn attention to the way literary priests—such as Fermín (*La Regenta*), Julián (*Los pa-*

zos de Ulloa), Gil Lastra (*La fe*), and even Serafín (a minor character in *Una cristiana*)—can function as a bodily site for exploring anxieties about gender and social change (Bieder 1990) or as a means of testing new ways of writing gender identities (Krauel 2001). My contention is that Casanova refines this strategy to employ the paradoxical figure of the Moorish priest as a means of probing not only gender but also racial anxieties. As a racial hybrid, Juan embodies the establishment fears about the breakdown of boundaries of gender, race, and class that were central to fin de siècle culture. In *Lo eterno* these fears are conflated with the fear of hereditary transmission of physical and moral degeneration that Casanova had already explored in detail in *Wolski*. *Lo eterno* explores the reactionary response to these fears as Juan is forced into the church by his mother and her bishop brother (1907, 16–17) in order to save him from the degenerative influence of his Moorish side, represented in the present day by his freethinker father (20).

Juan's story thus explores the consequences of the church's attempt to counter the "threat" of racial and moral degeneration through force. It traces his growing awareness that the church is the primary agent in an oppressive, patriarchal society that exerts power through the maintenance of firm boundaries between self and other, masculine and feminine, public and private. These boundaries are vividly represented in the novel through Casanova's careful portrayal of Juan's negotiation of the acutely gendered and racialized maps of modern Spain. Alayeto's observation that the novel contains "fine descriptive passages on Madrid's urban life" (1992, 59) draws attention, albeit only in passing, to the fact that *Lo eterno* is alone among Casanova's works in being set chiefly in Madrid. Furthermore, although we do not discover the fact until chapter 8, the action takes place in that pivotal year, 1898 (1907, *Lo eterno*, 102). Madrid is a city sharply divided along gender lines. Consuelo's story takes place entirely within the walls of the Villabrizo palace, a private, feminine space open solely to the widowed countess and her family—daughter Lola, niece Consuelo, a series of priests and friars, and a number of elderly relatives "que como la Condesa vivían del todo entregados a las exterioridades religiosas" (29) [who, like the countess, were completely in thrall to religious appearances]. Meanwhile, Juan's inner journey is paralleled by his journeys along and across the lines between the private and public spaces of the city. The narrative takes him from his native Andalusia to the enclosed world of the medieval palace in the Austrian quarter of Madrid (chapter 2 of the novel). For some time after he arrives in Madrid, we see him only inside the palace, but as he comes to question his priestly vocation and to rebel against the generic ambiguity that it imposes, Juan spends more and more time outside the palace, in Madrid's public spaces. He wanders the medieval alley-ways around the palace as he tries to come to terms with his doubts (chapter 6 of the novel); he follows the Carretera de Segovia to gaze at the sierra that reminds him of home (chapter 7 of the novel);[4] he takes the Calle de Alcalá to the Retiro, where he debates whether to transmit Consuelo's message to Álvarez (chapter 7 of the novel);[5] he visits Álvarez in the Salamanca neighbor-hood (chapter 7 of the novel); and finally he joins the crowds in the Plaza de la Lealtad, where, against the backdrop of the monument to those who have sacrificed themselves for Spain, he makes the momentous decision to sacrifice himself for Consuelo (chapter 8 of the novel).[6] Significantly, all mention of Madrid is excised from the 1926 edition, with the Villabrizo palace relocated from Madrid to "una escondida y medioeval capital de Galicia" (1926, *Lo eterno*, 153) [a remote, medieval Galician provincial capital], and most of the descriptive and symbolic scenes are simply cut. The effect of these changes, which I discuss in more detail as they arise, is to strip the novel of an entire layer of meaning. Perhaps most significantly, in the 1926 edition Juan loses his racial ambiguity to become a pure Galician hidalgo: "Moreno el enjuto rostro, pronunciadamente aguileña la nariz, garzos los ojos, entre soñadores y fieros, todo en aquella cabeza denotaba el hidalgo galaico" (140). [His narrow face brown, his nose decidedly hawklike, his eyes pale, somewhere between a dreamer's and a wild beast's, everything about that head denoted a member of the minor Galician nobility.] Paradoxically, however, although Casanova's revisions may have been intended to neutralize the critical view of church and nation in the original, their effect—at least for the scholar with access to both versions—is to throw the excised passages into even sharper relief.

Casanova's vision of Madrid as a city divided into public (masculine) and private (feminine) spaces can be read in terms of debates about the politics of space, as a valuable contribution to the still-hypothetical development of a female-authored urban literature in Spain. In *A Female Vision of the City*, Christine Sizemore observes that representations of urban life throughout early twentieth-century Western literature are inherently gendered and that until the "late modernist" period "it was the male imagination and the male experience that shaped the view of the city" (1989, 2). Based on a detailed reading of Casanova's works and an initial reading of those of many of her fe-male contemporaries, my postulation is that the *fin de siglo* is a time of transi-tion in female-authored representations of space and, particularly, of the city. With respect to the fin de siècle, Michael Ugarte has observed that "there is a dearth of urban women's literature of any kind" (1996, 19), and—with the major exception, as always, of Pardo Bazán, whose urban novels take in both

provincial cities (*La Tribuna*) and Madrid (*Insolación* and *Una cristiana*)—
this is as true of Spanish women's writing as of any other. On the whole, pre-
twentieth-century women writers in Spain as elsewhere focus on the domestic
spaces of home and church, keeping the city firmly in the background. Ugarte
suggests that "women represent the city according to its parts, its ecological
niches, rather than in its ever-expanding and incoherent wholeness" (1996,
20), whereas Sizemore argues that "the city . . . has been a confining factor
in women's experience in nineteenth- and early twentieth-century literature"
(1989, 3–4).

By the time Casanova wrote *Lo eterno*, the situation was changing. Public
spaces such as the Ateneo, the theaters, and even—to an extent—the universities were opening up to women, and Casanova (along with contemporaries such as Emilia Pardo Bazán, Concepción Gimeno, María Martínez Sierra, and Carmen de Burgos) took advantage of the rapprochement to map
out their own visions of Madrid. Female-authored representations of the city
would come to maturity in the 1920s and 1930s with the work of writers such
as Margarita Nelken and Rosa Chacel. Works such as Concepción Gimeno's
Una Eva moderna (1909); Blanca de los Ríos's *La niña de Sanabria* (1907),[7] *Las
hijas de don Juan* (1989 [first published in 1907]), and *Madrid goyesco* (1908);
many of the works of Gregorio and María Martínez Sierra, Carmen de Burgos's *El veneno del arte* (1910), *Los negociantes del la Puerta del Sol* (1989 [first
published in 1919), and *La rampa* (2006 [first published in 1917]); and Casanova's *Lo eterno* and *Más que amor* (1908), however, are among those that show a
growing awareness of the city's possibilities. Like so much literature by *fin de
siglo* women, the majority of these works remain largely unknown; where they
are studied, moreover, it is often in isolation from more general literary and
cultural trends. *Lo eterno* is a comparatively early example of detailed urban
representation in a female-authored novel; central to its vision of the city is its
assumption of a connection between masculinity and access to public spaces.

Casanova's telling of Juan's story plays on this assumption. As a priest who
occupies a position on the borders of race, class, and gender, Juan embodies
the fears about the breakdown of these borders that drove men such as Enrique Wolski. In contrast with *El doctor Wolski*, however, which focuses on the
downfall of a man who is supremely confident in himself and his vocation,
Lo eterno examines—through its protagonist's quest to become "a man like
any other"—the nature of the identity he is trying to assume. In other words,
whereas *Wolski* takes Enrique's androcentric version of Polishness as a given
(albeit an unpalatable one), *Lo eterno* describes and contests dominant concepts of both Spanishness and masculinity. Juan's difference from his peers
is clear from the novel's opening passage, in which the volatility of his fea-

tures denotes a certain ambiguity, a fluidity that sets him apart from his still, silent companions. This passage, set in the Episcopal palace of an unnamed Andalusian (or Galician in 1926) city, uses a device seen also in Pío Baroja's *Camino de perfección* and Azorín's *La voluntad*: the introduction of "descriptions of paintings to underscore certain philosophical tendencies," which Roberta Johnson suggests is "a practice doubtless inspired by the authors' reading of decadent literature" (1993, 52). We get our first glimpse of Juan as he waits silently for his uncle in an antechamber watched over by "una copia del Cristo del Velázquez, acentuando el carácter conventual y frío de la estancia" (Casanova 1907, *Lo eterno,* 9) [a copy of Velázquez's Christ, accentuating the cold, convent-like character of the room]. The description of Velázquez's *Cristo crucificado* "Christ crucified" (circa 1630) anticipates the chilly lack of sympathy that the church will show toward Juan's suffering.[8] Meanwhile the priests waiting with Juan are as static as works of art—one middle-aged and one elderly, the three generations suggesting the coexistence of past, present, and future or perhaps foreshadowing the life that awaits Juan within the church. Although "las figuras adquirían el relieve especial y casi negativo de las de segundo término en algunos lienzos religiosos de Zurbarán" (10) [the figures took on the special and almost negative relief of those in the background of some of (Francisco) Zurbarán's religious canvases], Juan lends a dissonant note to the portrait: "Aquella cabeza . . . copiada por el pincel o el buril resultaría dura—porque la movilidad de la fisonomía daba a las nobles facciones su encanto peculiar" (11). [That head . . . copied by the paintbrush or the sculptor's knife would seem rigid—for it was the mobility of the physiognomy that gave his noble features their peculiar charm.] It is this mobility, in a world where church and state set social roles and there is no room for negotiation, that is the driving force behind Juan's struggle. One could read the novel as the story of his quest for the self—the "tú propio"—that the church, in the shape of his uncle, has denied him. Juan becomes increasingly aware that the church is the primary agent in the maintenance of an oppressive, patriarchal society that exerts power through the construction of firm boundaries between self and other, masculine and feminine, and even good and evil and heaven and hell. Indeed, the first hint of the church's commitment to the patriarchal system occurs in the palace, when the bishop compares it to an army:

Para organizar y dirigir un ejército, todo general tiene que haber aprendido a obedecer. . . . Nuestra fuerza moral es una garantía de la victoria. Es con *la voluntad* y *la intención* con los que vencemos, no con actos exteriores solamente que a veces son fruto de la *costumbre* o de la *indiferencia*. (20, emphasis Casanova's)

[If he is to organize and direct an army, every general must have learned to obey. . . . Our moral strength is a guarantee of victory. It is with *will and intention* that we will win, not merely with superficial acts, which can sometimes be the fruit of *habit* or *indifference*.]

Catholic dogma privileges will over the degenerative menace of hereditary determinism; however, the bishop neither foresees the other (environmental) determinism that will affect Juan in Madrid nor appreciates Juan's conflict with the restraints that the church imposes on him. When he arrives in Madrid, Juan finds the Villabrizo palace not dissimilar to the Episcopal palace, where the imprint of history remains undisturbed and past and present coexist:

Álzase desde hace cuatro centurias en un silencioso barrio de Madrid viejo, inmediato a la histórica iglesia de Santa María. . . . [E]l soplo del progreso que da a las grandes ciudades modernas nerviosa y prosaica agitación no ha pasado aún por allí, y si ha pasado, lo ha hecho respetuosamente, sin remover casi el polvo del suelo que guarda la huella de históricas pisadas, y sin conmover los sillares de aquellas viviendas que nos muestran el deteriorado escudo señorial sobre el portalón de mohosos herrajes. (25–26)

[It has stood for four centuries in a silent part of old Madrid, just beside the historic church of Santa María. . . . The breath of progress that gives great modern cities a nervous, prosaic agitation has not yet passed through there, or if it has, it has done so respectfully, barely disturbing the dust on the ground that preserves the trace of historic footsteps, and without stirring the stones of the houses, each with its dilapidated coat of arms above the front door with its rusted ironwork.]

The suggestion of foreshadowing—or the coexistence of past and present—embodied in the novel's opening image of the three priests is even more explicit in Casanova's depiction of the Villabrizo palace. The Villabrizo family is in decline. Devoted Carlists, they donated their fortune to the beloved pretender Don Carlos and then withdrew from society (1907, *Lo eterno*, 29). The Villabrizo palace is a world of legend, history, and tradition; it is dominated by the church, but—significantly—it borders Madrid's old Moorish neighborhood, the *barrio de la Morería*. The Villabrizo palace represents conservative Spain, dogmatically Catholic but unable to distance itself from its Moorish antecedents. It evokes a history contained not in the deeds of politicians and statesmen but in la leyenda caballeresca, la emboscada por los celos urdida, las luchas y la existencia de muchas generaciones que han desaparecido en la eternidad, y que nos inspiran respeto y cariño porque representan ideas, transformaciones y hechos genuinamente nacionales. (26)

[chivalric legend, the jealousy-inspired ambush, the struggles and lives of many generations who have disappeared into eternity and who inspire in us respect and affection because they represent genuinely national ideas, transformations, and deeds].

The passage recalls Miguel de Unamuno's distinction between history (the series of chronological events that interest historians and journalists) and what he terms "intrahistoria" (the continuous, often-ignored essence of a people), which he compares with the difference between surface waves and the depths of the sea. For Unamuno, the sea of intrahistory—the lives of the silent masses—is where the eternal tradition and also, paradoxically, the nation's future are to be found. In *En torno al casticismo*, he writes, "Hay que buscar *lo eterno* en el aluvión de lo insignificante" (2000, 29, emphasis mine). [We must seek *what is eternal* amid the torrent of insignificance.] Thus, Juan's quest for meaning in his life takes place against a symbolically loaded background. The palace where his struggle is played out is a microcosm of conservative Spain, where the individual must contend with the weight of legend, oppressive social realities, and fears about the future.

In his meeting with his uncle, Juan observes, "Yo no debía ser cura" (Casanova 1907, *Lo eterno,* 16) [I should never have been a priest]; like his better-known contemporaries Antonio Azorín and Fernando Ossorio—the protagonists of two classic Generation of 1898 novels—however, he lacks any ideological or practical direction. He knows only that his instincts lead him toward the liberty and freedom of expression that the church denies him:

Yo no sé qué quiero. . . . [Y]o no sé qué me falta. Algo interior, inexplicable. . . . Nada de cuanto encierra el mundo apetezco, nada envidio. Sólo los breñales y la soledad de mi sierra me atraen: sólo una diversión me apasiona, la caza. ¡Si yo no quisiera ser rico, ni casado, ni feliz! . . . Pero tener libertad. . . . ¡Oh! Sí, tener libertad es lo que necesito. (22)

[I don't know what I want. . . . I don't know what I need. Something internal, inexplicable. . . . Nothing in all the world appeals to me; I covet nothing. Only the breeze and solitude of my native mountains attract me:

only one diversion impassions me, hunting. I never asked to be rich, or
married, or happy! But to have freedom. . . . Oh! Yes, to have freedom, that's
what I need.]

The freedom that Juan most desires is freedom of expression: "ser libre, libre,
para decir a los hombres que vienen a mí cuanto siente mi corazón, sin trabas
ni fórmulas" (22) [to be free, free, to say to the men who come to me everything I feel in my heart, without impediments or formulas]. This is a desire
that he shares with Consuelo and that he himself will deny her when he fails
to convey her message to Álvarez. As Juan comes to realize that his false vocation and public image deny him the freedom to express his love for Consuelo,
his inability to express himself freely obsesses him. If he were not a priest, he
believes, "al menos yo podría hablarla libremente, adorarla a gritos o en silencio" (62) [at least I could talk freely to her, adore her aloud or in silence]. The
gulf between Juan's public image and vocation as a priest and his desire for
freedom causes him increasing bodily discomfort, which he focuses on his
robes: "Yo puedo romper mis cadenas y llegar a ser libre. . . . Los hábitos me
queman como si fueran de hierro candente" (61). [I can break my chains and
become free. . . . The robes burn me as if they were molten iron.] At the same
time, he yearns for an escape from the oppressive atmosphere of the palace,
whose iron gates prevent his flight (67). When he finally manages to breach
the apparently impermeable boundaries of the palace, he is shocked to find
that he unthinkingly returns within minutes: "¿Cómo he podido volver aquí?
Es la costumbre, la ley de la costumbre, más fuerte que yo, que me trae a mi
capilla en la que durante meses y meses, a esta misma hora decía misa" (69).
[How can I have arrived back here? It's habit, force of habit, stronger than
I, that brings me to my chapel, where for months and months, at this very
time, I used to say Mass.] Once he has acknowledged the determinist forces
from which his uncle tried to save him, Juan gives himself up to them, asking, "¿Qué culpa tengo yo si las circunstancias de mi existencia me coloquen
en tan cruel alternativa?" (85). [What fault is it of mine if the circumstances
of my life offer me such a cruel choice?] He struggles to replace his priestly
identity—which he views as having been forced on him—with a new identity shaped by the discourse of Darwinism: He repeats again and again, "Soy
hombre como los demás. . . . Tengo el mismo derecho como los demás" (81).
[I am a man like any other. . . . I have the same right as any other.] He argues,
"Lucho por la existencia como lo hacen todos los seres de la creación" (87).
[I struggle for existence like every being in creation.] Taking up the military
images that the bishop used in chapter 1, he reimagines them not in terms of

the church's mission but in terms of the diametrically opposed evolutionist struggle for life:

> La guerra es la guerra y no todos los combatientes están en iguales condiciones. . . . Yo tengo, hoy por hoy, las mejores posiciones, estoy en mejores circunstancias para maniobrar con mi ejército. . . . Soy como el lobo que cae sobre el rebaño cuando está dormido. . . . Todos somos lobos en la vida. (82)

> [War is war and not all combatants are the same. . . . Today it is I who occupies the best positions, who is in the best situation to maneuver my army. . . . I am like the wolf that falls upon the flock while it is sleeping. . . . We are all wolves in this life.]

Still, in another example of the narration that probes the gap between religious appearances and hidden agendas, Juan is unwilling to give up the privileges that his priesthood affords him:

> ¿Cuándo podré desprenderme de ti, odiosa negrura, pregón mentiroso de mi estado, eslabón de mi cadena . . . ? Pronto, sí, pero todavía no. *Tú eres mi salvo conducto para entrar en casa de Álvarez.* . . . Los curas servimos para todo, enterramos a los muertos, casamos a los vivos, cristianamos . . . y hoy me toca a mí dar unas solemnísimas calabazas. Ja, ja, ja. ¡Cuándo digo que servimos para todo!
>   ¡Ea! Cúbreme bien y que bajo tus pliegues no se eche ver la piel del lobo. (89, emphasis mine)

> [When will I be rid of you, hateful blackness, lying herald of my state, link in the chain that holds me . . . ? Soon, yes, but not yet. *You are my safe-conduct to enter Alvarez's house.* . . . We priests are good for everything; we bury the dead, marry the living, carry out christenings . . . and today I am to perform a terribly solemn breakup. Ha, ha, ha. I did say we're good for everything!
>   Ha! Cover me well and make sure nobody can glimpse the wolf skin beneath your folds.]

As Juan begins to define himself as a man rather than a priest, he begins to move out of the palace, and we see him more and more often in public spaces. The novel's climax takes place in the Plaza de la Lealtad [Loyalty Square]—Madrid's monument to those who have died for Spain—where Juan's increasingly fractured self-image is mirrored by the way other people view him. Once again, the narrator appears to be questioning whether one can—or should—trust a priest:

[Muchacha 1]	—Las penas de los clérigos mejores serán de soportar que las nuestras. Al fin y al cabo van por otro caminito en el mundo. . . .
[Muchacha 2]	—Por otro caminito. . . . Sí . . . por el de su vocación, pero nadie les quita de ser hombres de carne y hueso.
[Muchacha 1]	—Pero son curas. . . .
[Muchacha 2]	—Pero son hombres. . . .
[Chulo] —	Ese, como todos los jesuitas habidos y por haber, será un mal tío. . . . ¡Pues si por ellos anda perdida España!
[Soldado] —	¡Mentira! (Casanova 1907, *Lo eterno,* 98–99)

[(Girl 1)	A priest's unhappiness must be harder to bear than ours. At the end of the day they take another path through the world. . . .
(Girl 2)	Another path. . . . Yes . . . the path of their vocation, but nobody's saying they aren't men of flesh and blood.
(Girl 1)	But they're priests. . . .
(Girl 2)	But they're men. . . .
(Jack-the-lad)	That one, like every Jesuit past and future, is likely a bad sort. . . . It's thanks to them that Spain's going down the drain!
(Soldier)	Liar!]

With this passage, the narration explicitly locates Juan's quest within debates about the role of the church and the clergy that were taking place in Spain at the time. While the girls recognize that the concept of the priesthood is problematic, the *chulo* and the soldier who springs to Juan's defense take up dogmatic positions on either side of the argument over anticlericalism. Juan is caught in the middle. Although the *chulo*'s anticlericalism reflects Juan's own frustration with the church, Juan is attracted to the patriotic, faithful Andalusian soldiers because their accents evoke memories of his childhood and of his life before Madrid. Ultimately, however, as the soldiers describe the effects of their experiences in Cuba—a description whose earthy realism contrasts sharply with more mystical interpretations of the defeat—he is disabused of his idealism:

Crea usted, padre, que si nos rendimos en Santiago, fue porque nos lo
ordenaron, y con las ordenanzas no hay bromas. . . . Se acabó la *huerga* y
ahora a trabajar el campo, si es que podemos, porque la verdad, los miembros
se nos han quedao como pajuelas, con la quinina. (102, emphasis Casanova's)

[Believe me, Father, if we surrendered in Santiago, it was because we were
ordered to, and you don't joke about orders. . . . The *party*'s over and now
it's off to work in the fields, if we can, because the truth is that our arms and
legs are like straws, from the quinine.]

Having made this statement, the soldiers disappear into the swell of people,
and Juan—unable to follow—realizes that he cannot emulate them. The soldiers ask him to accompany them. They tell him, "Usted también es hombre como los demás" (Casanova 1907, *Lo eterno*, 103). [You're a man like any
other.] He responds, however, "¡Un hombre como los demás! No. Yo estoy
solo en el mundo y me están vedadas la alegría, la familia, ¡hasta mi juventud
es un pecado!"(103–4). [A man like any other! No. I'm alone in the world, and
happiness, family, are forbidden to me; even my youth is a sin!] Juan's revelation is set against the triumph of the matador in the bullring behind him and
the ensuing series of cultural archetypes that signify glorious death:

Resonaba la música de la Plaza entonando una marcha triunfal, y con salvas
de aplausos saludaban allá dentro en el redondel a las cuadrillas, al frente
de las cuales iban los cuatro matadores, que sonreían levemente al público,
serenos, con la serenidad elegante de los gladiadores amaestrados a caer con
gracia. (106)

[The music from the plaza rang out in a triumphal march, and the assistants
were greeted in the ring with salvos of applause; in front of them were
the four matadors, smiling slightly at the public, serene, with the elegant
serenity of gladiators skilled at falling with grace.]

That Casanova considered this passage key to the alternative, "scandalous"
reading of the novel is clear from its virtual excision from the 1926 edition.
In the revised version, the entire conversation between the two girls and the
chulo is reduced to the first two lines of the original, changed only by the introduction of a single Galician idiom: "Filliña" (210) [Dearie]. At this point,
Juan experiences his revelation and goes straight home: The absence of the
soldiers, anticlerical *chulo,* and *toreadores* removes any symbolic element

from the passage and recasts the novel as a simple story of Juan's search for redemption.

In both versions of the novel, once Juan is forced to confront his treatment of Consuelo, he is plunged into a nervous depression from which he recovers only after he resolves to undo the damage he has done and bring Consuelo and Álvarez together. Casanova clearly uses the relationship between Juan and Consuelo to exemplify the relationship between men and women in the Spanish society in which *Lo eterno* is set. Initially, Juan empowers Consuelo by teaching her to understand and value the antiques and treasures that they find in the palace. As he struggles to take on a masculine identity, however, he begins to question her rationality and his behavior becomes increasingly oppressive—"¡Eh! Que saben a veces las mujeres lo que dicen y lo que desean" (Casanova 1907, *Lo eterno*, 84) [Ha! Women hardly know sometimes what they mean or what they want]—and then, through his abuse of his role as liaison between Consuelo and Álvarez, he takes away her voice. Only when he rejects the masculine identity that he has been trying to assume does he realize the significance of his actions and resolve to restore Consuelo's right to choose her own future. Interestingly, although both Juan and Consuelo are haunted by the lack of opportunity for self-expression that society affords them, it is in the passages about Consuelo that the authorial voice—a public voice, addressing a reader outside the text—is most in evidence.

Consuelo's entire story is played out within the walls of the Villabrizo palace. The room she and her cousin Lola occupy is an oasis of light and modernity enclosed within the walls of the gloomy, antique-filled ancestral palace. As the narrator points out, a room can be convenient literary shorthand for character: "Cada mueble, cada objeto en el cuarto de una mujer es un símbolo de sus gustos y de sus inclinaciones" (Casanova 1907, *Lo eterno*, 31). [Every piece of furniture, every object in a woman's room is a symbol of her tastes and inclinations.] This room, then, and those who occupy it appear to exemplify the popular conception of Spanish womanhood. There is a sewing box, a book of devotions, a rosary, and paintings; in short, as the narrator notes approvingly, "Todo hablaba de la mujer que hace del hogar su reino. . . . [B]ien podía decirse que la piedad y el sentimiento de lo bello *apacible* eran notas dominantes de quienes allí habitaban" (31, emphasis Casanova's). [It all spoke of the woman who makes of her home her kingdom. . . . It could certainly be said that piety and the feeling of *peaceful* beauty were the dominant notes of those who lived there.] Piousness and the passive appreciation of beauty are defining qualities of the sentimental protagonists of the domestic novel who survived into the early twentieth century—such as Carmencita in Concha Espina's *La niña de Luzmela* (1909)—and they are to be expected in the sort of work that Casanova (in the prologue) claims *Lo eterno* to be. Looking deeper into this passage, however, the reader will notice that all is not as it seems. The rosary is there, yes, but it is pushed to one side, "allí olvidado" (31) [forgotten there]. The paintings are not simply ornaments; the women are in the process of painting them: "Sobre un caballete había un lienzo sin terminar, y las rosas que copiaba parecían recién cortadas, tal era la frescura del color y la delicadeza de los detalles que acusaban la fina pincelada de una mano femenina" (30–31). [On an easel was an unfinished canvas, and the roses painted there seemed recently cut, such were the freshness of the color and delicacy of the details, which all suggested the subtle brush strokes of a female hand.] For Lola and Consuelo, confined to the palace, artistic creation is a form of self-expression during

> los días monótonos de la existencia sedentaria de la mujer española, que imaginativa y sensible cual ninguna consuela sus pesares o teje sus ilusiones inclinada sobre el bastidor, haciendo una de esas primorosas labores de aguja que revelan la paciencia hermana de la sumisión y la fantasía creadora del arte. (32)

> [the monotonous days of the Spanish woman's sedentary existence; imaginative and sensitive like no other, she consoles her sorrows or weaves her illusions as she leans over the tapestry frame, stitching one of those delicate needlepoints that reveal patience, sister of submission and the creative fantasy of art].[9]

The authorial voice here expresses clear dissatisfaction with the demands of a society that requires women to be little more than pious and passive bearers of children. This does not, of course, mean that we should read *Lo eterno* as an explicitly feminist text: Although the narrator criticizes the life that Consuelo and Lola—like the vast majority of middle-class Spanish women—are expected to lead, the characters themselves question neither this life nor the patriarchal system that confines them to the private space of the palace. Like Mara in *Wolski*, constantly scolded by Doña María for studying instead of performing her household duties, Consuelo is constantly under pressure (from herself and those around her) to act in a "feminine" way. She is not a feminist heroine in the modern sense, challenging the existing order and actively working for a female-centered alternative. In this sense, she differs from her predecessor, *Wolski*'s Mara, who leaves her oppressive, middle-class life and fiancé and founds a female community. Unlike Mara, Consuelo is initially cowed by the weight of tradition and expectation that the palace represents.

With Juan's help, however, she and Lola gain a semblance of control over the palace, cataloguing the many antiques and treasures that surround them:

> Las jóvenes descubrían entonces novedades y bellezas que no sospechaban siquiera que existían, porque ninguna de ellas gustaba de entrar en aquellos aposentos donde los retratos antiquísimos y los muebles del tiempo de los retratos, envueltos en húmeda penumbra, causábales viva impresión muy semejante al miedo. (34)

> [The young women then discovered new and beautiful objects whose existence they had never even suspected, for neither of them liked to enter the rooms where the ancient paintings and equally old furnishings, enveloped in dank shadows, inspired in them a vivid feeling very similar to fear.]

If the palace represents a society ruled by the church and the traditions and expectations that it defends, then Consuelo and Lola's newfound interest in its many treasures—which helps them to overcome their fears and to see the palace with new eyes—suggests a way for women to play an active role in society without threatening the system. The question is, of course, what that role might be. Just as Juan had to take up, try on, and ultimately discard the masculine roles made available to him within the national discourse, so Consuelo must confront a series of feminine roles, each of which reflects an aspect of "literaturized" Spanish womanhood: the Virgin, the fallen woman, the domestic angel, the poor spinster. Bieder has argued that the process of literaturization is characteristic of male authors of the period:

> As iconoclastic as they are in seeking to redefine the boundaries of authorship, genres, and reading in their fiction, they approach female characters principally through re-literaturization. That is, they suppress the individuality of most of their female characters and form them instead into familiar literary models, thus making the experience of reading the female one of repetition and recognition. (1992, 304)

Casanova's treatment of Consuelo in *Lo eterno* examines this process at work; significantly, it is self-imposed as much as outwardly imposed. The first time Consuelo appears in person, in chapter 3, she is virtually silent, listening—and occasionally reacting—to Lola's persistent attempts to define her. Lola, who sees Consuelo as both poor relation and domestic angel, tells her cousin, "Tu vida por ejemplo es mucho más penosa que la mía. Huérfana . . .

sin hogar. . . . Mira, yo no me hago ilusiones acerca de tu situación" (Casanova 1907, *Lo eterno,* 36). [Your life, for instance, is much more difficult than mine. Orphaned . . . without a home of your own. . . . Look, I'm under no illusions about your situation.] She tells Juan that Consuelo's reluctance to marry her suitor, Álvarez, can have only one motivation: "Es por abnegación, por deber hacia nosotros por lo que no se casa. . . . Quiere pagarnos la hospitalidad, el cariño que le tenemos, no separándose de mí, consagrándome toda su vida" (42–43). [It's from abnegation, from duty to us that she won't marry. . . . She wants to repay our hospitality, our affection for her, by not leaving my side, dedicating her whole life to me.] Consuelo protests this view weakly; however, like Lola and Juan, at this point the reader is still unaware of Consuelo's reasons for resisting her companions' insistence that "el matrimonio es la única carrera de una mujer" (41) [marriage is the only career for a woman]. There is a hint, nonetheless, of another possible outlet for Consuelo: the act of writing. Like the other female protagonists of Casanova's novels—Mara, María Cruz, and Laura—Consuelo uses letters to communicate her most intimate feelings. Unlike Casanova's other heroines, however, Consuelo suffers from what Gilbert and Gubar have termed "the anxiety of authorship" (1978, 55–92). Alone in her room, she begins a letter but she finds it difficult, crying, "Es imposible, no puedo. . . . ¿A qué ensangrentar su corazón con el relato de aquella farsa vergonzosa? . . . No puedo" (Casanova 1907, *Lo eterno,* 48). [It's impossible, I can't do it. . . . Why bloody his heart with the story of that shameful farce?] At this point, the authorial, "public" voice intervenes to give Consuelo's anguish significance beyond her own personal story:

> No hay punta acerada que penetre tan honda como los argumentos de una mujer honrada al acusarse de sus flaquezas, ni hay humano enemigo que luche tan despiadadamente, como lo hacen la conciencia y la voluntad, después de un desastre, al que asistieron aquélla dormida sobre rosas y ésta hipnotizada por el sentimiento. (50)

> [No steel blade can penetrate so deeply as the arguments of an honorable woman accusing herself of weakness, nor does any human enemy fight as pitilessly as conscience and determination after a disaster, which the former slept through on a bed of rose petals while the latter was hypnotized by emotion.]

This passage links Consuelo's personal "disaster" with the abstract subordination of conscience and determination to sentiment. In other words, although Consuelo has, in the past, played the role of sentimental heroine in her own "farce," she is now conscious that in doing so, she turned herself into a victim. Her attempt to write her own story might be read as mirroring the attempt of the woman writer to regain control over the figure of woman in literature. Consuelo's need to write is intimately linked to her sense of self, as the words are almost a physical part of her: "Y cada renglón fino, igual, parecía sobre la blancura del pliego hilo de negra sangre caída de una herida sin cicatrizar" (50). [And each neat, even line appeared on the white of the parchment like a thread of black blood dripping from an unhealed wound.] Once she has put into writing the story of how her cousin seduced her by tricking her into a sham nocturnal wedding ceremony presided over by a friend dressed up as a priest and then informed her that he would be marrying someone else, she reads the letter aloud to herself and tears it up, symbolically destroying her nascent role as subject. Immediately thereafter, she accompanies Juan to prayers with the countess, returning to a world where women must be pious and silent. Her intention is "expiar, hora tras hora, mi locura" (51) [to expiate my madness, hour after hour], and she views her only means of accomplishing this as imitating the countess, giving herself over to religion. The depiction of the countess that follows, however, highlights Casanova's suspicion of *beatería* [ostentatious devotion], at least in its officially sanctioned form:

> La Condesa, vestida de negro . . . bella con esa belleza de la demacración ascética que no llega al desmoronamiento de las facciones, tenía parecida de expresión y de actitud con la santa imagen.
>
> Bajo las tocas blancas de la Virgen los párpados caían sobre las pupilas llenas de lágrimas, y la boca fina contraíase expresando el más terrible dolor de una madre. . . .
>
> Bajo la cabellera blanca, los párpados fatigados de la Condesa, velaban los ojos húmedos, los labios descoloridos por el continuo suspirar de la penitencia, entreabríanse, apenados, y las manos de largos dedos de color de marfil cruzábanse como los de la imagen sobre la negra vestidura. (54–55)

[The countess, dressed in black . . . beautiful with the beauty of ascetic emaciation that all but obliterates the features, adopted an expression and pose similar to the sacred image.

Beneath the Virgin's white veil, her eyelids were lowered over tear-filled eyes, and her delicate mouth was pursed with the most terrible anguish of a mother. . . .

Beneath the countess's white mane, her exhausted eyelids, her dewy eyes were watchful; her lips, discolored from constant penitential sighing, half-opened painfully, and her hands, with their long marble-colored fingers, were folded like those of the image, above her black robe.]

Casanova's ironic comparison of the countess and the Virgen de los Dolores exposes how they differ in one significant way; whereas the Virgin is a symbol of maternal love, the countess is barely aware of her own role as a mother. For Consuelo, the consequences of accepting the church's dictates and following in the countess's footsteps unquestioningly are foreshadowed when she asks Juan to hear her confession and facilitate her effort to emulate her patron. Ironically, unaware that he is no longer what he seems, she trusts him implicitly: "Sólo usted, todo bondad y cristiana fortaleza, puede ayudarme a seguir el camino que debo seguir" (73). [Only you, sir, all goodness and Christian fortitude, can help me take the road I must follow.] The consequences of this misplaced trust are grave. As soon as Consuelo enters the chapel, like the countess, she loses all semblance of life and individuality: "Semejante a mortuoria aparición, vestida de negro y envuelta la cabeza en las ondas de un manto . . . en el sombrío y silencioso fondo del confesionario una rígida silueta negra, parecía un cadáver en entreabierta tumba" (76). [Like a deathly apparition, clad in black, her head enveloped in the folds of a scarf . . . a rigid black silhouette in the shadowy, silent depths of the confessionary, she resembled a cadaver in a half-opened tomb.] It is important to note, however, that this is not a rejection of faith; Casanova's description of the Villabrizo chapel carefully distinguishes (as in *Wolski*) between the church as an institution and individual places of worship and personal faith, for which she has an almost mystical respect:

De los centenarios muros emanaba la admósfera [*sic*] especialísima del templo húmeda, cálida, perfumada por los incensarios y los cirios olorosos; atmósfera peculiar de las iglesias españolas que penetra las almas haciéndolas vibrar con intensa emoción religiosa. . . . Inefable atmósfera de beatitud que predispone a místicos transportes. (75–76)

[From the centuries-old walls emanated the singular atmosphere of the damp, warm sanctuary, perfumed by incense burners and aromatic candles; an atmosphere peculiar to Spanish churches that penetrates the soul, making it vibrate with intense religious emotion . . . An ineffable atmosphere of devotion that prompts mystical elation.]

This is the last time Consuelo actively intervenes in the novel until the penultimate chapter. She transfers her agency to Juan and asks him to act as her public voice, since she is unable to leave the private space of the palace to visit Álvarez herself. Yet another example in which the narration probes the borders between appearances and what lies beneath is evidenced by the reader's awareness that Consuelo has no idea of the ever-increasing gap between Juan's public image as a priest and his increasingly fractured self-image and that her trust is therefore misplaced. Just as Casanova argues in *La mujer española en el extranjero* that the fate of Spanish women in entirely in the hands of Spanish men (1910, 37), from this point forward, Consuelo's fate is entirely in the hands of Juan. She has to trust that Juan will relay her message accurately, and, of course, he does not. The implication is that until women are permitted to speak for themselves in the public space, they can have no real power over their own lives.

The culmination of Consuelo's story provides the romantic resolution and restoration of moral order that a reader invested in the novel as a sentimental romance will have been expecting from the start. When she reappears in chapter 9 of the novel, it is to find out—now that Juan is recovered enough to talk—what happened in his interview with Álvarez: "Aunque esperaba el alejamiento definitivo de su pretendiente, ante la realidad tuvo momentos de desesperación invencible. Se le hizo insoportable la vida, sin ver, siquiera de lejos, el ser que más amaba en el mundo" (Casanova 1907, *Lo eterno,* 113). [Although she expected her suitor to distance himself for good, the reality caused her moments of insurmountable despair. Life became unbearable without seeing, even from a distance, the person she loved most in the world.] Her realization that she truly loves Álvarez means that marriage is an appropriate solution. As Lola observed, although "casarse sin amor es un pecado que Dios castiga con infinitos sufrimientos" (37) [marrying without love is a sin that God punishes with infinite suffering], this is not always the case: "Si se elige bien se halla la felicidad" (41). [If you choose well, you can find happiness.] Álvarez does seem to be a good choice. He appears in person only once—when Juan brings him back to the palace at the end of chapter 9—and he does not speak; he simply gazes adoringly at Consuelo. He is described first as a lawyer (37) but later as an engineer (81, 92, 111). Both are modern professions, symbolizing a world of business and science that is very different from the world of the palace, where the only men are either priests or (like Lola's brother) Don Juanesque seducers. Furthermore, Álvarez lives in Salamanca—the new and elite area of Madrid that had developed as part of the Castro urbanization project during the nineteenth century and was now home to the highest ranks of the bourgeoisie. Consuelo's decision to marry him represents a conscious decision to leave the stifling world of the palace for a modern future, where the reader imagines she will no longer have to rely on a priest to carry her voice to the outside world. Marriage is clearly plotted as not only a happy ending for Consuelo but also a vision of a happy future for the Spanish women she represents—in an imagined Spain where modernity means freedom from stifling social conventions and freedom to choose marriage from among other options.

Consuelo's happy ending, though, is not the whole story. In fact, in a graphic demonstration of DuPlessis's (1985) concept of "writing beyond the ending," Casanova offers multiple endings to *Lo eterno*, each of which unlocks a variety of interpretations. The penultimate chapter resolves the romantic story line, as Juan—having confessed to Consuelo and Álvarez—blesses them and asks their forgiveness. Had Casanova ended the novel here, the conclusion would have been satisfactory not only for readers invested in Juan's spiritual journey and Consuelo's sentimental journey but also for readers who recognized the text's criticisms of Spanish society but perhaps were not ready to see those criticisms made explicit. Instead, however, Casanova included a final chapter, which takes the form of a letter that describes Juan's death ten years after he left Spain to work as a missionary in Africa. This chapter is usually taken as further emphasis of his return to the church and thus the restoration of moral order. According to the anonymous priest who writes the letter, Juan traveled to Africa ten years earlier (that is, immediately after the conclusion of the previous chapter) as "un voluntario en el ejército del bien" [a volunteer in the army of good], entering "las tierras salvajes de las que sacaba con persuasión y dulzura sobrehumanas, tribus enteras de indígenas que hoy . . . alaban al Dios único" (Casanova 1907, *Lo eterno*, 117) [the savage lands from which he extracted with superhuman sweetness and persuasion entire tribes of natives who today . . . praise the only God]. The priest's account of Juan's death from drowning during an attempt to save a shipwrecked man is florid and all too familiar: "Venía envuelto en algas olorosas; en su faz serena, sonriente, como de dichosa mortal que vislumbra cercano el cielo, no había la menor huella de sufrimiento" (118). [He was enveloped in aromatic seaweeds; on his serene face, smiling like a fortunate mortal who glimpses heaven close by, there was not the slightest trace of suffering.] The effect is, of course, to reinforce the message of Juan's redemption. Just as ten years earlier Juan sacrificed his nascent masculinity and freedom for Consuelo's happiness, he has now given up his life for an unknown man. The moral of the story is explicitly set out in the novel's closing passage, on which most existing readings have turned: "Bienaventurados los que luchan y vencen; los que llegan a la presencia de Dios ensangrentados los pies y las manos por las espinas y las piedras del angosto camino. . . . Los fáciles senderos floridos no llevan a la altura" (118). [Fortunate are those who fight and win, those who reach the presence of God with hands and feet bloodied by the thorns and rocks along the narrow path. . . . The easy, flower-lined paths do not lead to heaven.]

To accept this reading at face value is, as ever, to do Casanova a grave disservice. According to DuPlessis, "One of the great moments of ideological negotiation in any work occurs in the choice of a resolution for the various services it provides" (1985, 3). In the case of *Lo eterno*, Casanova's refusal to commit fully to any one resolution raises many more questions than are resolved. The sudden change of narrative voice, from the implicitly female third-person narrator used throughout to the explicitly hegemonic voice of the priest, is not inconsequential. It is, I argue, key to recognizing the subversive interpretation encoded within the conventional reading of the novel. The "doubleness" (Lanser 1992, 13) hinges on the reader's recognition (or not) of this shift in narrative voice and the consequent dissonances that this provokes. This reading is reinforced in the closing pages of the novel, when we learn that this final chapter is not only singly but doubly mediated; the priest's letter is being read by Juan's uncle, the bishop who was responsible for forcing him into the church in the first place. It is the bishop, not the third-person narrator of the rest of the work, who utters the closing words that have proved so decisive for so many of *Lo eterno*'s readers. Moreover, by showing us the bishop reading the letter and then allowing him to voice, in his own words, his reading of the moral of Juan's story, Casanova unequivocally and literally depicts for us the officially sanctioned reading of her novel.

Leaving us with the bishop's interpretation is a clever move, because although it gives the appearance of a clear and unambiguous moral resolution, it also makes explicit what Lanser calls "the articulation between surface and subtext, the syntactic hinge that binds and finally transforms the whole" (1992, 12). The shift from the third-person narrator of the rest of the work to a pair of voices that represent, in a speech dominated by imperialist rhetoric, the very institution that is the focus of the novel's critique serves principally to highlight the dissonance between the figure in the official church account of Juan's last years and the character that we have come to know over the previous 120 pages. Because we hear only one side of the story, we are simply left to choose whether or not we accept the official version. It is my contention that Casanova deliberately exploits this dissonance as a strategy for questioning and destabilizing the notion of "Spain's African vocation," which forms the ideological basis for the renewed colonialist project, without drawing excessive attention to her criticisms. Her choice of Africa as a destination enables this effort, because Africa functions in the same way as Lithuania at the end of *Wolski*. As a "paradoxical space"—at once part and not part of the Spanish nation—it can be evoked, like Lithuania, in support of either reactionary or utopian arguments. As a result, a reader invested in the celebration of the dominant national discourse can see Juan's journey to Africa as a sign of his commitment to the neocolonial project and the realization of "Spain's African vocation." At the same time, a reader for whom the key to the novel lies in its critique of the church's treatment of women and other minorities can view Juan's journey to Africa (like Consuelo's move to the modern barrio of Salamanca or Mara's move to Lithuania) as an acknowledgment that the liberty he desires is unattainable within the inescapably gendered and *castizo* borders of modern Madrid.

Lo eterno continues the project that Casanova began in *Wolski*. It explores responses to fin de siècle fears about the breakdown of borders of race, class, and especially gender. Where the earlier novel incorporated specific strategies designed to mitigate any suspicions of overt authorship on Casanova's part, however, *Lo eterno*—as the response of the editor quoted by Casanova in the prologue shows—was far less accommodating of social mores. Gone are the distancing strategies, such as the exotic setting and the claims of modesty; a far angrier and more overtly critical novel, *Lo eterno* deals directly with issues of public concern in contemporary Spain. Far from being a distraction or a smoke screen, the sentimental plotline is essential; the great achievement of *Lo eterno* is that it provides an incontrovertibly female perspective on many of the burning intellectual debates of the *fin de siglo*. The novel's vision of a modern Spain in which the individual will enjoy freedom of expression and liberty to decide his or her own future is, like the conclusion to *Wolski*, essentially optimistic. In this sense, then, Casanova's novel bears out Johnson's observation that whereas many male intellectuals at the *fin de siglo* looked to the "homogenizing" idea of *intrahistoria* that "yearns for that mythical Golden Age when all was peace, unity, and harmony within the imagined national borders" (1996, 170), their female contemporaries "chose to depict a contemporary Spain, and to imagine a future for the nation in which new social configurations are possible" (172). That future would, however, be quite a long time coming; Casanova's extensive revisions to the novel two decades later—which entirely negated the symbolic dimension of the story through the elimination of all mention of Madrid or 1898—suggest that, for this author at least, the fear of scandal would ultimately supersede the desire for reform.

CHAPTER 4

Poland–Madrid–Poland

Más que amor: Cartas (1908)

El gran patriota director de la *Gaceta Codzienna*, de Varsovia, me dio la noticia sin que el desagrado amenguara la cortesana efusión del apretón de manos.

Una de las cartas de mi novela *Más que amor*, que publicaba su periódico, había sido multada con 500 rublos (1.500 pesetas), el máximum del castigo impuesto por los tribunales militares a los "crímenes" literarios. Y la sentencia del sumarísimo proceso verbal, decía así: "Por atentatorio al Estado imponemos," etc. (Casanova 1924, *En la corte de los zares,* 155)

[That great patriot, the director of the Warsaw *Daily Gazette,* gave me the news without allowing the unpleasantness to diminish the courteous warmth of his handshake.

One of the letters from my novel *Más que amor,* which his newspaper was publishing, had been fined 500 rubles (1,500 pesetas), the maximum punishment imposed by the military tribunals for literary "crimes." And the pronouncement in the most cursory minutes of the meeting was this: "For being prejudicial to the State we impose," etc.][1]

Compared with Sofía Casanova's own account of the storm that greeted her third novel, *Más que amor,* when it was published in Russian Poland (where it was swiftly denounced as a "literary crime"), contemporary readings of the novel seem to refer to a different book entirely. For late-twentieth-century Hispanists, *Más que amor* is "an epistolary novel chronicling the rise, decline, and fall of a long-distance idyll" (Alayeto 1992, 58), which "follows the traditional Romantic pattern from silence to spiritual compenetration" (Galerstein and McNerney 1986, 71) and is shaped by a "personal experience of solitude and pessimism concerning human relationships" (Pérez 1988, 20). All readers of Casanova since the Russian censors—or at least all of those who committed their thoughts to paper—have been united in their interpretation of the novel as a sentimental and only thinly veiled autobiography. These readings invite the question of how a novel that seems so straightforwardly "feminine" could have been considered "prejudicial to the State," a disjunction that is, I think, exactly what Casanova intended. Although *Más que amor* does, indeed, follow the sentimental model in many ways, it also makes some significant departures from the norm—most notably in that the expected restoration of moral order (to which Casanova had at least paid lip service in her earlier novels) does not occur. Unlike Mara (who devotes her life to social work), Juan (who becomes a missionary), or Consuelo (who marries the man she loves), María Cruz—the heroine of *Más que amor*—ultimately rejects her suitor's proposal of marriage, only to agree several months later (in what Kathleen Glenn sees as an "unconvincing" ending [1996, 49]) to resume their correspondence.

It is true that if we try to read *Más que amor* as a pure and simple romance, it is, ultimately, not only unpersuasive but also unsatisfying in its lack of explicit resolution. Inspired by the epistolary form and the coincidences between María Cruz's situation and Casanova's own, critics have nevertheless continued to read the novel as a semiautobiographical romance, thus illustrating the conventional expectation—of which Casanova cannot have been unaware—that epistolary fiction would be personal, sentimental, and autobiographical. As Amanda Gilroy and W. M. Verhoeven note in their revisionist study of the epistolary genre, *Epistolary Histories*, "The dominant critical tradition equates letters and love, women's writing and the writing of the heart" (2000, 3). That is, we as readers expect female-voiced epistolary novels to be both about love and profoundly personal—whether the epistolary heroine is written by a male or a female author. It is this expectation that seems to condition virtually everything that has been written about *Más que amor*. Carolyn Galerstein and Kathleen McNerney suggest somewhat gratuitously that "the language and events reflect a first-hand knowledge of correspondence and isolation" (1986, 71); Janet Pérez describes it as "an epistolary novel with possible autobiographical ingredients" (1988, 20). Both of Casanova's biographers consider the novel a thinly veiled autobiography and treat it almost exclusively as a roman à clef. Ofelia Alayeto wonders whether

> perhaps part of *Más que amor*'s inner-circle appeal was the knowledge that the star-crossed lovers were none other than Casanova herself and the

Madrid editor Alfredo Vicenti. Protected by distance, Casanova freely told her family in Warsaw that the book being published in Madrid was her correspondence with Vicenti, but she never showed the book to them. As of 1983 they were unaware of the letters' romantic focus. (1992, 58)[2]

Rosario Martínez offers two possible sources for the figure of Carlos de Vargas. Casanova's youngest daughter names Alfredo Vicenti, recalling, "Yo le tenía mucha simpatía de niña y mamá una gran amistad" (qtd. in Martínez 1999, 150). [I had great affection for him as a young girl, and he was a great friend of Mama's.] Casanova's granddaughter Krystyna Niklewicz believes that the character was based on the poet, journalist, and playwright Emilio Ferrari (Martínez 1999, 152). Both Martínez and Alayeto take the autobiographical element as read, and they place it at the center of their interpretations. According to Martínez, "La cantidad de datos y de detalles de la vida real que la escritora lleva al mundo de la realidad creada facilitan extraordinariamente [las] identificaciones [de los personajes]" (1999, 152). [The number of facts and real-life details the writer brings to the fictional world greatly facilitates the identification of the characters.]

Such readings result from the expectation that an epistolary novel—and particularly one written by a woman—is, by definition, deeply personal and sentimental. Indeed, two of the most salient—and misleading—features of epistolary writing are its often female-centered plots and the hazy line that divides it from autobiographical writing. Current scholarship is calling this expectation into question, arguing that the genre's personal, sentimental reputation is not the whole story and that "the most historically powerful fiction of the letter has been that which figures it as the trope of authenticity and intimacy, which elides questions of linguistic, historical, and political mediation, and which construes the letter as feminine" (Gilroy and Verhoeven 2000, 1). In fact, as recent research in the field confirms, women writers have always used the epistolary genre as a mask for transnational and political commentary. For example, Janet Altman points out that "women's letters were printed alongside men's [in eighteenth-century French letter manuals] as examples of verbal art cultivated and circulated in private, but which ultimately served to record, conduct, and criticize the state" (1995, 114). In other words, by reading beyond the established epistolary canon (*Letters of a Portuguese Nun*; *Les liaisons dangereuses*; *Clarissa*; *Pamela*) to consider both other literary texts and the nonliterary writings of (among others) Catherine of Siena, Christine de Pizan, and Mary Wollstonecraft, scholars such as Altman have shown that even eighteenth-century epistolary writings by women were neither always about love nor necessarily deeply personal. Extending Altman's work, Susan

Lanser reads the use of epistolary features as narrative strategies that women writers can employ to appropriate narrative authority. She argues that the letter's most significant feature is that it "is defined not by its content but by its rhetorical frame; it can embrace virtually any topic and encompass virtually any discursive mode" (1992, 46). In other words, the rhetorical frame of the epistolary narrative masks its content "so that male discursive hegemony in a manifestly public arena is at least titularly maintained. While the epistolary novel is not literally a private discourse, in other words, what it models for women is a private voice" (33). In this way, far from being a limitation, use of the epistolary framework can be an empowering strategy.

This is true too of *Más que amor*. Like *Wolski* and *Lo eterno*, the novel ends with a journey, as María returns to her adopted Poland, which—existing only in imagined form—is, like Lithuania and Africa, a symbolically charged "paradoxical space." This journey, like Juan's to Africa or Consuelo's to the new barrio of Salamanca, stands for María's rejection of traditional Spain and its restrictions, in favor of an uncertain, unsettled future in a place whose boundaries—political and social—remain to be drawn. What my analysis shows is that in *Más que amor*, as in *Lo eterno*, Casanova deliberately plays on the divide between public and private discourse, using the expectations that arise from her use of the traditionally private and feminine epistolary romance genre to mask her intervention in the public sphere of social and political commentary.

Más que amor was published in 1908, first as a serialization in the Warsaw newspaper *Gazeta Codzienna* [Daily Gazette] and then in book form in Madrid and in Kraków, where its title was translated literally as *Więcej niż miłość*. It would be republished only once, in 1931 in Madrid, under the new title *Idilio epistolar* [Epistolary Idyll]. It is a radical departure from Casanova's previous novels in two principal ways: (1) As the title suggests, it is in epistolary form, and (2) it is focused on a female protagonist, María Cruz, who is also Casanova's first married heroine (in fact, she is widowed). A long novel, approximately the same length as *Wolski*, it consists of a prefatory poem dedicated by Casanova to her friend Ela Balicka[3] and ninety-five letters spread over nearly three years during the first decade of the twentieth century.

The principal plot can be summarized briefly as follows: María Cruz is a Spanish woman whose mentally ill Polish husband has recently died in a Swiss sanatorium. Although she is nostalgic for Spain, she remains in Poland with their two sons, whom she has promised to bring up as good Poles. Over the course of a year, she develops an epistolary relationship with Carlos de Vargas, a Madrid politician and poet. Carlos falls in love with María, and—after he has a serious car accident that she foresees in a dream—she is moved to reciprocate. Although he is already married to Elisa, who is mentally ill, Carlos becomes increasingly irritated by María's reluctance to return to Spain to spend the rest of her life with him. María, in turn, becomes increasingly frightened by Carlos's violent behavior and his attempts to force her into submission. Nevertheless, she represses her fears and agrees to meet him in Spain. Just as they are making the final arrangements, Elisa dies, and María moves her journey forward by a month. Carlos sees this as a signal that she is planning to marry him and stay in Spain permanently. When they finally meet, María realizes that her fears were justified. Carlos is domineering and resentful of her refusal to marry him. Eventually they argue, and María leaves without telling Carlos. Initially, Carlos is furious, but in the end they decide to rekindle their epistolary relationship, which Carlos describes as "más que amor" [more than love] (Casanova 1908, *Más que amor,* 248).

My reading of *Más que amor* takes as its starting point Altman's concluding remarks in *Epistolarity,* her structuralist analysis of the epistolary form:

> Epistolary fiction tends to flourish at those moments when novelists most openly reflect upon the relation between storytelling and intersubjective communication and begin to question the way in which writing reflects, betrays, or constitutes the relations between self and other, and experience. At those crisis moments the letter form foregrounds—in its very consciousness of itself as a form—questions that are basic to all literature. (1982, 212)

Altman introduces the concept of "the epistolary mosaic," which she explains as follows: "Awareness of the arrangement of letters within a narrative work involves consciousness of the hand that arranges—that of the fictional 'editor,' or the epistolary novelist" (167). This concept provides a framework for my discussion of the relationship between public and private, political and sentimental discourse within *Más que amor.* Since it has no fictional editor, our assumption must be that it is the implied author who is responsible for arranging the letters in the novel. By extension, the distribution of letters, the decision to include some and to withhold others, must respond to a pattern that, we might assume, reflects Casanova's authorial mission. As Altman suggests, "Careful analysis of the pattern formed by the distribution of letters among the various correspondents of an epistolary work is a basic step in interpretation" (178).[4] The novel's structure illustrates Altman's point and supports the notion that Casanova is exploiting the reader's expectations about the boundaries between public and private discourse. Although the romantic plot provides the dynamic for *Más que amor,* the correspondence between

María and Carlos does not begin until the seventh letter. Instead, the novel's introductory letters (which critics rarely mention) elaborate Casanova's dearly held theory—frequently expressed in her nonfictional work—that the oppression of women is one of the central impediments to national progress, and the future of the nation is therefore dependent on the emancipation of women.

María's letters to her "master and friend" (Casanova 1908, *Más que amor*, 9) Daniel Olivar and to the Andalusian novelist Rafael Solares introduce the abstract element of her argument. Playing on the Spanish and Polish fears of sexual and therefore social anarchy that Casanova had already critiqued in *Wolski* and *Lo eterno*, María applies the highly gendered discourse of medicine to what (in both Spain and Poland) was widely described as the "national malady." She describes the "sick" nations of Poland and Spain in feminized terms, as neurotic and hysterical, respectively:

Las circunstancias trágicas de Polonia han perturbado muchas de sus facultades anímicas. El alma polaca, soñadora, nostálgica, viviendo desde hace más de cien años en condiciones que coartan su expansión y su vitalidad, cae en las lobregueces del mesianismo; la neurosis cunde entre la juventud; y tiemblo por mis hijos. (11)

[Poland's tragic circumstances have greatly disturbed many of her spiritual faculties. The Polish soul, dreamy, nostalgic, living for more than a century under conditions that restrict its expansion and its vitality, is falling into the shadows of messianism; neurosis is taking hold among the young; and I tremble for my sons.]

Desde lejos no puede percibirse si el latido de su corazón [de España] es de decrépito o de adulto vigoroso. . . . [S]uelo preguntarme si la sana organización de mi patria no está cercana a un desequilibrio antitético al de Polonia, pero igualmente deplorable; el de la risa inconsciente parecida al cascabeleo del tirso que lleva en Carnaval, por esas calles de Dios, la locura. (12)

[From a distance it is impossible to tell whether the heartbeat (of Spain) is that of an old man or a healthy adult. . . . I often wonder whether the healthy organization of my homeland is not approaching an imbalance that is the antithesis of Poland's, but equally deplorable; that of unconscious laughter, echoing the clattering bells on the sticks carried by madness through these streets of God during Carnival.]

María's point is that the stifling effects of partition in Poland that have led to the messianistic tendencies that Casanova criticized so strongly in *Wolski*, like the enforced gaiety of Spanish popular culture, have their equivalent in the private sphere. When she asks Olivar, "¿No cree usted . . . que los defectos de una raza acentúanse y se desarrollan implacablemente, si por largo tiempo vive en condiciones contrarias a su naturaleza?" (9–10) [Don't you think a race's defects are accentuated and inexorably developed, if it lives for a long time in conditions contrary to its nature?], she is also asking about the implications for the women on whom the nations are modeled. This implicit question gradually becomes more explicit throughout the novel, as María's letters reveal the extent to which the stifling everyday life of the middle-class woman exposes her to the risk of succumbing either to nervous illness—neurosis—or hysteria.

Early in her correspondence with Carlos, María observes that her life has been overshadowed by repressed creativity. As a child she was musically gifted; however, out of a concern for her health, her parents—advised by "los tontos de los médicos" (Casanova 1908, *Más que amor*, 81) [those idiot doctors]— "me tasaron el estudio, redujeron al mínimo las lecciones de música que yo adoraba, y preservándome del esfuerzo mental de la lectura, de la emoción intensa que me daba la música, me salvaron" (82) [rationed my study, reduced to a minimum the music lessons I loved, and by protecting me from the mental strain of reading, from the intense emotion music caused me, they saved me]. In consequence, she has become an example of the masochistic feminine figures that people nineteenth-century Spanish literature: "Lo perdido en sabiduría fue ganado en fortaleza. Una fortaleza extraña y negativa que me hace soportar a pie firme el dolor y desfallecer de contento" (82). [What I lost in wisdom I gained in strength. A strange, negative strength that makes me stand firm before pain and faint away from happiness.] Even today, she remains at the mercy of the doctors, who continue to force her into the role of an invalid: "No me dejan escribir hoy, no me permiten pensar. Recluida en mi cuarto casi a obscuras, extendida en mi chaisse-longue [*sic*], me fuerzan a que no me mueva, a que no hable. . . . [M]e prohíben pensar" (82). [They won't let me write today, won't allow me to think. Shut up in my room, almost in darkness, reclined in my chaise longue, they force me not to move, not to speak. . . . They forbid me to think.] As Kathleen Glenn observes in her study of the novel, this was not an unprecedented reaction to the creative woman, either in life or in literature: "Readers of Charlotte Perkins Gilman's 'The Yellow Wallpaper' will remember another woman who was not allowed to write and for whom total emptiness of mind was prescribed as the remedy for her supposed abnormality" (1996, 53). That woman, of course, ultimately went insane, and María is acutely aware that she runs the same risk. As a remedy, she has been conditioned to suppress her creative urges and with them her opportunity to speak for herself. On one occasion, she admonishes herself, "No están los nervios en orden y hay que volver a echar la llave al piano y a la boca" (41). [My nerves aren't in order, and I must once again lock up the piano and my mouth.] Increasingly, however, she rebels, crying out, "Yo no estoy enferma, no me duele nada" (83). [I'm not ill; nothing hurts at all.]

In the novel, the consequences of perpetual repression are played out in the suffering of Carlos's hysterical wife, Elisa, who functions as María's "dark double." Elisa is the embodiment of the "madwoman in the attic" who inhabits nineteenth-century writing by and about women, most notably in the many "mad antiheroines who complicate the lives of sane heroines" (Gilbert and Gubar 1978, 80).[5] Elisa's existence—dismissed by Carlos as "un gran cero" (Casanova 1908, *Más que amor*, 176) [a big nothing]—provides María with a buffer against Carlos's plans for their future, and Elisa's sudden death sets in motion the chain of events that leads to the breakdown of María and Carlos's relationship. There are hints that Elisa, like María, is frustrated in her desire for self-expression, a frustration that is manifested in her obsession with dancing: Carlos tells María, "De los trescientos sesenta y cinco días del año, doscientos se baila o se inventan jolgorios aquí, el resto en otras partes, y en todas ríe, ríe como un autómata hecho para lanzar carcajadas la alegre persona trágica" (51). [Of the 365 days of the year, 200 she spends dancing or inventing festivities here, the remainder elsewhere, and every day she laughs; the joyful, tragic woman laughs like an automaton made only to emit cackles of laughter.]

Unlike Elisa, María does not, in the end, become mad, although she certainly comes close to it. The avoidance of this fate can, in part, be attributed to the fact that, like her predecessors Mara and Consuelo, she succeeds in finding an intellectual outlet through writing. The act of writing and the possibilities of the epistolary form are all the more important for María because of her expressed belief in the Romantic notion that "el poeta, el artista, es el tabernáculo del alma de la patria" (61) [the poet, the artist is the tabernacle of the national soul]. The parallel that she draws between her own situation as a frustrated artist (who is both considered "sick" because of her desire to express her art and made "sick" by her inability to do so) and that of the Polish and Spanish nations (each of which was undergoing its own *fin de siglo* crisis of identity) sets up an allegorical framework for the novel that takes it far beyond the simple romance. Through her letters, María increasingly undertakes to challenge the widely held contemporary belief that for women to aspire to anything more than domesticity was inherently dangerous given that, as

Elaine Showalter puts it, "women's conflicts over using their gifts . . . would doom them to lives of nervous illness" (1991, 40). In its self-reflexive engagement with the question of female creative independence, the story of María's struggle thus provides a perfect illustration of Altman's contention that the nature of the epistolary novel "foregrounds . . . questions that are basic to all literature."

How, then, are we supposed to read this deceptively challenging novel? Interestingly, in addition to offering a theoretical argument, the opening letters supply us with a case study. This is María's reading of a novel that, she tells Solares, has been the source of much controversy in Poland during the past year: *Popioły* [Ashes], by Stefan Żeromski (1864–1925), first published in 1904 (Casanova 1908, *Más que amor,* 14).[6] The controversy over *Popioły,* which Casanova does not explain for her Spanish readers and María does not explain for her Spanish correspondents, arose from its overt questioning of the official narrative of Polish history as celebrated in the works of contemporary canonical authors such as Maria Konopnicka and the Nobel laureate Henryk Sienkiewicz. Debate centered on "the author's struggle with Sienkiewicz's populism and the messianic elevation of the sacred Polish cause" (Eile 2000, 158) and, in particular, Żeromski's criticism of the glorification—and mythification—of Polish participation in the Spanish campaigns of the Napoleonic Wars. These campaigns, especially those that culminated in the sieges of Zaragoza and the Battle of Somosierra in 1808, were—and remain today—a central element of Poland's national history. This is evident in the following passage, in which María's son Yerzyk tells his mother:

> Yo no quisiera nunca salir de Polonia, ni vivir en otro sitio que en Kalinowo,[7] donde vivieron mis antepasados . . . pero a veces me agita un vivo afán de ser hombre para recorrer los lugares donde ocurrieron nuestras grandes batallas. Me gustaría ir al desfiladero de Somosierra, cerca de Madrid, en el cual nuestros soldados tan heroicamente vencieron. Muchos quedaron allí y deseo recorrer las alturas y traer un puñado de aquella tierra que empaparon con su sangre. (Casanova 1908, *Más que amor,* 191)

> [I never want to leave Poland or live anywhere but Kalinowo, where my ancestors lived . . . but sometimes I'm stirred by a strong desire to be a man so I can travel to the places where our great battles took place. I'd like to go to the pass at Somosierra, near Madrid, where our soldiers triumphed so heroically. Many of them remained there, and I want to go up to the peak and bring back a handful of the soil they drenched with their blood.]

Popioły deconstructs the glorious military history taught to schoolchildren like Yerzyk, replacing stereotypical depictions of military heroes and great victories with "scenes of savage brutality and rape, accompanying the conquest of Saragossa by the Polish troops" that force the reader to question the moral basis of Polish participation in the wars and, therefore, of the Polish national myth (Eile 2000, 158). As a result, although María is sympathetic to Yerzyk and glad that he wants to visit Spain, she is also wary of the possible consequences of his blind adherence to a patriotic myth that, following Żeromski, she can see only as brutal and tyrannical.

The choice of a contemporary, foreign novel, especially one that is as radical as *Popioły*, signals Casanova's intention to bring to the literary debates of the current moment in Spain—albeit indirectly (as we might surmise from her decision not to explain the controversy around the novel)—the new perspective embodied in María. As much as an Azorinian discussion about the role of classic literature and historical "types" in defining the national identity, both *Popioły* and *Más que amor* provide a critical—even metacritical—examination of the way that histories are told. *Popioły* is a radical break with the past, in terms of not only subject matter but also form, as Żeromski moved away from the linear, realistic approach of Sienkiewicz and his school, interweaving lyrical fragments and moral and philosophical digressions into what has been described as a "roman experimental" (Krzyżanowski 1978, 524).[8] Żeromski's formal experimentation, unusual in a purportedly historical narrative, provides a precedent for Casanova's own formal and metacritical experimentation in *Más que amor*.

Although the formal and metacritical parallels between *Popioły* and *Más que amor* are left for the reader to discover independently, María is completely straightforward about her principal interest in the novel. Her reading highlights the sentimental element of the plot that has not figured highly in Polish readings of the novel. She observes:

> La inspiración del novelista se afina y se perfecciona al describir el amor, o, mejor dicho, el enamoramiento de sus personajes, que va haciéndole pasar por los contradictorios estados de la melancolía a la alegría vehemente; de la duda tímida a la tristeza y el delirio. (Casanova 1908, *Más que amor*, 15)

> [The novelist's inspiration is polished, perfected by describing the love, or, rather, the falling in love of his characters, which takes him through the contradictory states of melancholy and intense joy; from timorous doubt to sadness and delirium.]

This reading supports her belief—paraphrasing the French bohemian poet Arsène Houssaye—that love is central to the expression of identity: "Las dos manifestaciones más sintéticas del individuo son su religión y sus amores. . . . 'Dime en qué crees y como amas, para que yo pueda conocerte' " (16). [The two features that most intimately characterize the individual are his religion and his love affairs. . . . "Tell me what you believe in and how you love, so that I may know you."] Most significantly, she goes on to suggest that the study of literature means that what is true of the individual can just as easily be applied to the nation as a whole:

> Aplicado este axioma a los grandes pensadores de una nación, a sus poetas, a sus místicos, representantes de ella, descúbrese la infinita escala de las diferencias de raza, que, dando color propio a los pueblos, variedad a las costumbres, formas diversas a la cultura, ofrecen tan ancho campo a los estudios etnográficos puramente, y a los más complicados y atractivos de la psicología comparada. (16)

> [If you apply this axiom to a nation's great thinkers, its poets, its mystics, all its representatives, you will discover the infinite range of racial differences, which, giving each people a color of its own, creating a variety of customs, of diverse cultural forms, offer such a great subject not only for purely ethnographic studies but also for more complicated and attractive studies of comparative psychology.]

The logical extension of María's argument is that *Popioły* is as valuable for its depiction of a peculiarly Polish type of "*enamoramiento*" (17, emphasis Casanova's) [*falling in love*] as for its depiction of military episodes from Poland's history and thus that the "personal" sphere of romance is as necessary as the "public" sphere of politics and military action to the telling of the national narrative. She offers a new and radical reading of *Popioły* as a novel that straddles the boundary between public and personal, between politics and sentiment. Her interpretation points out the "feminine" element in a text that has generally been read as a political commentary and offers a model against which to read *Más que amor*. The implication is that *Más que amor*, a text that has normally been read as feminine and therefore of limited, private appeal, can also—must also—be read as an intervention into public debate. María's firmly held belief that art is central to the development of national identity, and her assertion (through her reading of *Popioły*) that "masculine" and "feminine" forms of art are equally necessary to that process, makes clear her proposition that it is only when the female artist is allowed to speak that the nation will be able to progress. The story that is about to unfold in María's correspondence with Carlos, ostensibly one of *enamoramiento* and, eventually, *desenamoramiento* [falling out of love], is also a story of national significance, as it dramatizes the difficulties inherent in the realization of this dream.

The conflict between the sentimental rhetoric that characterizes *fin de siglo* writing about women and the desire of women such as Casanova to question and contest that rhetoric, which drives the development and ultimate disintegration of María's relationship with Carlos, is made explicit in an early exchange between Carlos and María:

María, mi hermana, mi doble yo . . . [a]unque la llevo siempre conmigo, hay horas en las que mi solicitud, queriendo preservarla de la realidad tediosa o bárbara, prefiere dejarla en el bosque encantado donde me espera. (1908, *Más que amor*, 67)

[María, my sister, my double self . . . although I always carry you with me, there are hours when my solicitude, wanting to protect you from tedious or barbarous reality, would rather leave you in the enchanted forest where you await me.]

Hay exageración en esa manera de expresarse, Carlos. (69)

[There is exaggeration in that way of talking, Carlos.]

As these two quotations show, María is acutely aware of the unequal—and gendered—relationships of power that underpin the rhetoric on which Carlos tries to build their relationship, and she warns him early in their correspondence not to overdo it:

Hallo hiel [*sic*] en sus mieles, Carlos, porque me parece que su dormido instinto de galanteador es quien ha movido ese tumulto de su fantasía. . . . *Y si mi alma, cansada ave de paz, es acogida con la descarga cerrada de sus ansias de conquistador*, mi amigo, hagamos de esta correspondencia . . . un recuerdo del atardecer de nuestra vida. (71–72, emphasis mine)

[I find ice in your honey, Carlos, because it seems to me that it is your latent instinct as a seducer that has provoked this torrent of fantasy. . . . *And if my soul, a weary bird of peace, is received with the volley of your aspirations to conquer*, my friend, then let's make this correspondence a memory of the twilight of our lives.]

Always aware of the gulf between his image of her and the reality, she cautions, "La comunicación epistolar, por efusiva y sincera que sea, no reemplaza la conversación, no pone en contacto más que ciertos lados del alma que solo se abre y se expande enteramente en la reciprocidad del trato personal" (122). [Epistolary communication, however effusive and sincere, cannot replace conversation, can connect only certain aspects of the soul, which fully opens and swells only with shared personal contact.] However, Carlos fails to listen, and his willful misunderstanding of the evidence in front of him allows the novel to deconstruct the acutely gendered balance of power that is at the root of his worldview.

This shift in the balance of power is reflected in the presentation of the protagonists. Unlike Mara and Consuelo, whose stories are secondary to those of Enrique and Juan, María Cruz is the central figure of *Más que amor*. In Rachel Blau DuPlessis's terms, she is a hero not a heroine, and this is the story of her quest (1985, 6–7). That María, and not Carlos, is the focus of the novel is reflected in its structure. As Kathleen Glenn has observed, "Seventy-three pages of the text are devoted to his communications, one hundred eighty-nine to hers. Her voice rings loud and clear" (1996, 48). In fact, María writes every one of the first ten published letters, which—together with the novel's prologue poem—establish a strong female voice and perspective from the outset. This liberty of expression is both enabled and enforced by María's social and geographical position: As a widow and an exile, she is beyond the confines of not only the bourgeois marriage contract but also the Spanish nation itself. Furthermore, her only means of communication is the letter, which, as we have already seen, could be a powerful tool in the establishment of a female voice. Whereas in Casanova's earlier novels the move to a liminal or "paradoxical" space was seen as a resolution, allowing the protagonists to escape the restrictions enforced within the hegemonic national space, *Más que amor* begins with a protagonist who has already made this journey. Adding another dimension to DuPlessis's concept of "writing beyond the ending," the novel examines the hegemonic response (represented by Carlos) to the perceived threat to national unity of María's relative liberty—and, by extension, the liberty of the female artist to speak (or write) her own mind.

If the dominant worldview silences and excludes women who challenge, subjecting them to the unrealistic demands of "femininity," Carlos is the personification of this worldview in *Más que amor*. As a politician and a poet, he represents the two most powerful means of controlling women in life and art. In other words, he is the guardian and promoter of the romance plot and its associated rhetoric in literature and the guardian of marriage and the associated civil restrictions on women in society. He can imagine no ending for María other than marriage to him, and he will do anything in his power to ensure that this is the outcome. If Carlos's romantic fantasy is to succeed, however, he must turn María into a model of femininity. The nature of epistolary discourse facilitates his self-deception, illustrating Altman's observation that "the imagined dialogue . . . has an advantage over the real conversation: one can manipulate one's partner" (1982, 139). Carlos takes full advantage of this possibility, bolstered by his belief that "la inspiración del artista precede a la obra que patentiza su existencia; pero solo la obra, que es lo material fijando la divina inmaterialidad de la idea, nos revela al artista y nos revela el genio" (Casanova 1908, *Más que amor,* 171–72) [the artist's inspiration precedes the work that makes its existence visible; but only the work, a material object fixing the divine immateriality of the idea, reveals to us the artist and reveals to us the genius]. That is, art (and remember that he is a poet) fixes the intangible (he would very much like to pin María down) and bathes the artist in reflected glory. As María points out, there is certainly very little advantage to her becoming the epitome of "femininity." Carlos's relationship with María follows this pattern: He first creates an imagined María and then tries to force the real María into the mold he has created, telling her at one point, "Tú me apareces como te necesito y te anhelo" (77). [You appear to me as I need you and want you.] The very first words we hear from him, quoted by María, are a horrified response to her philosophical musings about the nature of sentiment: "Oyéndola definir y sentenciar, me recuerda usted ciertas mujeres de [Henrik] Ibsen analizadoras y frías. . . . Y usted no es así" (31). [Hearing you make definitions and pronouncements, you remind me of some of (Henrik) Ibsen's women, analytical and cold. . . . And you aren't like that.]

Carlos's certainty about María's nature contrasts very strongly with María's own uncertainty, which stems largely from her removal from the comforting certainties of the social and national order of her homeland. Initially, María struggles against her liminal position. She compares her exile in Poland to a living death, believing that as far as her friends in Spain are concerned, she may as well be dead (Casanova 1908, *Más que amor,* 12, 29). Her widowhood is a significant factor in her feelings of uncertainty and abandonment. It is a state, as Sandra Gilbert has observed, that locates a woman in the limbo between life (her own) and the death of her partner:

> According to the *OED* the word *widow* is from the Indo-European *widhewo-,* meaning 'to be empty, be separated,' to be 'destitute' or 'lack.' Death has entered the widow, this etymology implies, and she has entered

death, for she is filled with vacancy and has dissolved into a void, a state of lack or nonbeing that is akin to, if not part of, the state into which the dead person has journeyed, fallen, or been drawn (2001, 559).

This is certainly true of María. She believes that she does not exist as a fixed entity, that she is held together only by her public identity as a woman in mourning: "Toda entera soy un compuesto de incoherencias y flaqueza que se muere dentro de un vestido muy largo . . . muy negro" (Casanova 1908, *Más que amor*, 12). [All in all I'm a composite of incoherences and weakness, dying inside a very long . . . very black dress.] These incoherences initially constitute her self-image. Early on, she tells Carlos that she is "impulsiva, vehemente" (30) [impulsive, passionate], directing him to take her "*tal como soy*, o como las circunstancias me han hecho: fastidiosa, rara, exigente, discurridora [*sic*], ¡qué horror!" (31, emphasis mine) [*just as I am*, or how circumstances have made me: fastidious, strange, demanding, argumentative, what a fright!"]. A few pages later, her mood is the reverse, as she begs him to receive her "*tal y como soy*; una insignificante criatura apenada y sola" (34, emphasis mine) [*just as I am*; an insignificant creature, afflicted and alone].

Carlos's response to María's uncertainties is to provide her with a strong indication of the woman he would like her to be, even though this frequently necessitates his actively rejecting the woman she really is. Like Miguel de Unamuno, who claimed that a woman writing was as unnatural as a woman wearing trousers, Carlos needs to neutralize María's intelligence (note his use of the diminutive): "En sus cartitas . . . se me aparece usted como un esgrimidor que desconoce el juego de su contrario" (Casanova 1908, *Más que amor*, 33). [In your dear little letters . . . you appear to me like a swordsman who is ignorant of his opponent's game.] When she backs down and soothes him, he answers gratefully that she is "tan mujer, tan terriblemente mujer, que por su excesiva feminilidad [*sic*] me hace gracia" (36) [so womanly, so terribly womanly, that you charm me with your excessive femininity]. His love for María is based on his vision of her as the epitome of femininity. He loves her "vocecita" [dear little voice] and her "declaraciones tan naturalmente femeninas en lo del miedo" (57) [such naturally feminine declarations of fear]. Her physical fragility makes her even more attractive to him:

Tu frágil cuerpo y tu alma fuerte me cautivan. Soy tuyo. Tu debilidad física, que es exceso de sensibilidad moral, me acongoja y acrecienta mi ternura. . . . Me gustas infinitamente en los desmayos de tu impresionabilidad. . . . Es lo cierto que la debilidad femenina tiene su

encanto peculiar, el más subyugante. . . . Tu debilidad tiene algo de
. . . graciosa flaqueza infantil. (102)

[Your fragile body and strong soul captivate me. I am yours. Your physical
weakness, which is an excess of moral sensibility, touches me and increases
my tenderness toward you. . . . Your swoons and impressionability are
infinitely pleasing to me. . . . It's true that female weakness has a charm
all its own, the most overpowering of all. . . . Your frailty has some . . .
charming childlike weakness about it.]

Having worked himself into a state of passionate frenzy with these images of
helpless femininity, Carlos reveals what it is that he really desires: "Lo que yo
anhelo es ocupar tu pensamiento con exclusivismo tiránico" (103). [What I
want is to be the sole tyrannical occupier of your thoughts.]

Carlos's reference to the "tyrannical" nature of his desire for María illustrates the master-subaltern relationship between the sexes that *Más que amor*
seeks to question. It reflects the fact that his self-image as a Spanish man is
built on stereotypical images of masculinity, which are authorized only in opposition to the images of femininity that he seeks to impose on María. That
is, unless María is a "real woman," Carlos cannot be a "real man." Carlos's
idea of a "real man," however, is predicated on literary types that provide
only a degraded model for his relationship with María. He sees himself as a
Romantic hero cursed—like Lord Byron's Manfred—to be unhappy in love.
He believes that his life is inevitably shaped by "la tragedia de mi existencia,
el *ananke* fatídico" [the tragedy of my existence, the fatal *ananke*], which he
explains as follows: "Yo he hecho llorar, he menospreciado, he dado muerte,
a veces, a cuantos seres me amaron y amé" (Casanova 1908, *Más que amor*,
49).[9] [I have brought to tears, I have scorned, I have even, at times, taken the
lives of all the people who loved me and whom I loved.] In a scene that evokes
Manfred's incestuous relationship with his sister Astarte and her subsequent
suicide, Carlos confesses to María that a former lover committed suicide at his
feet when she discovered that he was about to elope with her sister. He uses
the "curse" to justify his cruelty:

En muchas ocasiones las circunstancias me forzaron a ser cruel, verdugo.
. . . En muchísimas más lo fui por invencible rebeldía interior; por súbita
repugnancia de lo apetecido. Por piedad, a veces, de un alma que con
ciego impulso venía a enlodar su albor en la negra fatalidad de mi destino.
(49–50)

[On many occasions circumstances forced me to be cruel, an executioner.
. . . On a great many more occasions I acted that way from an invincible
inner rebelliousness; from a sudden repugnance toward what I had wanted.
From compassion, at times, for a soul that blindly, impulsively came to soil
its whiteness in the black misfortune of my destiny.]

Initially, María (who has, of course, been brought up on the sentimental celebration of marriage) is captivated by Carlos's colorful and romantic reputation, "la leyenda de su vida de estudiante poeta" [the legend of your life
as a student poet] and "su empaque de gran señor del renacimiento" (25)
[your gravity in the style of a great renaissance gentleman]. She recalls, "En
mi adolescencia soñadora, mirando a la luna, he repetido versos suyos, los
desgranados de aquel poema que usted quemó inédito" (46). [In my dreamy
adolescence, gazing at the moon, I repeated your verses, from that poem you
burned unpublished.] She recalls avidly reading his poetry as an adolescent
and dreaming of him as

> Príncipe encantador, que se aproximaba para caer a mis pies y realizar mis
> sueños. Y el Príncipe tenía las manos pálidas, los ojos altivos y las curvas
> pestañas negras como tú. . . . El Príncipe de mis sueños existe, me ha
> tendido la mano. (96–97)

> [Prince Charming, coming to fall at my feet and make my dreams come
> true. And the prince had pale hands, haughty eyes, and curling black lashes
> like you. . . . The prince of my dreams exists; he has held out his hand to
> me].

Carlos, too, sees their relationship in literary terms, but whereas María acknowledges from the start that stories of Prince Charming and fair princesses
are inadequate models for an adult relationship, Carlos persists in his role-
playing game. Turning to the imagery of the fairy tale that can "state and
enforce culture's sentences with greater accuracy than more sophisticated literary texts" (Gilbert and Gubar 1978, 36), he worships María as his "dulce du-
rmiente en el bosque" (Casanova 1908, *Más que amor,* 31) [sleeping sweetheart
in the forest], imagining her awaiting him, like Sleeping Beauty, in a state of
suspended animation. Significantly, the power to awaken her belongs only to
him, and he is perfectly willing to abuse this power if it means keeping her
subdued. Mixing his fairy stories somewhat, he later tells her that his mission is to rescue her from her "torre de marfil" (168) [ivory tower]—meaning,

presumably, her exile in Poland. Carlos's insistence reflects the prevalence of images of sleeping and dead women in fin de siècle art and literature, which formed one response to fears about the rise of feminism as they allowed the artist to subdue the dangerous female symbolically (Dijkstra 1986, 68–69). María is well aware of the peril of playing along with Carlos: Writing to Halina from Spain, she complains, "A fuer de amoroso y solícito me ha convertido en una princesa de sus pensamientos encerrada en las cuatro paredes de este castillo roquero" (Casanova 1908, *Más que amor,* 224). [Loving and solicitous as he is, he has turned me into a princess of his dreams imprisoned within the four walls of this stone castle.]

As Carlos and María's relationship progresses, María develops strategies to counter his fantasies and attempt to anchor him in the real world. The conflict between them comes to a head toward the middle of the novel, in a series of letters that form a transition between the exposition of Casanova's thesis that the oppression of women impedes national progress (in the first half of the novel) and the rapid, dramatized deconstruction of the assumptions that underpin this oppression (in the second half).

This transitional section begins as, trying to distract Carlos from his fantasy of kissing her (XL),[10] María responds with a series of apparently unconnected digressions (XLI, XLII, XLV, and XLVI) that lead into a political discussion that, in turn, ends with Carlos's announcement of his resignation from his government post. The discussion includes the letter (LXVII) for which Casanova was fined by the Russian government when the novel was being serialized in *Gazeta Codzienna* (a situation that Casanova described as "una humillación impuesta a mi libertad intelectual" [1924, *En la corte de los zares,* 156] [a humiliation to my intellectual freedom]).[11] In light of Altman's observation about the importance of the "epistolary mosaic" to the interpretation of the epistolary text, the central position of this letter, as forty-seventh out of ninety-five letters in the novel, is significant. In an obfuscating move on Casanova's part, the letter is attributed to Carlos, who suddenly seems to have become an authority on the Polish situation in general and Polish literature in particular. Carlos criticizes Poland as "un país de ambiciones desequilibradas y de anárquicos" (1908, *Más que amor,* 133) [a country of unbalanced ambitions and of anarchists] and the Poles as "inconsistentes, inquietos debilitándose en la vacilación o la autocrítica" (135) [inconsistent, restless, weakening themselves through vacillation or self-criticism]—criticisms that were common currency both in endlessly self-conscious Poland and abroad. In an extensive passage that recalls opinions that Casanova expressed in other works and that Carlos excuses with the comment "He dejado correr la pluma y no sé lo que he escrito" (136) [I've let my pen run free and don't know what I've written], Carlos claims that the key to Poland's subjugation lies in the Romantic self-absorption of its artists:

> La juventud, los artistas, lo más exquisito de la raza, es como la describen sus novelistas y sus poetas. . . . Quien se extasía en sí mismo, quien se goza en sí mismo, no va adelante, no progresa. . . . El descontento psicológico de los polacos es anómalo. . . . Plosowski [*sic*][12] y Polaniecki,[13] las dos antítesis del tipo polaco, tienen el mismo defecto de origen: no saben lo que quieren, y cuando lo saben, caen en la melancolía de lo ya conocido. (135–36)

> [The youth, the artists, the most exquisite representatives of the race, are just as their novelists and poets describe them. . . . A person who is captivated by himself, who delights in himself, doesn't move forward, doesn't progress. . . . The psychological discontent of the Poles is anomalous. . . . Ploszowski and Polaniecki, the two antitheses of Polishness, have the same fundamental defect: They don't know what they want, and when they do know, they sink into the melancholy of overfamiliarity.]

These opinions, although not very flattering to the Poles, were probably not what attracted the attention of the "Asociación de los 'buenos rusos' " (Casanova 1924, *En la corte de los zares*, 160) ["Good Russians" Association] and thus of the Russian governor. The charge, which Casanova denied, was having spoken "mal del Gobierno ruso" (162) [ill of the Russian government], and it must have resulted from the passage in which Carlos refers to the affair between Catherine the Great of Russia and Stanisław II August Poniatowski, the last King of Poland, which gave rise to the first partition of Poland in 1773:

> La hedionda Catalina, con el primer beso dado a Poniatowski, hizo lo que Judas; entregó maniatada a Polonia. . . . Seguro estoy que cuando se hunda la hegemonía prusiano (no hay hegemonía que dure más de dos, tres siglos) y se disgregue en pequeños grupos bárbaros el núcleo moscovita, Polonia continuará su historia, reforzada por los pequeños focos eslavos de Hungría y los Balkanes que se unirán a ella, y a orillas del Vístula surgirá blanca y potente la Atenas del Norte. *Amor, patriae, vinxit*, proclamará la inscripción de su Acrópolis. (Casanova 1908, *Más que amor*, 133–34)

> [The repugnant Catherine, with the first kiss she bestowed on Poniatowski, did the same as Judas; she handed Poland over, chained and bound. . . . I'm

sure that when Prussian hegemony eventually falls (no hegemony lasts more than two, three centuries) and the muscovite nucleus disperses into little groups of barbarians, Poland's history will continue, reinforced by the little Slavic enclaves in Hungary and the Balkans that will join her, and on the banks of the Vistula will arise, white and powerful, the Athens of the North. *Amor, patriae, vinxit,* the inscription on its Acropolis will say.]

Recounting the incident in her biography of Roman Dmowski (the right-wing Polish nationalist politician with close ties to the Lutosławski family), Casanova's second daughter, Izabela Wolikowska, corroborates this interpretation:

Matka moja drukowała w "Gazecie warszawskie" około 1910 roku pewna nowele. Nagle, po kilku odcinkach, censura rosyjska nałozyta wysoką grzywnę za jeden ustęp w którym znakomita poetka hiszpańska zarliwie oddana polsce, przepowiadała przyszlą Polskę. (1961, 99)

[My mother was publishing a certain novel in "Gazeta Warszawska" in about 1910. Suddenly, after several installments, the Russian censor imposed a large fine for one paragraph in which the superb Spanish poet, passionately devoted to Poland, predicted an independent future for Poland.]

Although the analysis of the Spanish political situation that follows the central letter seems tame by comparison—and, indeed, this may even have been the intention—it is no less critical. The dialogue concerns María's reaction when Carlos announces, "Me esperan días duros; estoy en desacuerdo con mi partido, que intenta llevar a las Cortes un absurdo proyecto coercitivo de las órdenes religiosas" (Casanova 1908, *Más que amor,* 149). [Dark days await me; I'm in disagreement with my party, which is trying to take before the Cortes an absurd project to coerce the religious orders.][14] Troubled and concerned with his moral integrity, she asks, "¿Qué compromisos, qué amistades, qué programa político, o qué falsos pudores pueden obligar a un hombre a hacer algo contra sus convicciones éticas?" (147). [What commitments, what friendships, what political program, or what false modesty can oblige a man to act against his ethical beliefs?] Her response is masked by conventional claims of a "feminine" inability to understand politics: "¿Me equivoco? Es probable. Las mujeres no entendemos de esas cosas, y yo menos que todas ellas" (147). [Am I wrong? Probably. We women don't understand these things, least of all me.] However, María's response reveals, in fact, a profound and knowledgeable cynicism about political maneuverings:

Y no me explico que los sociólogos, los reformadores o los políticos más
serios, hasta los más puros de intención y de vida, dejen en casos dados
arrinconada la ética, para poner en pie y en movimiento una ley, una teoría,
un proyecto oportunista, suerte de autómata que haciendo piruetas y dando
tumbos recorre un breve camino y cae al fin. (147)

[And I can't understand why sociologists, reformers, or the most serious of
politicians, even those with the purest intentions and lives, can leave ethics
aside on some occasions, to set in motion a law, a theory, an opportunist
project, like an automaton, which, twirling and lurching around, travels a
short distance only to fall over in the end.]

Again voicing opinions that Casanova had recorded elsewhere, María explains
why women are vital to the nation's future: "En lo que tenemos voz y voto,
es en defender lo bello y lo justo: en querellarnos por la moral, sobre la que
pasan los hombres ocupados y preocupados de otros altos problemas" (147).
[Insofar as we have a voice and a vote, it is to defend the beautiful and the
just, to argue for the moral, which men disregard, busy and concerned about
other, higher problems.] To criticize the seemingly futile party infighting that
dominated Spanish politics, Casanova again assigns the most biting analysis
of the situation to Carlos. He describes his own Liberal Party as "un partido
que cuenta varios caciques y no tiene jefe" [a party with several caciques and
no leader] and dismisses their policies as "esos que hacen de un serio programa político un cartel de espectáculos populares" [the sort that turn a serious political program into a poster for popular spectacles]. Then he concludes
despondently, "No es difícil presentar y hasta aprobar leyes cuando se cuenta
con la mayoría parlamentaria: lo difícil es legislar para bien del país" (155–56).
[It's not hard to present and even pass laws when you have a parliamentary
majority; what's difficult is to legislate for the good of the country.] Disil-
lusioned, he resigns the next day. Perturbed by the possibility that his resignation is motivated by his love for her rather than by his conscience, María
rereads their entire correspondence only to discover that she has profound
reservations about their future together:

He releído todas, todas tus cartas, y me asombra el camino que hemos
andado juntos en el tiempo relativamente corto que dura nuestra
comunicación. ¿A dónde vamos, mi amigo del alma? Si me dejo conducir
por tí, ¿a dónde me llevas? (166)

[I've reread every single one of your letters, and I'm horrified by the road we've taken together in the relatively short time our correspondence has lasted. Where are we going, my dearest friend? If I allow myself to be led by you, where will you take me?]

María's revelation is a turning point in terms of both her relationship with Carlos and the novel's negotiation of personal writing and public authorship. If the first part of the novel establishes that oppression of women impedes national progress, the second part breaks down the images that underpin that oppression. There are no further digressions or anecdotes as Carlos intensifies the pressure for María to come to Spain and marry him. He admonishes her, "Comienza a ser molesto, molesto y doloroso, que no respondas a mis llamamientos . . . Lo que me das es menos de lo que tienes para darme. . . . ¿Por qué, amándote cual te amo, no he de tenerte toda mía?" (Casanova 1908, *Más que amor*, 167–68). [It's becoming annoying, painful and annoying, that you won't respond to my pleas. . . . What you're giving me is less than you have to give. . . . Why, loving you as I do, can't I have you all for myself?] His reaction to her resistance eliminates any doubt that his sense of his own masculinity is predicated entirely on her feminine submission. When he makes his decision to resign from his government post, he explains, "Tus cartas han *virilizado* mi voluntad" (157, emphasis mine). [Your letters have *virilized* my will.] When she refuses to visit him in Spain, however, he remarks irritably, "Quien *castra* el amor o *hace abortar* sus sueños, que envejezca aislado y muera solo" (176, emphasis mine). [Let those who *castrate* love or *abort* its dreams grow old by themselves and die alone.] His outstandingly petulant response to her reminder that her duty to her sons and his duty to Elisa impede their marriage convinces María once and for all that Carlos has no understanding of her moral and religious beliefs:

Tus hijos representan para mí, en el proceso de las dificultades que debemos vencer, un gran cero. ¿Lo entiendes? Un gran cero, exactamente igual al que representa mi mujer. . . . ¿Que no tenemos porvenir? ¿Por qué? ¿A causa de dos muñecos y una loca? ¡Desvarío! . . . ¿Crees tú que en el Vaticano no hay soluciones para un hombre como yo? Pues te equivocas. (176–77)

[Your children are to me, in the context of the difficulties we must overcome, a big nothing. Understand? A big nothing, just like my wife. . . . You say we don't have a future? Why? Because of two little dolls and a madwoman? That's insane! . . . Do you think the Vatican has no solutions for a man like me? Well, you're wrong.]

After he threatens to travel to Poland, María agrees to visit Spain. Confronted with the prospect of a face-to-face meeting, and quailing at the thought of the inevitable clash between Carlos's image of her and the reality, she asks Halina:

> ¿Y si mi personita insignificante desagrada a Carlos? Él es, ante todo, poeta, y tengo miedo que me haya embellecido imaginariamente y que, desencantado, se inmute al encararse conmigo. (188)

> [And what if my insignificant little person displeases Carlos? He is, after all, a poet, and I'm afraid he might have built me up in his mind and, disenchanted, he may shudder to look upon me].

When they meet and she sees that her fears are justified, she complains to Halina that Carlos conducts their conversations "como si en vez de contestarme se contestara a sí mismo" (Casanova 1908, *Más que amor,* 211) [as if instead of answering me, he is answering himself]. Worse still, echoing Enrique Wolski's treatment of the unfortunate Gelcha, he tells her what to do: "Carlos ha organizado mi vida, ha marcado horas a mis paseos y, naturalmente, no doy cuatro pasos sin la tutela de mi escudero leal [Carlos's manservant, who attends María in Carlos's absence]" (224). [Carlos has organized my life, has set times for my walks, and, naturally, I can't go four paces without the watchful eye of my loyal page.] Unlike Gelcha, however, María is vociferous in her objection, protesting, "Las mujeres españolas no tenemos libertad, no podemos prescindir de dueñas y rodrigonas" (224). [We Spanish women have no freedom; we can't get away from chaperones and lady's maids.] Armed with "bravura de soldado impaciente de entrar en combate" [the courage of a soldier itching to go into battle] and "cierta dureza interior inexplicable, una sensación acre de animosidad hacia Carlos" (193) [a certain inexplicable inner hardness, a bitter feeling of animosity toward Carlos], María sets about regaining her independence and destroying what Carlos himself refers to as "la jaula dorada de mis planes concretos, definitivos" (247) [the gilded cage of my solid, definitive plans]. Over a weekend in Madrid, the two clash continually: in the Prado over artistic taste and at the Teatro Español over social niceties (LXXXV), in the cemetery over Carlos's past (LXXXVI) and in the Paseo de la Florida over his attempt to kiss her (LXXXVII). The distinction between masculine/elite and feminine/popular approaches to culture at the heart of the novel comes to a head in the contrasting responses to the paintings in the Prado. María describes how Carlos enters the museum "grave con la gravedad del devoto que entra en un templo" (230) [grave with the gravity of a believer entering a temple] and how "su refinamiento estético se extasía solamente ante la obra depurada, genial" (229) [his refined aesthetic taste rejoices only before elaborate works of genius]. In comparison, she is not inspired by the aesthetic doctrine of *l'art pour l'art* but by the materialist world of history and faith: "Me embobo con [obras] que reviven un momento de nuestra historia; con una escena caballeresca, con la romántica soledad de un claustro, con una cabeza ascética, extática, o una Virgen místicamente hermosa" (229). [I'm crazy for works that revive a moment of our history, with a chivalric scene, the romantic solitude of a cloister, an ascetic, ecstatic bust, or a mystically beautiful virgin.] María acknowledges the incompatibility of their worldviews—"cada uno de nosotros aborrece lo que al otro seduce" (230) [each of us despises what seduces the other]—but Carlos is unwilling to do so, and their visit ends abruptly.

The final blow to María's idealization of Carlos comes with the juxtaposition of her sudden realization as they leave the theater that he enjoys his public image as "el envidiado héroe de leyendas Donjuanescas" (Casanova 1908, *Más que amor*, 233) [the envied hero of donjuanesque legends] and her unwitting discovery of the tomb of his dead lover at the cemetery. Just before their confrontation in the Paseo de la Florida, María accepts that the man she loves is not the man in front of her. She tells Halina, "Asómbrate, atérrate, mi leal consejera; aquel 'Carlos mío' no era el que enamorado y trémulo estaba a mi lado, sino *el otro*, el de las cartas . . . el que de lejos amé—¡Qué absurdo!" (244, emphasis Casanova's). [Be amazed, be afraid, my faithful counselor; that "Carlos of mine" was not the same man who stood enchanted and tremulous at my side but *the other one*, the one from the letters . . . the one I loved from afar—how absurd!] When she turns her head as Carlos tries to kiss her, he grabs her by the neck, shouting, "¡Te aborrezco!" (245). [I despise you!] All pretense vanishes: "Nos miramos un instante frente a frente, como dos enemigos irreconciliables" (245). [We gazed at each other for a moment face to face, like two irreconcilable enemies.] Nevertheless, Carlos makes one more overture. He writes María a letter threatening to imprison her "pobre almita . . . en la jaula dorada de [sus] planes concretos, definitivos" (247) [poor little soul . . . in the gilded cage of (his) solid, definitive plans]. In their subsequent interview, he attempts to intimidate her into marriage, chillingly remarking, "Cuando el pajarillo caído del nido no sabe buscar su alimento, hay que abrirle el pico y darle de comer" (249). [When the fledgling fallen from the nest can't find its own food, you have to open its beak and make it eat.] As Kathleen Glenn observes of this scene, "The violence implicit in the image of force-feeding and the words *tomará*, *forzará* and *de viva fuerza* make this sound suspiciously like a threat of rape" (1996, 52). For María, this is the end. She feels "quebrantada de cuerpo y espíritu, rendida, sin saber qué hacer" (248) [broken in body and soul, worn out, at a loss as to what to do]; she feels suffocated, as his plans "oprimen como un nudo corredizo" (249) [press like a slippery knot]. As Carlos accuses her of being un-Spanish, "contaminated" by her time in Poland, María determines to fight against the nervous exhaustion—the result of her conditioning—that threatens to engulf her. A week later, fortified by letters from her children that remind her of her maternal duties and a visit from a society acquaintance who reaffirms Carlos's public image as an amoral seducer (XC), María grants Carlos a final interview, submits passively to a kiss, allows him to imagine that her silence is acquiescence, and flees without a word that same night (XCI). For the remainder of the novel, we hear only Carlos's words, first cursing María, threatening to kill her, and accusing her of being "medio muerta" (263) [half dead] and then, after a lapse of some months, agreeing to resume their correspondence.

How, then, are we to read the end of *Más que amor*? In her discussion of what she calls the "dynamics of literary closure," Altman identifies two major categories of closure in epistolary narrative: "motivated state of arrested equilibrium" and "lack of resolution due to the enigmatic silence of one writer" (1982, 148–49). *Más que amor* fits the second of these categories, which—according to Altman—is the rarer of the two. The distribution of the last letters of the novel is as follows:

> XCI: May 8, Madrid. María's last letter, addressed to Halina.
> XCII: May 11. Telegram from Carlos to María.
> XCIII: May 12. Letter from Carlos to María.
> XCIV: September 12. Letter from Carlos to María.
> XCV: October 13. Letter from Carlos to María.

Significantly, María's last letter is addressed to Halina, emphasizing the importance of their friendship. The pattern of the beginning of the novel, where María wrote the first six letters in sporadic bursts, is partially mirrored at the end, where we see only Carlos's letters to María. In both letters XCIV and XCV, Carlos refers to correspondence he has received from María, paraphrasing (but not quoting from) them, but the letters themselves are withheld from the reader. Why might this be? Kathleen Glenn suggests that "if Carlos is given the last word, it is only so that he can confess that he is still irresistibly drawn to María, perhaps because of her inaccessibility and "el misterio de lo no desflorado" (1996, 49 [quoting Casanova 1908, *Más que amor*, 264]) [the mystery of what hasn't been deflowered]. Carlos's confession suggests that he persists in seeing María as an example of conventionally feminine mystery. Has he learned nothing? Glenn does not directly address the issue of María's sudden silence, or its possible motivation, but several readings are suggested. If we read the end of the novel as a reversal of the beginning, where María's voice was dominant and Carlos remained silent (the first of his letters that the reader sees firsthand is XI), then it would seem that María has been silenced—as a punishment for her "transgressions"?—and returned to the conventional feminine role of passive object of affection. Or perhaps it reflects an active withdrawal from Carlos and a refusal to invest in the relationship. The key, I think, lies in Carlos's paraphrase in his final letter. María has asked him to explain the rules of distant attraction to her. Could this be a test? Could it be a chance for Carlos to prove that he does, in fact, understand what she has been trying to tell him all along? Glenn believes this to be the case: "Unconvincing as the ending may be, it is an acknowledgement that María was right and that she has won Carlos over to her point of view" (1996, 49). Glenn's reading of the novel's conclusion emphasizes its inherent paradox. Carlos appears to have come around to María's point of view about the merits of a long-distance relationship; in fact, however, he has learned nothing. He is persisting in his imagined dialogue with an imaginary María who is nothing whatsoever like the very real woman who has eluded him.

The denouement of *Más que amor*, like that of *Wolski* and *Lo eterno*, is consciously ambiguous. The novel ends with what appears to be the beginning of a renewed relationship, but what is its basis? Has anything changed between Carlos and María, or are they condemned to continue talking at cross-purposes? Is there any hope of men and women understanding each another? The ending that Glenn has described as "anticlimactic" (1996, 49) is deliberately so. Casanova emphatically does not resolve the many questions that Carlos's last letters pose. Does he give up his "masculine" mindset and come around to María's way of thinking? Is it a victory for "feminine" ways of thinking? Why does María disappear at the end of the novel? What does her silence mean? In DuPlessis's terms, María has found a way to "writ[e] beyond the ending" that Carlos, representing Spanish society, prescribes for her. She has successfully eluded marriage, but—just as in *Wolski* Mara had to choose Lithuania over Poland and in *Lo eterno* Juan had to leave Spain for Africa— she has had to leave Spain in order to do so. In the context of my reading of *Más que amor* as a dramatization of the female artist's struggle for freedom of expression, the novel's conclusion suggests that Spanish society is so hostile that she can survive Spain only by leaving it. If María does not leave, she faces the prospect of sharing the fate of her "dark double" Elisa, who is trapped and dies insane. In light of the analogy between the "sick" female artist and the "sick" nation that underpins *Más que amor*, this conclusion suggests that if it is to progress, Spain (like Poland) must detach itself from the assumptions and preconceptions that underpin its current position.

Más que amor is an unusual and ambitious text. Casanova uses the possibilities of the epistolary genre to test out a wide range of narrative voices other than the intimate and a variety of cultural models other than the romance, among them regenerationism, politics, literary criticism, nationalism, feminism, popular tale, oral confidence, travelogue writing, and the Gothic. Among these, the central position of the most controversial letter, followed by political discussion that is virtually unmediated by sentimental formulas, is profoundly significant. The self-consciousness of the epistolary form allows Casanova to treat questions of authorship and the relationship between public and private, politics and literature. Thus, María's reading of *Popioły* at the start of the novel foregrounds the role of art in the construction of nation, which is reflected both in the figure of the poet-politician that María believes Carlos to be and in Casanova's own intervention (through the characters of María and Carlos) into the very public world of national politics.

CHAPTER 5

Madrid–Galicia

Princesa del amor hermoso (1909)

The breakdown of Sofía Casanova's marriage to Wincenty Lutosławski so swiftly followed her literary success with both the Spanish and Polish versions of *Más que amor* that a cynical reader might be tempted to connect the two events. Casanova never openly acknowledged Lutosławski's remarriage (he began a new family with a former student). She managed to turn this personal ordeal into a great professional opportunity, however, by taking advantage of her success and focusing once again on her writing career. To this end she traveled to Madrid several times during 1907 and 1908, paying extended visits to her mother and younger brother, Vicente (now a published poet and editor). Until her permanent return to Poland in 1914, her principal mission was to reestablish herself in Galician and Spanish literary and intellectual circles (now with the added motivation of making a living, since she could no longer rely on financial support from her husband). Her two elder daughters, who were now adults (María was nineteen and Izabela eighteen), spent a great deal of time in Poland; only ten-year-old Halina remained with her mother. In the winter of 1907, moved—as she recalled in the 1916 *ABC* article "Diario de viaje"—by her "secreta ansia de *no morir aún* en la memoria de los poetas" (n.p., emphasis Casanova's) [secret desire *not to die yet* in the memory of other poets], she decided to visit Carlos Fernández Shaw, the president of the literary section of the Ateneo de Madrid, to propose a poetry reading. Although (after some prodding) Fernández Shaw agreed, Casanova found the experience traumatic. Later (in the same *ABC* article) she recalled, "Salí del Ateneo temblando con una pena de soledad en mi alma" (n.p.). [I left the Ateneo shaking and with a lonely pain in my soul.]

When the poetry reading at the Ateneo finally took place, it led to a series of collaborations, including the 1910 lecture *La mujer española en el extranjero* (see Chapter 1 herein). Still, Casanova soon realized that in order to make a living, she would need to expand her professional horizons beyond occasional lectures and readings and that to do so would require a concerted change in direction. The financial considerations combined with the social and personal freedom that she seized (even if she had not sought it out) resulted in more determination and, perhaps, less scrupulousness in the choices she began to make. Where she had previously focused on prestigious literary forms—full-length novels and poetry—she now turned her attention to the mass market, playing the game of marketing and publicity that she hoped would raise her professional profile and, crucially, earn her enough money to maintain her independence in Madrid. At the same time, however, as her lecture at the Ateneo shows, she remained committed to her critical, feminist perspective on Spanish society and culture.

In this chapter and the chapter that follows, we follow Casanova's career during the six subsequent years she spent in Madrid, a period during which—in an attempt to exploit the new audiences brought about by the diversification of the literary market—she made the decision to rebrand herself as a popular, regional (Galician) writer. Especially interesting are the textual consequences of the tension between Casanova's evident desire to continue her feminist intellectual project and the very real aesthetic and editorial demands of the mass market. These demands were fueled by the explosion in popular fiction linked with the development of the new *novela corta* [short novel] genre in the first decade of the twentieth century, to which Casanova contributed with her *Princesa del amor hermoso* (1909).

After Casanova's disagreeable first experience with the demands of the new genre when she was trying to place *Lo eterno* for publication (see Chapter 3), she appears to have become much more willing to balance her feminist commitment with the limitations imposed by commercial and editorial demands by the time she wrote *Princesa*. The novel also reveals her participation in the Galician cultural scene then emerging from the *rexionalista* political movement headed by her great friend from A Coruña, the writer, politician, and historian (and husband of Rosalía de Castro) Manuel Murguía. This new cultural scene and Casanova's most high-profile contribution to it in the short story compilation *El pecado* (1911) are the subject of Chapter 6. I mention this new dimension to Casanova's work here because of its bearing on my reading of *Princesa*. Although the original edition of the novel was illustrated by the caricaturist Castelao (Alfonso Daniel Rodríguez de Castelao), soon to become a key figure in the Galician nationalist movement, this was not its only Galician connection. Perhaps more pertinently, Casanova's penchant for repackaging old works for new markets (as with *Wolski, Lo eterno,* and later *Más que amor*) meant that the novel itself would soon be retitled, rebranded as a *novela gallega* [Galician novel], and reprinted along with several other newly Galicianized works in El *pecado*. In other words, not even two years after first publishing *Princesa*, Casanova was already nudging her readers in a particular direction and, perhaps more significantly, ensuring that she retained control of the novel's place (and with it her own) in the rapidly evolving Iberian literary ecosystem.

Little of this peculiar context has hitherto been addressed in critical studies of *Princesa*. Thanks to its 1989 reprinting in Ángela Ena Bordonada's anthology *Novelas breves de escritoras españolas, 1900–1936*, the novel (in its original incarnation) has received rather more critical attention than most of Casanova's other works. Partly, perhaps, as a result of the exceptionalizing effect of anthology, however, critics have tended to consider it in isolation from not only the overall trajectory of Casanova's life and work but also the material conditions of its composition and publication. In consequence, the *novela* has often been seen as highly conventional, "un relato basado exclusivamente en una historia de amores y desamores" (Bordonada 1989, 35) [a story based exclusively on a tale of love and loathing] or "un texto de tipo realista y de intención eminentemente didáctica . . . que se aboga por la acción femenina reducida a la domesticidad" (Paredes 2003, 93) [a text with realist features and eminently didactic intentions . . . which defends the reduction of female activity to domesticity]. We have already seen that to take Casanova's fiction purely at face value is almost always to do her a great disservice and that her pragmatically subtle manipulation of literary and cultural convention has led her works to be greatly underestimated by even the most sympathetic critics. Casanova's use of these conventions as scaffolding is evident from the following plot summary of *Princesa,* which, as we will see, appears to justify Bordonada's reading of the novel as a text where "se localizan abundantes elementos de origen romántico, con ocasionales aproximaciones al tono enfático y melodramático de la novela folletinesca del siglo XIX" (1989, 36) [there are abundant elements of romantic origin, with occasional hints of the emphatic, melodramatic tone of the serialized novels of the nineteenth century].

Princesa is the story of Laura de Medina and the consequences of her decision to forgo marriage to her unfaithful fiancé to begin a new life for the sake of "divertirme . . . *flirtear* . . . ver pasar junto a mí las emociones que inspiro y no comparto" (Casanova 1989, *Princesa del amor hermoso*, 160) [enjoying myself . . . *flirting* . . . watching the passage of emotions that I inspire but do not share]. The plot can be summarized briefly as follows: Having discovered that her fiancé of ten years, the diplomat Fernando Insáuriz, has been unfaithful to her with her own married sister, Laura writes him a long letter in which she breaks off their engagement and declares her intention to forgo marriage to live a flirtatious life in which she does not take men seriously (chapter 1 of the novel). She spends the following summer at the Galician *pazo* [country house] of some distant relatives, accompanied by a small group of socialites who cynically comment on her every move (chapter 2). While at the *pazo*, she attracts the attention of her cousin's sickly son, the twenty-five-year-old poet José Luis, and they begin an intimate friendship (chapter 3). Shortly thereafter, Fernando joins the house party and proposes a midnight walk (chapter 4). José Luis becomes sick from the night air, and as he convalesces, his feelings for Laura undergo a series of profound changes, from poetic reverence to erotic desire to neoplatonic ecstasy (chapters 5 and 6). On the visitors' last afternoon, Fernando and Laura talk, she offers him a final rejection, and he warns her that she is making José Luis her victim (chapter 7). Over the following five days, Laura, who has remained at the *pazo*, is stricken by guilt and resolves to confess to José Luis that she cannot return his love and that, indeed, she has never loved him. Still in ecstasy, he replies that it does not matter, as his love is eternal. Then he dies, leaving Laura and his mother, María, united in grief (chapter 8). The final chapter takes the form of an epilogue, with a peasant couple (who appeared briefly in chapter 3) commenting on the death of José Luis (chapter 9).

Casanova's debt to the sensational, melodramatic, sentimental genre is evident, above all, in the plotting (the love triangle ending in tragic death) and the cast of stereotypes, but the sentimental novel is not the only cultural model against which *Princesa* is written. *Princesa* resembles Casanova's earlier works in that it is a complex narrative constructed from a series of cultural models, among them the sentimental novel, Galician regionalism, and the Don Juan archetype. Like the earlier works, moreover, the text explicitly encourages the reader to move beyond the overt but superficial reading of *Princesa* as an "eminently didactic" story of "love and loathing." Although the straightforward moral denouement understood by María Paredes is clearly present, therefore, it is unsettled by a number of hints and clues that make other readings available to an attuned reader. What is more, because of the conditions of its publication and dissemination, the novel brings a new dimension to Casanova's ongoing critique of the questions of gender and national identity and women's position in society that we have viewed at the center of her work so far. Because understanding these conditions is key to understanding the novel and Casanova's intentions for it, I preface my analysis of the text with a brief analysis of the *novela corta* form itself, particularly the gendered dimensions of its production and reception.

Casanova's interest in the *novela corta* seems to have begun very early in the life of the new genre. In 1907 Eduardo Zamacois founded *El Cuento Se-*

manal [The Weekly Story] in Madrid, and we know from the prologue to *Lo eterno* that Casanova's novel was rejected by a publisher (most likely Zamacois) that same year. It is hardly surprising that Casanova was so keen to take advantage of a genre that not only offered unprecedented financial and commercial possibilities but also was fast becoming a forum for artistic and literary experimentation. Its greatest innovation was that it did not depend on existing media for dissemination but was a commercial enterprise in itself. Everything about it—from its length (usually between sixteen and thirty-four pages) and the low-quality paper used to print it to its accessible language and urban, middle-class scenarios—was designed to aid its rapid consumption by large numbers of urban, middle-class readers who were unable or unwilling to invest the necessary time and money in long, convoluted, and expensive realist novels. *El Cuento Semanal*, the first of the collections, produced a complete, original illustrated novel at a low price every Friday. The regular publication schedule meant that it was in the best interest of each collection to retain its *colaboradores* [authors], many of whom signed contracts, were treated as employees and given much the same status as journalists, and followed a (broadly conceived) house style. The result was a radical change in the writer's social and economic status that proved attractive to not only most of the best-known Spanish writers of the late nineteenth and early twentieth centuries but also a great many others who—like Casanova—have subsequently been forgotten.

The *novela corta* may have brought radical changes to the production and dissemination of narrative at the *fin de siglo*, but like other less-prestigious media, it rarely finds a place in conventional histories of *fin de siglo* literature. As Carmen de Urioste observes, it was seen as "un género inferior, menor o marginal, en cualquier caso literatura popular" (1994, 593) [an inferior, lesser or marginal genre, and certainly popular literature]—a view that, of course, presumes the existence of a genre that is considered better, more important, central, and elite. At least insofar as prose fiction is concerned, this position was occupied during the late nineteenth century by the realist novel, which gave way in the early twentieth century to the so-called Generation of 1898 novel. The contrast between this elite fiction and popular narrative, including the *novela corta*, was intrinsically gendered, not only in terms of authorship. As Alda Blanco has argued, canonical novelistic theory was based on "the retrieval and recirculation of the traditional idea of 'lo castizo' which came to function in the discourse as the symbolic representation of 'masculinity' in opposition to the 'femininity' of imitation and sentimental writing" (1995, 133). Blanco shows that realist and Generation of 1898 writers and intellectuals celebrated their own narrative as *viril* [virile] and *castizo* [pure-bred Spanish] whereas they dismissed popular literature as "tainted" by femininity and foreign influence. The *novela corta*—with its roots in popular literature, its sentimental themes, and its large female readership—was, by its very nature, a hybrid genre and therefore perceived as potentially threatening (and of course inferior) to the "true" Spanish novel.

One might expect that the reputedly inferior status of the new genre would cause elite intellectuals to disregard it; in fact, however, it appears to have caused them a surprising amount of anxiety. This anxiety was expressed primarily in moral terms, as canonical critics such as Azorín sought to discredit the new genre by focusing on a single type of text: the *novela galante* or *sicalíptica*. With regard to these erotic stories published by young male authors such as Felipe Trigo and Antonio Hoyos y Vinent, Azorín wrote with some disgust in 1910:

> La nueva generación . . . está completa y desenfrenadamente entregada al
> más bajo y violento erotismo; no transcurre una semana sin que aparezca en
> las librerías una nueva novela pornográfica; se ponen a estos libros los títulos
> más provocadores y llamativos; se los anuncia con grandes carteles por las
> esquinas; se describen en ellos las más torpes aberraciones humanas. (Qtd. in
> Granjel 1968, 35)

> [The new generation . . . is completely and unrestrainedly given over
> to the basest and most violent eroticism; not a week goes by without a
> pornographic novel appearing in bookshops; these books are given the most
> provocative and attention-seeking titles; they are advertised with enormous
> posters on street corners; they describe the crudest of human aberrations.]

Azorín's horror (which seems to have been inspired at least as much by the concept of advertising the novels with enormous posters as by the content of the novels themselves) would be shared in later decades by Francoist critics, who also focused heavily on the sexual content of what was, in the end, a relatively small corpus of texts. In consequence, the perception remains that the *novela corta*, in addition to being a popular genre, was pornographic, aberrant, and (if not downright dangerous) morally and intellectually inferior to the "serious" works of Azorín and his peers. As a result, it has been largely excluded from the Spanish cultural narrative and the self-named Generación de 1907 has fallen into virtual oblivion.[1]

One of the most serious consequences of this obsession with the relatively limited corpus of erotic *novelas cortas* is that it has helped to obscure the significant role that the genre played in opening up publishing to new types of authors. The *novela corta* certainly provided opportunities for Casanova and other female authors, but decades of critical resistance have prevented the extent of its influence from being fully uncovered. Since the late 1980s, a small but growing interest in the female-authored *novela corta* has emerged, in anthologies (e.g., Bordonada 1989), in studies of the period (e.g., Hurtado 1998), and in studies of individual authors (e.g., Imboden 2001). They all agree that the new genre provided new opportunities for women writers and "les proporcionó . . . fama y dinero" (Hurtado 1998, 151) [afforded them fame and money]. If the social and economic aspects of professionalization that the new genre provided were attractive to women authors, so too was the freedom from the social and narrative strictures of the late nineteenth century—what Azorín describes as "una época en que la novela era simetría y ordenada composición" (1959–1963, 863) [a time when the novel was symmetry and ordered composition]. Although certainly the *novela corta* created vital opportunities for women writers, the lack of comprehensive bibliographical information about the female-authored *novela corta* and the inaccessibility of texts have made it difficult to draw informed conclusions about its contribution to women's negotiation of national culture. We see the impact of our limited contextual knowledge when, for example, Ámparo Hurtado and Rita Imboden come to markedly different conclusions in their analysis of Concha Espina, whom Hurtado considers radical (1998, 153) but Imboden dismisses as producing sentimental, melodramatic texts that anticipate the popular and romantic *novela rosa* of the 1940s and 1950s (2001, 74).

Bibliographical research gives us some idea of the opportunities that the *novela corta* offered to Casanova and her peers at the *fin de siglo*, but the critical narrative does not always reflect these facts. In her study of the women she calls the "escritoras de 1898" [women writers of 1898], Hurtado argues that "todas, prosistas y dramaturgas, escribieron *novelas cortas*" [all of them, novelists and playwrights, wrote *novelas cortas*] and that "independientemente de su producción individual la novela corta destacó entre sus obras como un género literario común" (1998, 151) [quite apart from their individual production, the *novela corta* stands out among their works as a shared literary genre]. In fact, research shows that only a small number of women published *novelas cortas* in the first decades of the twentieth century, and many of the writers Hurtado considers to be part of the female Generation of 1898—such as Isabel de Palencia, María Goyri, María de Maeztu, and Carmen Baroja— published none at all. As far as I can ascertain, out of a total of 263 *novelas* in *El Cuento Semanal*—the collection that published Casanova's *Princesa*—14 are by women writers:[2] 3 each by Emilia Pardo Bazán and Carmen de Burgos; 2 by Blanca de los Ríos; and 1 each by Concepción Gimeno, Sofía Casanova, Ángela Barco, Sidonie-Gabrielle Colette Willy (in translation), Concha Espina, and Gloria de la Prada. Of the other collections in existence before World War I, *Los Contemporáneos* published 5 by Pardo Bazán (up to 1914), and 1 each by De los Ríos, De la Prada, and Casanova (*La madeja*). *El Libro Popular* included only 6 *novelas* by female authors: 1 by Pardo Bazán, 4 by Burgos, and 1 by Casanova (*El crimen de Beira-mar*).[3] These bibliographical details show that of the few women writers who published *novelas cortas* in the first decades of the twentieth century, the majority (Burgos, Casanova, Colette, De los Ríos, Gimeno, and Pardo Bazán,) were already established writers. Only Barco (whose *novela* was published for winning an honorable mention in a competition) and De la Prada could be said to have made their first—and, in Barco's case, only—literary impact with the *novela corta*.[4]

With the exception of the *novelas* by Pardo Bazán and Burgos, the vast majority of female-authored *novelas* remain unread, unstudied, and—where they are remembered at all—dismissed (like *Princesa*) as "conventional." For example, despite the importance that she ascribes to the *novela corta* in the careers of *fin de siglo* women, Hurtado mentions the names of only four authors, whom she divides into two "tendencies." In one group, she places Casanova and De los Ríos, whom she considers largely traditional (1998, 153). In the other group, she places Burgos and Espina because "fueron más allá y contaron . . . una historia femenina no convencional, otorgando a sus protagonistas femeninas capacidad para opinar y actuar en el dominio público" (153) [they went much further and told . . . unconventional stories of women, giving their female protagonists the ability to speak and act in the public domain]. This interpretation is, at the very least, unorthodox: Any reading of Espina's works, especially those written before 1916, shows her female protagonists to be largely passive and conformist, whereas (as my reading of *Princesa* shows) Casanova's Laura is anything but a traditional heroine.

More important, other writers unmentioned by Bordonada, Hurtado, or Imboden used the *novela corta* in highly creative ways. For example, Gimeno's *Una Eva moderna* is an explicitly political, feminist tract with only the most superficial sentimental framework. The protagonist, Luisa, is an intellectual who pushes her politician friend Lavistal to promote legal reforms based on the conviction that "los Códigos son la ley del varón, y es preciso que sean ley de la humanidad" (1909, chap. 2) [the Codes are the law of men, and they ought to be the law of all humankind]. In a number of closely argued passages, Gimeno sets out the bases of her feminist beliefs through conversations between Luisa and her friends (male and female). The *novela* closes with Luisa's decision to dedicate herself to her daughter's education, which may, of course, be read as supporting her return to the domestic sphere but may also (in the spirit of the *novela*) be read as actively promoting the importance of a feminist education for the future of Spanish women (chapter 9). De la Prada's 1912 *El cantar de los amores* takes a similar approach. Its pivotal moment is when the protagonist, Ana María, burns all the mementos of her past relationships so that she can move forward into a modern, egalitarian relationship with Rafael. The impulse toward the future is symbolized by the novel's climax: a train speeding through the Castilian countryside from historic Burgos to Madrid, where the couple's new life will begin. In this fascinating but almost entirely forgotten novel, De la Prada intentionally juxtaposes the "feminine" discourse of sentimental convention with the "masculine" discourse of Spanish history to propose a future for Spain (and its women) that is free from the baggage of the past.

These necessarily cursory readings of two texts that deserve far more critical attention demonstrate that Casanova was not alone in her use of the sentimental conventions of the *novela corta* to address issues of much wider importance. Furthermore, they reinforce the conviction that existing models for reading *fin de siglo* literature simply do not function for these complex and often contradictory texts. In my attempt to establish a model for reading the *novela corta*, I have found Maryellen Bieder's 1990 article "Between Genre and Gender: Emilia Pardo Bazán and *Los pazos de Ulloa*" both interesting and useful. Bieder argues that because in 1886 Pardo Bazán was standing "at the confluence of [competing] literary impulses, some in ascendancy, others on the wane," her novel is shaped from "the diversity of competing genre models." That is, she "forges her novel from the conjunction of *costumbrista* set pieces, realistic portrayal and plotting, sentimental exaltation of motherhood, and naturalist observation of man and nature" (1990, 131). Bieder's convincing argument is that the competing models that underpin *Los pazos de Ulloa* allow Pardo Bazán to raise "radical questions about the stiflingly rigid definitions of gender identity inscribed in the generic modes that [she] reworked" (143)—notably "male-voiced *costumbrismo*" and "the female-voiced sentimental novel" (131).

My analysis of *Princesa* is based on the hypothesis that twenty years later, Spanish literature again found itself at a "confluence of [competing] literary impulses," brought about by the emergence of the *novela corta*. As a hitherto unmarked space on the border between "high" and "low" fiction, novel and sentimental romance, "male-voiced" and "female-voiced" discourses, the *novela corta* offers an ideal locus for imagining social change. Although it is true that some (but by no means all) male writers of *novelas cortas* used their newfound authorial freedom to produce the famous *novelas sicalípticas*, we still know comparatively little about how their female peers used the genre.

The apparent incongruity of Casanova's decision to relaunch herself through this relatively unprestigious and undoubtedly marginalized genre may have been a deliberate strategy. I contend that the works she published after 1908, beginning with *Princesa*, offer us a model not only for reading the massive but critically untouched body of popular and regional writing (much of it by women) but also for reframing the conventional narrative of Spanish and Galician literary history to include these marginalized voices. Casanova—like Gimeno and De la Prada—took advantage of the newly fluid generic boundaries to introduce her questions about *fin de siglo* constructions of gender and nation, in life and in literature, to the wider audience provided by the *novela corta*.

The briefest glance at the cultural references that Casanova weaves into the tapestry of *Princesa* reveals the fact that, as David Herzberger has argued, "texts are always infected with meanings derived or appropriated from other texts" (1998, 126). The variety of "infections" that riddle the novel reveals not only Casanova's fascination with the key tropes of *fin de siglo* Spanish cultural discourse but also her determination to challenge them at the most fundamental level. This challenge is most evident in her treatment of the familiar figure of Don Juan, which has provided the focus of most existing critical readings. As Ann Davies persuasively argues, a key aspect of Don Juan's significance for Spanish cultural criticism is that he embodies "a [Foucauldian] form of sexual discourse, historically constructed," which "has allowed different writers and dramatists . . . to give their own account of what sexuality entails" (2001, 160). In the case of *Princesa*, the highly gendered connotations of the Don Juan figure provide Casanova with a potent starting point for her critique of the norms of Spanish gender and sexual relations. Through the character of Fernando Insáuriz, a diplomat by profession (and thus a public representative of the Spanish nation), she presents her own take on the contemporary Spanish obsession with this legendary figure and, in particular, with his modernist incarnation in the works of her fellow Galician Ramón del Valle-Inclán.

Casanova was not the only woman writer to perceive the fascination with Don Juan as an opening, and the connection has not gone unnoticed by critics. In "The Domestication of Don Juan in Women Novelists of Modernist Spain," reading *Princesa* alongside texts by De los Ríos, Burgos, and Espina, Roberta Johnson argues that, like her contemporaries, Casanova enters "into a dialogue with Valle-Inclán's contemporary treatment of the [Don Juan] figure" (1998, 223). As Johnson shows, the points of contact between *Princesa* and Valle-Inclán's *Sonatas* are undeniable. Still, I contend that the function of the Don Juan allusion in Casanova's novel goes beyond simply challenging "the legendary Don Juan with a contemporary female 'Doña Juana'" (229), since both narrator and protagonist are concerned not only with confronting such stereotypes but also with actively dismantling them. In other words, Don Juan is not the center of the text, although (in what may be another tactical move by Casanova) his familiarity means that we instinctively focus in on him. In fact, Fernando occupies only a marginal position in the novel. He does not appear in person until chapter 4 (after all the other characters), and he disappears at the end of chapter 7 along with the other houseguests. Most tellingly, he is, like De los Ríos's "personaje—no me decido a llamarle héroe" (1989, 67) [character—I can't bring myself to call him hero], a Don Juan in decline. In her opening letter, Laura points out to Fernando that although he considers himself a seducer *par excellence*, in truth—at nearly forty—he is getting on in age and will soon need a nurse rather than a lover:

> Tu insistencia es soberbia, entreverada de fatuidad donjuanesca. Tu amor propio se siente alfilerado por mi alejamiento; sin contar con que, como te acercas a la cuarentena, entiendes que te conviene tomar mujer dócil que te cataplasmee los achaques futuros—acaso inmediatos. (Casanova 1989, *Princesa del amor hermoso*, 157)

> [Your insistence is pride, interpolated with Don Juanesque presumption. Your self-regard is wounded by my withdrawal; not to mention that, as you approach forty, you understand the benefits of a docile wife who will cosset you through future—even imminent—illnesses.]

We later discover through some society gossip that Fernando's donjuanesque reputation is on the wane in public as in private. It has been noted that he gets tired during polo and is making a habit of going to bed early in a bad mood (185). Nevertheless, the Don Juan image is fundamental to Fernando's self-esteem. He tries to justify Laura's accusation of his "odiosa *flirt* con [su] propia hermana casada" [hateful flirtation with (her) own married sister] with the time-honored excuse that "la infidelidad en nosotros los hombres no excluye el amor: a veces hasta lo aviva" (156–57) [unfaithfulness in us men doesn't exclude love: sometimes it enlivens it]. Laura, however, is no longer prepared to play the willing and submissive female on whom Don Juan depends for his masculinity (and thus his very existence). Her decision to leave seriously affects Fernando's self-image, not to mention his self-control. A couple of days into her visit, he appears (uninvited) at the *pazo*, vainly attempting to needle her with such snide comments as "Veo que te has hecho una *modern women* [sic] *my dear*" (173) [I see you've become a modern woman, my dear] or flirting with another houseguest (Camila), who willingly plays the submissive role that he desires and thus restores his dignity (174).

As the embodiment of Spain's public face, Fernando represents the dominant concept of "Spanishness" that the text calls into question, but he is not alone as a target for Casanova's critique. In an interesting and deceptively significant move, she aligns him not with the principal protagonists Laura and José Luis but with the houseguests, who see themselves as bastions of polite society but who, like Fernando, in fact represent degenerate versions of well-known Spanish stereotypes. The second chapter of the *novela* is devoted to this "grupito de personas aviesas" (Casanova 1989, *Princesa del amor hermoso*, 161) [nasty little group of people] who function as a chorus, providing society's view of Laura and the unfolding events: the Cuban millionairess Camila de Valdés, a cynical magistrate called Rafael, and the elderly Marquesa de Vivar. By presenting these characters in particularly damning terms, Casanova neatly stimulates the reader into questioning the conventional views that they espouse. Camila, "la churrigueresca damita" (161) [the befrilled and furbelowed little lady], is married (to a rather shady businessman), but she is hardly a conventional devoted wife; she has led a life of "domestic liberty" in Madrid, where "todo lo criticaba; de todo el mundo decía pestes, y hacía allá y aquí lo que se le antojaba" (161) [she criticized everything; said dreadful things about everybody, and went here and there doing as she pleased]. She makes great play of appearing moral and devout, but, as Rafael remarks, this is but one example of her hypocrisy: "*¡Pardon!, prude* y sensible hija del trópico. Se me olvidó que usted se escandaliza de todo . . . y de nada" (163). [*Pardon, prude* and sensitive daughter of the tropics! I quite forgot how you are scandalized by everything . . . and nothing.] Her flirtation with Fernando, which leads to a midnight walk (proposed by Fernando with the express intention of further irritating Laura), is presented as profoundly unnatural: As they walk, "las luciérnagas de las veredas blandas—antorchas en los transportes del sano y fuerte amor campesino—apagaban las fosforescencias de sus alas al paso de aquella pareja sensual y frívola" (176) [the fireflies along the soft footpaths—torches illuminating the course of healthy, strong peasant romance—extinguished the glow of their wings as the sensual and frivolous pair passed by]. Similarly, the magistrate is sarcastically described as quite the opposite of compassionate, impartial justice: "Afirmaba que el género humano lo componen, casi sin excepción, criminales en la víspera de cometer el crimen, y su alto espíritu de justicia satisfacíase cuando la desgracia ejercía de verdugo derribando a los hombres" (161). [He insisted that humankind is composed, almost without exception, of criminals on the verge of committing their crime, and his lofty spirit of justice was satisfied whenever misfortune played the part of executioner, cutting men down.] The Marquesa de Vivar, whose name recalls that other Vivar, El Cid, embodiment of the Castilian hidalgo tradition, is not the august noble lady we might expect. Instead, we learn, she is quite overdressed and (in a rare pun from Casanova) "aún con ánimos para echar una cana al aire (y como tenía el buen gusto de no teñírselas, había canas de sobra que dar al viento)" (161) [still spirited enough to let her (gray) hair down (and as she had the good taste not to dye it, there were still plenty of [gray] hairs to let down)].

The members of this group, which represents the most powerful branches of Spanish society—the aristocracy, the judiciary, and the bourgeoisie—embody the expectations that Laura struggles against, in both life and literature. Their observations provide not only a barometer of polite society's attitudes but also a reminder of the way the events of people's lives are played out before and interpreted by that society. On their first appearance, they compare themselves to gleeful spectators at a bullfight, as Camila remarks to the *marquesa*, "A mí me divierten [los duelos de amores] y mucho más en la vida real que en las comedias o los libros" (Casanova 1989, *Princesa del amor hermoso*, 165). [I find lovers' tiffs so very diverting and even more so in real life than in plays or books.] When the group discovers that Fernando is to arrive shortly, the *marquesa* whispers excitedly, "De aquí va a salir algo gordo" (173) [something juicy is going to happen]. Camila too rejoices, "Un drama . . . es lo que hace falta para que no nos entierren de aburrimiento" (173). [A drama . . . is what we need so that we don't die of boredom.] Meanwhile, Rafael predicts, "Vamos a tener diversión. Luchas . . . encuentros . . . equivocaciones, y cuchilladas, quizá, como en los novelones, que dicho sea de paso tenían—no mucho—pero más sentido común que los modernos" (164). [We're going to have some entertainment. Skirmishes . . . assignations . . . misunderstandings, and stabbings, perhaps, like in those great long novels, which I must mention in passing had—not much—but more common sense than the modern ones.] Rafael's allusion to the "common sense" of the "novelones" refers to the framework of intertwined social and literary convention that was embodied in the romance plot on which these long melodramatic novels were based and that still dominated much early twentieth-century writing. His forecast that, despite Laura's reservations, "la boda sería el sainetesco final previsto" (164) [the wedding will be the farcical preordained conclusion] emphasizes the convention that a woman's story must end in marriage, however incongruously this conclusion might sit with what has gone before. The weakness and hypocrisy of the characters who identify themselves with the moral and narrative structures that underpin this worldview suggest that, in a reaction against the expectations of Spanish social and literary convention, Casanova is aligning herself with "los modernos." In this instance, we might understand "los modernos" as a reference to the *novela corta*, whose novelty and flexibility make it the ideal location for Casanova's biting, if underplayed, criticisms.

Casanova's conviction with respect to the need to break with old models of gender and national identity and with respect to the search for new models in both literature and life is the driving force behind *Princesa*. It is represented very clearly in her decision to move Fernando and the other representatives of the establishment to the periphery of the text and to bring José Luis and Laura into the center. We see it also in her calculated focus on the role of the reader in constructing meaning, a device that she had used to great effect in previous works (most strikingly in the final chapter of *Lo eterno*). Her determination to influence the attuned reader is made clear in a key early passage of *Princesa* that not only dramatizes a feminist reading of canonical literature but also signals the radical (and, at the time, largely unconsidered) potential of female-authored writing to effect social and cultural change. As they sit together in the *pazo*'s rose bower, Laura asks José Luis to continue to read the poetry they had been studying the previous day. He begins to read the following verse:

> Non sai
> Che smisurato amor, che affanni intensi,
> Che indecibili moti e che deliri
> Movesti in me; ne verrà tempo alcuno
> Che tu l'intenda . . .
> (Qtd. in Casanova 1989, *Princesa del amor hermoso*, 167)

> [You never knew
> What immense love, what intense breathlessness,
> What unspeakable trembling and what deliria
> You inspired in me; there will never be a time
> When you do understand . . .]

Then Laura cuts him off, exclaiming, "No estoy para oír esas jeremíadas de Leopardi" (167). [I'm not in the mood for Leopardi's lamentations.] Her explanation for the outburst is this: "Es desesperante en esa poesía su desprecio a la mujer. Amar y despreciar, ¡qué absurdo!" (167). [His disdain for women in this poetry makes me despair. How absurd, to love and disdain!] Casanova's choice of Giacomo Leopardi (1798–1837) is significant, since he was considered not only Italy's greatest Romantic poet but also its second-greatest poet of all time (after Francesco Petrarch). His popularity in *fin de siglo* Spain was such that Casanova's friend and contemporary Carmen de Burgos would publish a biography of him just two years later (1911). Whereas Leopardi clearly stands for canonical literary tradition in the context of *Princesa*, the poem that Laura and José Luis are reading—"Aspasia," from the *Canti* —carries its own coded message. Aspasia not only was the wife of Pericles in classical literature but also was recognized in her own right as a rhetorician, famous for her intellect (C. Glenn 1994). In the intertextually loaded context of *Princesa*, the reference to Aspasia suggests yet another layer to Laura's textualized persona, intensified by the fact that Leopardi's Aspasia is not an eloquent and serious intellectual but a silent object of worship and, moreover, a mother. Laura's rejection of Leopardi can thus be read as a rejection of the Romantic discourse that not only ignores women's intellectual capacities, revering their maternal role while scorning them as weak and silly, but also deforms the inspirational female figures women might look to as role models.

As a thinking, writing woman with a voice of her own, Laura has no time for the Romantic poets and their silent objects of affection. Instead, she asks José Luis to read her "versos de nuestra Rosalía, el más humano de sus lamentos" (Casanova 1989, *Princesa del amor hermoso,* 171) [some of our Rosalía's verses, the most human of her laments]:

> ¿Qué di a meiguiña?
> ¿Qué di a traidora? . . .
> Corazón que enloitado te crubes
> c'os negros desprezos qu'a falsa che-dona,
> ¿por qué vives loitando por ela?
> ¿Por qué, namorado, de pena salouzas?
> (Qtd. in ibid., 171)

> [What says the enchantress? What says the traitoress? . . .
> O, heart who wears the mourning garb
> of the false one's black disdain,
> why do you spend your life fighting for her?
> Why, beloved, do you sob so pitifully?]

The verse Laura chooses is from *Cantares gallegos,* the first collection of poetry by her Galician compatriot Rosalía de Castro (1837–1885), originally published in 1863. In contrast to Laura's rejection of Leopardi's verses, both Laura and José Luis react instinctively to Castro's: "La intensidad de la estrofa emocionó a ambos; latían sus corazones, persiguiendo en la difusa verdad de la poesía algo de sus almas, de su esencia sentimental, que el verso despertara y esparcía" (171). [The stanza's intensity moved them both; their hearts beat, pursuing through the diffuse truth of the poetry something of their souls, their sentimental essence, which the verse had awakened and now dispersed.] Both poet and poem are significant: Initially known as a fervent Galician nationalist, Castro had been (re)discovered by the Generation of 1898 and was celebrated in turn-of-the-twentieth-century Spain as "uno de los más altos poetas contemporáneos" (Azorín 1959–1963, 852) [one of the greatest contemporary poets] (note Azorín's use of the gender-neutral term *poeta* rather than *poetisa*). Her complete works were published in Madrid in 1909, the same year as *Princesa*. For Casanova, however, Castro was important both as a Galician and as a woman who wrote: Four years later, Casanova would give a lecture on her predecessor at the Ateneo, as part of the series "Florilegio de poetas castellanos" (Azaña 1913, 24) [Anthology of Castilian Poets].

Casanova's choice of the poem that Laura and José Luis read is no accident and in itself provides an alternative model to the Leopardi poem that Laura had so vehemently dismissed. In fact, "¿Qué ten o mozo?" [What Ails the Lad?] is a dialogue between a pair of lovers, with a female protagonist who is not a silent object of affection but a speaking subject. Furthermore, like Laura, she is cynical about her lover's attitude. Foreshadowing what will happen to José Luis throughout *Princesa* (in the part of the poem not reproduced by Casanova), the lover swings from intense devotion ("canciño de cego / por onde eu andare seguíndome vai" [a blind man's dog / wherever I go he follows me"]) to extreme domination ("parece que pasa soberbo, / mandando nos homes su real maxestá" [Castro 1990, 134] [he seems beyond proud / his royal majesty commanding men]). The passage that Casanova quotes forms the transition between the two voices, questioning the (male) lover's Petrarchan protestations of misery ("¿Por qué vives sofrindo por ela?" [Castro 1990, 135] [Why do you live suffering for her?]). After the end of the quotation reproduced by Casanova, the male lover replies, accusing his beloved of being as changeable as he is ("Tamén es cal raiola de marzo, / que agora descubre, que agora se entolda" [Castro 1990, 136] [You too are like sunbeams in March, / now revealed, now concealed]). The poem ends as the male voice assures the female voice, "Iguales semos, / nena fermosa" (Castro 1990, 136) [We are the same, / beautiful girl], just as *Princesa* ends with José Luis's assertions that he and Laura are as one. Through this passage, Casanova opens up a dialogue with her Galician foremother that has as much impact on the text as does the dialogue with Valle-Inclán's *Sonatas* that Johnson has observed. The poem that Casanova quotes, as an alternative to the Romantic paradigm of man-subject-poet creating woman-object-ideal, offers a direct model both for the relationship between Laura and José Luis and for female authors at the turn of the century. At the same time (although it was an aspect that Azorín and his peers disregarded), Castro's Galicianness and her commitment to social change offer both Casanova and Laura a potential solution in the search for a viable future.

Through the story of Laura and José Luis, Casanova addresses the possibilities and limitations of this search in the *fin de siglo* Spain that she was only beginning to understand. If Fernando, the aging Don Juan, stands for decadent, masculine Spain, José Luis represents the other end of the spectrum: As Camila comments, they are complete opposites (Casanova 1989, *Princesa del amor hermoso,* 162). José Luis is first introduced to us through the eyes of Camila, Rafael, and the *marquesa*, who describe him as "ese pobre muchacho . . . ese pálido poetilla . . . jovenzuelo . . . pipiolo" (162–64) [that poor lad . . . that pale little poet . . . so young . . . a callow youth]. Although he is twenty-five years old, he is almost always referred to in diminutives, neutralizing his position as an adult male. His sexuality is further undermined by Camila's physical description: "Sus labios rojísimos no ríen, se entreabren dolorosos sobre los dientes deslumbrantes, y hay en ellos hálito de fiebre, de fuego" (164). [His red, red lips don't laugh; they half open painfully to show his glittering teeth, and they have a breath of fever, of fire.] As Johnson suggests, José Luis is "a character feminized not only by his disease [tuberculosis] but by the intensity of his gaze and the redness of his lips" (1998, 230). Nevertheless, the seeds of the man he might become are there from the start. When Camila claims that he has achieved nothing, great or small, the *marquesa* reminds her that they heard him speak in the Madrid Ateneo: "Eran ideas muy monas las suyas; un poco demasiado cargadas de igualdad y fraternidad, pero expresadas con elocuencia" (164). [His ideas were very sweet; a little heavy on the equality and fraternity, but eloquently expressed.] The reference to "igualdad y fraternidad" clearly recalls the ideals of the French Revolution—anathema to the "polite society" that Camila and the *marquesa* represent. At the same time, according to Rafael, the young man displays all the features of the stereotypical Romantic artist: "Tiene ojos de suicida—que son los criminales mansos—y efervescencias de reformador, de artista. . . . Los artistas son unos imbéciles que suelen hacer grandes cosas" (164). [He has the eyes of a suicide—the quiet criminals—and the effervescence of a reformer, an artist. . . . Artists are imbeciles who tend to do great things.] José Luis himself confirms his mission in life: "Es ésta: inmortalizar[me] en el amar y el laborar" (169). [It is this: to immortalize myself through love and work.] José Luis's reforming spirit is intrinsically connected with his identity as an artist and thus, in the context of the world that Casanova creates in *Princesa*, with his power over the female image. The question, of course, is how he will choose to use that power.

Initially, and rather like Juan in *Lo eterno*, José Luis's love for Laura leads him to try to inhabit the role of the dominant lover that he has seen Fernando play so well. He declares, "Te amo como hombre que soy, con exclusivismo absoluto" (Casanova 1989, *Princesa del amor hermoso,* 178). [I love you as the man I am, with absolute exclusivity.] Faced with Laura's coldness, however, the façade crumbles: "Se disipó su energía, la vehemencia del varón que con su voluntad domina y con su pasión subyuga. Allí estaba la débil alma que se arrastra de amor (180). [His energy, the vehemence of the man who dominates with his will and subjugates with his passion drained away. The fragile soul was revealed, dragged along by love.] Again echoing the lover in Castro's poem, he resembles "la mísera criatura que, como el can, besa la mano cruel que lo mata" (180) [the miserable creature who, like a dog, kisses the cruel hand that kills him].[5] By the end of the novel, José Luis has reverted to his initial generic ambiguity: He ends up being neither exclusively masculine nor exclusively feminine. On his deathbed, he evokes the many images of dying women that permeated European art around the fin de siècle, and his final protestations of love for Laura suggest that he has reached a neoplatonic state that transcends earthly bonds: "Te adoro tanto, que ya ni tu presencia necesito. Estás en mí, eres yo mismo en mi espíritu y mi sangre" (191). [I adore you so much that I no longer need your presence. You are within me; you are me myself in my spirit and my blood.]

If José Luis is the generically ambiguous counterpart to Fernando's ultra-masculine Don Juan, he is also placed in opposition to the equally gendered centralizing discourse that dominated *fin de siglo* intellectual debates. Where Fernando, a diplomat, represents the public face of Spanishness, José Luis represents one of Spain's barely repressed others—Casanova's native Galicia. The Galician element of *Princesa* has been noted by previous critics, such as Bordonada, who observes, "La parte más destacada de la acción se localiza en Galicia y lo gallego ocupa un lugar importante: abundantes referencias a elementos ambientales, frecuentes galleguismos, presencia de la poesía gallega, popular o culta (Rosalía de Castro)" (1989, 36) [The majority of the action takes place in Galicia, and Galician elements play an important part: abundant references to environmental factors, frequent linguistic Galicianisms, the presence of Galician poetry, both popular and elite (Rosalía de Castro)]. Bordonada is quite correct, as far as she goes (although to call Castro an elite poet is rather to miss the point). *Princesa* draws on a wide range of Galician symbols, from Bishop Gelmírez and the Cruz de Santiago to (as we have seen) Rosalía de Castro and the popular *alborada* "Dos namorados." A typical example is the opening paragraph of chapter 3 of the novel, which draws on heavily stylized elements of not only the pastoral tradition but also, in its evocation of the landscape, the emerging Galician narrative genre:

> Frescura de los pinares, claridad infantil de la mañana, suave humo de las queiroas ardiendo en los viejos lares campesinos; prados de azulado verdor, en los que un pastorcillo imberbe remeda en su rústica flauta de áloes los lentos compases de una alborada triste, ¡qué plácido fondo ofrecéis a una escena de bienaventurados geórgicos amores! (Casanova 1989, *Princesa del amor hermoso*, 165)

> [O freshness of the pines, childlike clarity of the morning, soft smoke of the brambles burning in the peasants' ancient hearths; meadows of bluish verdancy, where a beardless shepherd lad imitates on his rustic aloe flute the slow rhythms of a melancholy alborada, what a peaceful setting you offer for a scene of happy georgic romance!]

Like many of Casanova's critics, Bordonada accepts the Galician element of the *novela* uncritically, relegating it to the position of background decoration. However, Casanova does not simply reproduce Galician imagery. Rather, as befits someone who was closely linked with the Galician *rexionalista* movement, she engages with Galician cultural discourse and its relationship with the Spanish state from a committed and critical (if deliberately underplayed) perspective. There are textual hints of a vision of Galicia beyond the simplified pastoral world. For example, the *pazo*'s name—Lugriz—is an alternative spelling of the Galician name Lugrís. Manuel Lugrís Freire was a contemporary of Casanova's whom Xusto Beramendi and Xosé Núñez Seixas consider to be one of the most influential of the *rexionalistas*: "Será sobre todo Lugrís Freire quen personifique mellor a confluencia de *rexionalismo* liberal e republicanismo, establecendo un claro elo entre o nacionalismo progresista e o federalismo de raigame pimargalliana" (1995, 69). [It is Lugrís Freire above all who best personifies the confluence of liberal *rexionalismo* and republicanism, establishing a clear link between progressive nationalism and the federalism rooted in the thought of (Francisco) Pi y Margall.] Casanova and Lugrís certainly knew each other. He was one of the signatories of the parchment presented to her by the *Liga Gallega* in 1898 (Martínez 1999, 116), and she inquired after him fondly in a November 29, 1903, letter to Galo Salinas, the editor of the regionalist journal *Revista Gallega*. As the secretary of the Liga

Gallega, Lugrís was an emblematic figure in Galician *rexionalismo;* thus, Casanova's appropriation of his name could, conceivably, be a subtle admission of solidarity with the movement and its principles.

This background is essential for a full understanding of José Luis's story. He comes from a long line of Galician nobility, but his relationship with his past is ambiguous. His ancestral home, where all chapters but the first are located, fulfills a function similar to that of the Villabrizo palace in *Lo eterno*. It is famed for its archaeological collection and the enormous surrounding oak wood (Casanova 1989, *Princesa del amor hermoso*, 161–62), but for José Luis it is filled with "sombras de guerreros y pesadillas lúgubres de frailes y almas en pena" (168) [shadows of warriors and gloomy nightmares of friars and souls in torment]. The *pazo* represents Galicia's *fidalguía* [petty nobility], dominated until well into the twentieth century by the church and the army. A hitherto unexamined thread of *Princesa* is the bildungsroman narrative of José Luis's journey: from fear of the *pazo* and the stifling Galician tradition that it represents to adoption of a dynamic, modern Galician identity. This thread opens up new possibilities for linking the novel with the largely unstudied corpus of *fin de século* Galician narrative (which I discuss in more detail in Chapter 6). The key for the alert reader lies in José Luis's acceptance of his heritage, symbolized by the red and purple flag (166) that flies over the *pazo* de Lugriz: red, in the language of heraldry, often signifies the theological virtue of charity (Gage 1993, 84, 87), and purple often signifies the cardinal virtue of temperance (Brewer 1898). José Luis's decision to adopt these virtues can be read, in part, as a tribute to the *celtista* vision of Galicia and the Grail legends that formed a central part of the discourse of *galeguistas* such as Casanova's friend Murguía. His story echoes that of the young knight Percival who, according to Grail legend, devoted his life to the search for the principal axiom of the age of chivalry in which he lived: *compassion* (shown in the heraldic diagram as the link between red and purple, or between charity and temperance). Like Percival, José Luis is a widow's son who has been sheltered from the world by his mother. Both are popularly believed to be fools, but in their innocence they reach the Holy Grail that more accomplished knights could not find. Like Percival, too, José Luis decides to dedicate his life to the compassion that (according to his family flag, at least) is his innate duty. As he awakens to his Galician heritage, he realizes, "He pensado mucho y he trabajado poco" [I have done a good deal of thinking and rather less working], and he resolves to remedy this: "Hay que repartir [mi caudal] profusamente, en esta Galicia idolatrada. . . . En las cárceles y en los hospitales remediaré lo que pueda. . . . Recogeré a los presidiarios de la región, que, excarcelados, la sociedad abandona" (Casanova 1989, *Princesa del amor hermoso*, 183). [I must

dispense my wealth throughout my beloved Galicia. . . . I will do what I can
in the prisons and the hospitals. . . . I will gather up the region's prisoners,
who, once released, are abandoned by society.]

José Luis's decision to put his money to work in the prisons and hospitals
recalls, of course, the charity and compassion of the great Galician prison reformer Concepción Arenal (1820–1893). It evokes, too, the socialist vision of
Rosalía de Castro, less widely acknowledged at Casanova's time of writing but
clearly visible in the prologue and many of the poems from *Cantares gallegos*
and its successor, *Follas Novas* (1880). In the context of *Princesa* as a testing
ground for new social and cultural roles, the fact that it is the male (albeit not
conventionally masculine) José Luis who makes the shift from poet to social
campaigner seems to imply support for a parallel shift, in national (and, inevitably, gendered) terms, from Romantic individualism to socially grounded
philanthropy. Is Casanova suggesting that Spain may have something to learn
from its smaller neighbor, with its strong female-centered tradition of social
reform? José Luis's new mission also allows Casanova to comment on a contemporary political issue in Galicia: the problem of the "pleito de los foros"
[lawsuit regarding the traditional legal codes], which Bordonada acknowledges as a real-life problem (1989, 36–37). As the narrator explains:

> José Luis habíase puesto del lado de los aldeanos, considerando acto de
> justicia la redención de las gabelas ominosas, y animaba a los campesinos
> recelosos, incitándoles a que perseveraran en su actitud de protesta, a que
> resistieran y lucharan para librar a sus hijos de las cargas serviles que los
> empobrecían de generación a generación. (Casanova 1989, *Princesa del amor
> hermoso,* 189)

> [José Luis had taken the side of the peasants, considering the redemption
> of the abominable taxes an act of justice, and he encouraged the distrustful
> peasants, urging them to persevere in their protest, to resist and struggle
> to free their children from the burden of servitude that impoverished them
> from generation to generation.]

José Luis's solidarity with the peasants clearly evokes the aims of the new
Galician political party Solidaridad Gallega, founded in 1907, whose main
area of influence was Casanova's native A Coruña, where it won six out of the
thirteen seats in the 1909 local elections (Beramendi and Núñez Seixas 1995,
66). The movement's newfound interest in the previously marginalized peasantry is evident in a text that Murguía published in 1907:

Hoy como entonces sigo creyendo firmemente en el triunfo de nuestros ideales que ahora se me presenta de inmediato. . . . Ahí están para demostrarle las asociaciones agrícolas que con tanta rapidez se están propagando por Galicia entera[6] ¿no es esto una prueba fehaciente de que los campesinos están ávidos de encontrar alguien que pueda proporcionarles su liberación? (Qtd. in López Aydillo 1907, 67)

[Today, as then, I firmly believe in the triumph of our ideals that now seems imminent. . . . Look at the agricultural associations that are spreading so rapidly throughout Galicia; are they not faith-inspiring proof that the peasants are desperate to find someone who can give them their freedom?]

Despite her documented links with the *rexionalista* movement, Casanova rarely makes direct reference to *galeguismo* in her texts, fictional or journalistic. The story of José Luis's journey from isolation and uncertainty to peace with the past and the discovery of a vital social and political role, however, weaves a thread of political commentary into the sentimental tale. Can the same be said about Laura's attempts to challenge the images of femininity that society and literature want to force on her?

Laura de Medina has a great deal in common with Casanova's previous protagonists. Like Mara, Consuelo, and María Cruz, she is apparently motherless: Although her motherless state is never mentioned directly, one of the excuses she gives José Luis for her return to Madrid is that she cannot leave her father alone (Casanova 1989, *Princesa del amor hermoso*, 178, 190). Like her predecessors, too, she is educated, but she is not as overtly intellectual as such contemporary *novela corta* heroines as Gimeno's Luisa (*Una Eva moderna*) or De la Prada's Ana María (*El cantar de los amores*). Finally, like Mara, Consuelo, and María Cruz, Laura conveys through her correspondence the life-changing decision that she hopes will distance her from the romance plot and its seemingly inevitable resolution in marriage. It is Laura's letter to Fernando, breaking off their ten-year engagement, that introduces the theme that underpins the *novela*: women's awareness of the way that men, and a patriarchal society, construct the feminine. As the epigraphs to the chapter suggest, the impossibility of living up to the prevailing models of femininity preoccupied Casanova and many of her peers in the early decades of the twentieth century, and the most formidable model of all was that famous literary object of affection, Petrarch's Laura. In *Una Eva moderna*, Gimeno's *novela corta* published the same year as *Princesa*, she writes, "Los poetas fingen para sus trovas Lauras o Eleonoras [y] la musa que les inspira no es humana" (1909, 3). [The poets invent Lauras or Eleonoras for their songs, and the muse that inspires them is not human.] Different women react to the limitations of these models in different ways, but those who, like Casanova's Laura, are able to express themselves through speech or writing seem better able to cope. De la Prada's Ana María, heroine of *El cantar de los amores*, who is seen by society as the embodiment of the Petrarchan *dame*, "una linda muñeca de nieve y oro" (1912, 5) [a pretty doll of snow and gold], secretly writes her own verses. In contrast, because Gabriela—the heroine of Barco's *Fémina*, whom society sees as "la ideal mujer con su postura de muerta, casi rígida" (1910, 6) [the ideal women, with her corpse-like, almost rigid bearing][7]—lacks any such means of expressing her frustrated subjectivity, the only solution she can perceive is her secret plan of suicide.

In her letter to Fernando, Laura compares herself to another literary heroine: Penelope, the wife of Odysseus, whose long years of weaving and awaiting her husband's return equate her name with fidelity. Laura reminds Fernando that she has awaited his return for ten long years: "He esperado la vuelta de tus viajes, tejiendo en el retraimiento mi esperanza de ser tuya, la inacabable madeja de días de esperanza que ha roto en mis manos tu traición" (Casanova 1989, *Princesa del amor hermoso,* 157). [I've awaited your return from your travels, weaving, in seclusion, my hope of being yours, the endless bobbin of days of waiting that your betrayal has snapped off in my fingers.] The breaking of the bobbin thus represents the breaking of the pattern that Laura has hitherto felt condemned to follow and enables her to make the decision that sets the events of *Princesa* in motion. It also highlights (1) the importance of breaking with old models of gender and national identity and (2) the consequent need to identify new models in both literature and life. This need is particularly pressing for Laura at this point in her life, acutely aware as she is that if she wants to remain a valued member of society, she has few options other than marriage and motherhood. In her letter to Fernando, she acknowledges that her decision not to marry means that she will be virtually useless in the eyes of society: "Me quedo para vestir imágenes, agria solterona que será capaz de fundar una sociedad protectora de gatillos y perros para darles pan, cariño y abrigado hogar en invierno" (158). [I'm left to dress (holy) images, a bitter old spinster who might just found a society for the protection of cats and dogs to give them bread, love, and shelter in the winter.] She recalls that Fernando himself has previously warned her, "Si llegas a olvidarme, te harás beata" (159). [If you ever forget me, you'll turn into a beata.] The warning makes no difference, however, as Laura defiantly rejects the roles that Fernando and society make available to her: "No me haré beata, no. Eso sería lo que tú quisieras, verme beata o monja, cuando menos, ya que no muerta por tus lindos ojos. . . . Va a ser, te lo aseguro, todo lo contrario" (159–60). [I certainly won't turn into a beata. That's what you'd like, to see me as a beata or a nun, at the very least, if not dead from longing for your beautiful eyes. . . . It will be, I assure you, quite the reverse.] Instead, she declares her intention to take her destiny into her own hands and throw herself headfirst into a new life, paradoxically encouraged by Fernando's past flatteries. In her response to Fernando, the hyperbolic discourse of love and romance that celebrates woman's attributes only as long as she remains passive and submissive is turned firmly on its head:

> Como tus madrigalescas epístolas me han convencido de que son
> fascinadores mis encantos, voy a divertirme, a *flirtear*, a ver pasar junto
> a mí las emociones que inspiro y no comparto. . . . Voy a coquetear, sí, a
> coquetear, que es jugar a los dados con los ojos y las almas. (160)

> [Since your madrigalesque letters have convinced me of the fascination of
> my charms, I shall enjoy myself, flirt, watch the passing of emotions that I
> inspire and do not share. . . . I shall flirt, yes, flirt, which is to play dice with
> the eyes and souls.]

Johnson reads this passage as evidence that Laura's decision is tantamount to the creation of a "Doña Juana" (1998, 229), and this is certainly one of the many layers of the text. However, consistent with the ambivalence of Casanova's earlier works, it is not the whole story, as both *Princesa*'s author and main character take pains to reassure their nervous readers that the world is not necessarily about to change and that, ultimately, "las aguas volverán a su cauce" (Casanova 1989, *Princesa del amor hermoso*, 160) [the waters will return to their course].

Despite this concession to convention, however, there is little sign in the text that a return to normality is ever really an option. Laura vigorously rejects conventional models of unmarried femininity, refusing the role of the poetic muse and dismissing the faithful Penelope, the *beata,* and the eccentric spinster running a home for cats and dogs. Instead, she announces her intention to take an active role in her own destiny, but where does this take her? Does she, like José Luis, find a secure identity and an alternative social role? I would argue that she does not and that, in fact, she becomes a victim of the pervasive power of the imagery that she so forcefully rejects. From the very beginning of the text, as Bordonada has noted (1989, 36), the twin discourses of modernist decadence and the sentimental romance are juxtaposed, locating the text—and Laura's experience—in an unmarked space between the two.

In fact, the second paragraph of *Princesa* can be read almost as a parody of decadent writing, with image piled on image and adjective on adjective:

> En la soledad, un murmurio vago del atardecer, y un rayo póstumo del día, fundiéronse un momento en melancólico acorde. . . . La tristeza crepuscular metíase en aquel cuarto donde una mujer sufría. La tristeza de una tarde diáfana, de esas que llenan de lágrimas los ojos y las ayudan a caer suave, lentamente, horas largas. (Casanova 1989, *Princesa del amor hermoso*, 155)

> [In the solitude, a vague murmur of dusk and a posthumous ray of daylight mingled for a moment in melancholy accord. . . . The sadness of twilight entered the room where a woman suffered. The sadness of a diaphanous evening, the sort that brings tears to the eyes and helps them to fall softly, slowly, for long hours.]

Alongside this image is that of Laura, opulently dressed—"enguantada, puesto el negro sombrero de plumas y en los hombros echada la estola de ci-belina" (155) [gloved, in her black feathered hat and her sable stole around her shoulders]—gazing at the blue envelope with a golden ribbon that contains her love letters from Fernando (156). Similar descriptions of fashionable hero-ines and elegant accessories, designed to appeal to an aspirational (and largely female) readership, are characteristic of not only the contemporary sentimen-tal romance but also *fin de siglo* lifestyle publications. As Paredes notes, the description of Laura recalls the kind of fashionable woman who read Burgos's magazine columns and perused the style pages of magazines (2003, 97). By juxtaposing these descriptions with the language of decadent modernism—a juxtaposition that continues throughout the text—Casanova locates *Princesa* in the space between two discourses that both offer very limited possibilities for women. As Laura will learn at great cost, although she may reject the roles that these discourses prescribe for her, to escape them will be a much harder task.

The bind in which Laura is caught is emphasized through recourse to cultural images of women, such as Ophelia and Lady Macbeth (Casanova 1989, *Princesa del amor hermoso*, 184), which reinforce the difficulty of Laura's position. These two Shakespearean characters were enjoying a renaissance in fin de siècle discourse as contemporary manifestations of what Johnson calls "literature's long tradition of casting women in the antithetical roles of evil schemers and idealized objects" (1998, 230). In *Princesa* we see this antithe-sis evoked through the connection between woman and flower (and, in particular, the rose), which, as Bram Dijkstra demonstrates in *Idols of Perversity*, could be employed for very different ends. On one hand, there was

> the "pure" woman . . . with her passive, submissive, imitative, tractable qualities [who] seemed to share with the flowers all the features characteristic of the plant life of the domestic garden [and] came very generally to be seen as a flower herself, to be cultivated in very much the same way a flower ought to be cultivated in order to thrive. (1986, 16)

José Luis's persistent idealization of Laura in terms of a rose—despite her reminders that his version of her does not correspond in any way to her real self (Casanova 1989, *Princesa del amor hermoso*, 170–71)—reflects this aspect of the flower-woman. On the other hand, as many of the images that Dijkstra reproduces in his study make abundantly clear, the flower-woman was also perceived as dangerous and seductive and a serious threat to man—rather as Fernando accuses Laura of making José Luis her victim (187). However, these artistic and literary images created by men, which connect women with passive elements of the natural world, are accompanied in the text by a distinctively feminine discourse that turns this passivity on its head: the "language of flowers."

The "language of flowers," which was a fundamental part of nineteenth-century romantic etiquette, imbued each flower with a particular meaning that could be deciphered only by those in the know (of course, this meant primarily women). During the nineteenth century, dictionaries of the "language of flowers" were popular throughout Europe and America, and any self-respecting etiquette book also contained a chapter on the subject. In a society that frowned on contact between men and women, even during courtship, secret languages were a vital means of communication: The title of one work published in Havana in 1880 illustrates the rich (if rather overwhelming) range of possibilities: *El consultor de los enamorados: Manual completo de cartas de amor, en el lenguaje de las flores, colores, frutas, emblemas del abanico, de las piedras, del pañuelo, horario de Flora, etc.* [The Lover's Guide: Complete Manual of Love Letters, in the Language of Flowers, Colors, Fruits, Motifs for the Fan, for Jewels, for the Handkerchief, Timetable for Flora, Etc.]. Casanova was certainly aware of the potential of this language for rhetorically empowering women, as she demonstrates in her short story "Flores de acacia" [Acacia Flowers] (published in El *pecado* in 1911), which engages many of the same questions as *Princesa*.

In "Flores de acacia," the Parisian painter Moulin recounts the story of his stay with a family of minor Russian nobility in St. Petersburg. Moulin finds it difficult to see women with anything but an artist's eye, and he cannot comprehend that they might have an existence independent of the feminine stereotypes that he imagines for them. He is particularly troubled by the affection that his hostess, Princess Chamiloff, and her sister-in-law display for each other, which appears to contradict the paradigm of the heterosexual couple to which all women are supposed to aspire (Casanova 1911, *El pecado*, 144). His lack of imagination means that his relationship with the women is entirely predicated on an erotic desire that only he experiences. Amused by his obsession, the two women mock him by leaving a bouquet of acacia blossoms in his room. Moulin takes this as a secret message suggesting that he is about to get lucky and spends a delicious night wondering which of the two is his secret admirer (148). When both women appear the following day adorned with acacia, he is disappointed and embarrassed and furiously denigrates them as "crazy" for not playing their allotted role in his romantic game. The key to the story is the meaning of acacia, which, in the language of flowers, was used to signify chaste love and friendship. In other words, Moulin would have saved himself a great deal of humiliation had he been conversant in this language—or, by extension, had he been able to see the women on their own terms rather than simply as the objects of his desire.

In *Princesa* Casanova uses flowers much more subtly to provide an oblique rhetorical layer, perceptible only to those familiar with this particular form of expression. Even then, the intrinsic ambiguity of this informal meaning system allows for multiple layers of interpretation that only increase the rich texture of the novel. For example, Laura writes her letter to Fernando at a bureau adorned with a vase full of headily scented roses and tuberoses, which Casanova describes as "the flowers of passion" (1989, *Princesa del amor hermoso*, 155) and which Kate Greenaway's illustrated dictionary *The Language of Flowers* defines as representing "dangerous pleasures" (1884, 41). In chapter 3, Laura and José Luis are in the rose bower, surrounded by roses entwined with myrtles (1989, *Princesa del amor hermoso*, 166). According to Greenaway, myrtle represents "love" (1884, 29); however, it has many other associations, including, popularly, its use as a funeral plant: Could this be a presage of the *novela*'s denouement? Then, after the couple has left, we learn that the roses are yellow (1989, *Princesa del amor hermoso*, 171). In Greenaway, yellow roses, unlike red or pink roses, have negative connotations, such as "decrease of love" or jealousy (1884, 37). Whatever their connotations, the roses provide a constant thread throughout the novel: In chapter 6, Laura and José Luis are reunited after she has stormed out in irritation at his passionate declaration of love, and he tells her how he dreamed she was "deshojando rosas y nardos en la inmensidad" (1989, *Princesa del amor hermoso*, 181) [plucking petals from roses and tuberoses in infinity]. The image recalls Valle-Inclán's *Sonata de otoño*, when during Bradomín's meeting with Concha in the palace garden, she shows him "su falda donde se deshojaban las rosas, todavía cubiertas de rocío" (1994, 54) [her skirt where the roses were shedding their petals, still covered in dew]. As Robert Weber has pointed out, the death of Concha's roses is parallel to, and predicts the denouement of, Bradomín's renewed passion for Concha (1968, 186). José Luis's dream, too, represents a moment of crisis in his love, suggesting that he subconsciously understands that Laura does not love him.

The differences between Laura and Valle-Inclán's Concha are encapsulated in their interaction with the ever-present roses. Significantly, whereas Concha's roses are shedding petals of their own accord, in José Luis's dream Laura deliberately plucks them. That is, she plays an active role in her love affair, whereas Concha is largely passive. In chapter 8, Laura awaits José Luis in the rose bower, but he is too sick to come down so she goes in the library to see him. At his side is a dying bunch of the yellow roses that they gathered together in the rose bower; he asks Laura to give them to him, believing that "su aroma vivifica" (Casanova 1989, *Princesa del amor hermoso*, 192) [their scent is life-giving]. Breathing in their scent, he begins to slip away, telling Laura of his dream that she is plucking rose petals in infinity and begging her, "Echa sobre mi pecho las rosas del cenador. . . . Conservan partículas de nuestra aurífera tierra madre. . . . Y ellas son tú, mi *Princesa del amor hermoso*" (192, emphasis Casanova's). [Cast the roses from the bower onto my breast. . . . They retain particles of our golden motherland. . . . And they are you, my Princess of Beautiful Love.] In Roman Catholic iconography, of course, roses often represent the Virgin (as in the carol "There Is No Rose of Such Virtue"), and José Luis's final speech identifies Laura with another of the Virgin's titles, Madre del amor hermoso [Mother of Beautiful Love]. In other words, his idealized vision of her persists, despite all evidence to the contrary, and even shifts closer to that employed by Valle-Inclán, who (as Weber has demonstrated) links Concha and the rose together with religious symbolism (1968, 183). Like Valle-Inclán, Casanova uses the image of the rose to parallel her heroine's story, but whereas Valle-Inclán's Concha is the passive object of the hero's sexual and spiritual desire, the perfect example of the idealized flower-woman-virgin, Laura challenges the bonds created by both image and desire. Although in José Luis's dream Laura is seen destroying the roses that represent these bonds, she cannot in the end destroy the bonds themselves. Her inability to escape from, or at least find an alternative to, woman's romantic destiny is symbolized in José Luis's dying vision of her as one with the rose that represents all that she has tried to resist.

José Luis's death indubitably provides not only the dramatic plot climax but also the moral resolution expected by contemporary readers. The tableau of female grief that concludes chapter 8 is both vivid and predictable: "María echó los brazos al cuello de Laura y, unidas, lloraron las dos solitarias mujeres. . . . La madre lloraba por amor . . . Laura, por no haber amado" (Casanova 1989, *Princesa del amor hermoso,* 193). [María threw her arms around Laura's neck and, together, the two solitary women wept. . . . The mother cried for love . . . Laura, for not having loved.] The overt interpretation of this ending is clearly explicated by Paredes, who reads it as a warning that Laura's actions have succeeded only in isolating her and endangering the future of the nation: "El grupo familiar y la nación a través de él carecen de futuro. . . . [L]a rebelión de la mujer, su renuncia a los papeles que la sociedad sanciona como posibles, sólo puede traerle trastorno a la comunidad" (2003, 116). [The family group and through it the nation have no future. . . . The woman's rebellion, her renunciation of the roles sanctioned by society, can only bring disruption to the community.] Laura's story has, it seems, come full circle: She ends it as she began, in tears. Significantly, however, this is not the end of the *novela*. The brief final chapter shifts the focus to the melancholy scene outside the *pazo*: As the purple and red flag is lowered, "el lento son de una campana austera rememoraba que la vida es efímera" (Casanova 1989, *Princesa del amor hermoso,* 193) [the slow tolling of an austere bell recalled that life is fleeting]. A young peasant couple, a milkmaid and a shepherd boy, who appeared as distant figures in the idyllic landscape at the start of chapter 3 (166), comment on the denouement of José Luis and Laura's story:

> —O pobriño morreu—dijo ella en su dialecto melodioso.
> —Sei que o matuo [*sic*] una muller ingrata. . . . Asin vasme matar ti.
> —¡Santa Martiña!
> —Vas, muller, vas, si non me queres.
> Y el mozo, envalentonado con la actitud sumisa de ella, púsole los labios al oído. (194).

> ["The poor thing has died," she said in her melodious dialect.
> "I know an ungrateful woman killed him. . . . That's how you'll kill me too."
> "Good Lord!"
> "Go on, woman, go away if you don't love me."
> And the lad, emboldened by her submissive attitude, put his lips to her ear.]

This exchange appears to reinforce Paredes's reading, as the idealized couple exemplifies the traditional gender roles that the main cast of *Princesa* undermines. That is, this passage provides a comforting and familiar resolution to a potentially unsettling text, as Laura is condemned as an "ungrateful woman" and unequivocally blamed for José Luis's death. In common with Casanova's previous novels, however, the ending is not as simple as it appears: If we look at the passage again, another reading suggests itself. In this interpretation, the peasant couple performs the same function as the bishop in the final chapter of *Lo eterno*, dramatizing the officially sanctioned reading of the text. As in *Lo eterno*, it is essential to keep in mind that the moral of the story is not spoken by the narrator; rather, it is mediated through a character or characters whose significance within the text is acutely loaded. *Princesa* differs from *Lo eterno* in the reappearance of the narrator in the final lines of the text, where she affectionately rejects the idealism of the peasant lad as a "mentirosa, pero insustituible, quimera de la juventud" (194) [deceptive, but irreplaceable, chimera of youth]. That is, his faith in conventional gender roles (note that it is her submissive attitude that emboldens him) and his belief in the inherent dangers of departing from these roles might be seen as reflecting a certain childlike naïveté. The implication is that the world outside, the world of real people and grown-up relationships, necessitates a more flexible approach to gender roles than Spanish society, perhaps, can currently tolerate.

In the story we have just examined, both José Luis and Laura, in different ways, have passed beyond this naïve acceptance of the status quo. They have grown up to discover that life and love are complex and dangerous. However, whereas José Luis transcends the limitations of conventional national and gender roles, embraces his Galician heritage, and finds a role for himself in political and social activism, Laura's ending is less certain. Her Spanish suitor leaves her, her Galician suitor dies, and as she is left comforting his bereaved mother, we do not know what the future holds for her. Will she be punished for her transgression, or can she look forward to an independent future? Although, within the limits of the text, as Paredes suggests, no alternative is explicitly suggested, ultimately the reader has no way of knowing, and the narrator reveals nothing. The new title that graced the *novela* in the 1911 and 1926 editions of *El pecado*—"El triunfo"—clarifies this ambiguity, shifting the text's focus from Laura, the "Princesa del amor hermoso," to José Luis and thus, by extension, from the unsettling of models of genre and gender to the underlying socially and politically safer moral purpose.

Princesa, like Casanova's three previous novels, has a consciously ambiguous ending, in which the author exploits reader expectations and generic conventions to open up a variety of interpretive possibilities. In her allusions to modernist discourse and the sentimental novel in the opening paragraphs of the text, the author effectively manipulates her readers' expectations regarding the kind of plot they will find in *Princesa*. Modernism is, as Bieder has written, "a singularly male movement" (1992, 314), whereas the sentimental novel was intrinsically "feminine." By linking them from the start, Casanova plays one against the other and thus, like Pardo Bazán, locates her text in a space "between genre and gender" (Bieder 1990, 131). A central feature of the *novela corta* that *Princesa* exploits is the impossibility of its confinement within the boundaries of any one genre. Casanova's text dialogues with a series of cultural models, including the sentimental romance, the nineteenth-century novelistic tradition, early twentieth-century modernism, "new woman" fiction, the pastoral idyll, and Galician regionalism, and it questions them all. In its radical (for the time) celebration of the transformative power of female-authored literature, exemplified in the works of Rosalía de Castro, *Princesa* consciously intervenes in the *fin de siglo* transformation of traditional literary and cultural models, disproving the claims of Azorín and his followers that such renovation was limited to a tiny group of intellectuals. Ultimately, however, *Princesa* is more pessimistic than any of Casanova's previous works about women's ability to escape the influence of social and cultural images of femininity. Despite its unequivocal criticism of the limited roles available to women in life and literature, the text—like its protagonist—seems caught in the web of allusion and conflicting generic conventions inherent to the *novela corta*, to the extent that, for Laura at least, there is no immediately obvious way out. The principal source of optimism, although Casanova does not fully develop it here, appears to lie in the generically and nationally ambiguous character of José Luis and his pursuit of an ungendered social activism with its roots not in *castizo*, nationalist Spain but in the Galician periphery. The conviction that change can be imagined only from the national and social margins would drive Casanova's work during her last five years of residence in Spain.

CHAPTER 6

Madrid–London–
St. Petersburg–Galicia–America

El pecado (1911) and *El crimen de Beira-mar* (1914)

> Es un libro fragante, perfumado de cosas galicianas, así como un bello
> ramo de flores recogidas en los campos húmedos de nuestra amada Suevia.
> (Canitrot 1911, 15).

> [It is a fragrant book, perfumed with Galician things, like a handsome
> bouquet of flowers gathered in the damp fields of our beloved Suevia.]

> ¿Qué problemas van a resolverse? ¿Con qué nuevas formas va a surgir de la
> concepción la belleza? ¿Cuál de esos pensadores hará brotar de las cenizas
> que en el corazón lleva la escéptica juventud el fuego de un ideal que la
> fortalezca? (Casanova 1911, "Una ervingista," *El pecado,* 132–33)

> [What problems are to be resolved? What new forms of beauty will arise
> from this thinking? Which of those intellectuals will bring forth from the
> ashes that our skeptical youths carry in their hearts the fire of an ideal that
> will strengthen them?]

The success of *Lo eterno, Más que amor,* and *Princesa del amor hermoso* certainly aided Sofía Casanova's decision to establish herself permanently in Madrid. The deciding factor, however, may well have been her discovery (when she returned to Warsaw early in 1909) that Wincenty Lutosławski had sold the family house, leaving her no place to live (Martínez 1999, 160). Fortunately, with her rising professional profile, consolidated by the publication of *Princesa,* the prospect of setting up her own household near her family in Madrid and supporting Halina and herself through her writing was no longer unthinkable. Increasingly a fixture on the Madrid salon circuit, after nearly ten years' absence, Casanova was now also able to renew her contacts with such Galician friends and colleagues as the two Manuels, Murguía and Lugrís. It was an exciting time in Galician intellectual circles: The proto-nationalist cultural project that had begun with the mid-nineteenth century *Rexurdimento* [Renaissance] was now beginning to develop into a full-fledged political movement, and Casanova's friends were at the heart of it all. Even while she was in Poland, her support for the increasingly high-profile *rexionalista* movement had been officially recognized: In 1906 she was made a corresponding member of Murguía's newly founded Real Academia Gallega. Her involvement intensified after her return to Spain, although, careful as ever, she never openly addressed the issue in her journalism. In her fiction, however, it was another story: *Princesa* is evidence of Casanova's ability to weave a political thread—of implicit support for Murguía's new political party Solidaridad Gallega—into what was ostensibly a popular, mass-market romance. Her next project offers an even greater insight into the dynamics of the shifting cultural and political maps of *fin de siglo* Iberia. Once again, however, a combination of reader expectation and clever marketing has led few readers to discern its complexities.

The project, the short story collection *El pecado*, originated soon after Casanova's return to Spain, when the opportunity arose to collaborate on a new cultural initiative: the Biblioteca de Escritores Gallegos (BEG) [Library of Galician Writers]. Not surprisingly, it was an opportunity that Casanova seized enthusiastically. Now more than ever, her motives were as much financial as they were patriotic or intellectual, since she was responsible for supporting Halina and herself in their Madrid establishment. The project would prove to be a good investment: *El pecado*, like so many of Casanova's writings, worked hard for its author. The economic need to publish and republish resulted in two subsequent editions after the initial 1911 edition: First *El pecado* was reissued, with minor alterations, as part of the *La Novela Corta* series, which partly financed Casanova's post–World War I return to Spain between 1919 and 1920, and then it appeared again, considerably revised, as volume 3 of her *Obras completas* in 1926. The first edition, which is the focus of this study, contains eleven stories, at least five of which had been previously published: "El pecado" [Sin], "O campaneiriño" [The Little Bell Ringer], "El triunfo" [Triumph], "Una acuarela" [A Watercolor], "Más triste que el amor" [Sadder than Love], "El ladrón" [The Thief], "¡Qué tonta!" [How Silly!], "En la casa de enfrente" [In the House Opposite], "Luz en tinieblas" [Light in the Darkness], "Una ervingista" ["A (Female) Irvingite], and "Flores de acacia" ["Acacia Flowers]. In later years, individual stories would reappear with some frequency in journals and anthologies, both in Spain and Poland.

The proposal that arrived on Casanova's desk sometime in 1910, from the

BEG's two young directors, Luis Antón del Olmet and Prudencio Canitrot, was for the author to prepare a Galician-themed anthology of her published and unpublished short stories. *El pecado* would be the tenth volume in the BEG series, and the only one by a woman; the invitation suggests not only that Casanova's literary career had acquired renewed energy but also that audiences had acquired (or reacquired?) an appetite for her work, old and new. In fact, the collection is just one of a range of what were effectively "best of" compilations that Casanova published between 1911 and 1913. In 1911 she published an anthology of poetry, *El cancionero de la dicha*, which (like *El pecado*) included new work alongside a selection from the previous two decades. It was followed, two years later, by the first of several collections of her journalism, *Exóticas* (1913), which amassed a selection of newspaper articles published over the previous five years. In 1913 she would also see her only play—*La madeja*—produced by Benito Pérez Galdós at Madrid's prestigious Teatro Español (Simón Palmer 1989). It was not until the following year that she would publish her first original novel in five years, as part of the weekly *El Libro Popular* series. *El crimen de Beira-mar* (1914) would also be the work that brought this stage of Casanova's career to a close. At the outbreak of war later that year, Casanova left Spain to be with her family in Poland. It would be five long and traumatic years before she returned to Spain or to writing fiction.

The increasing focus on Galicia in the works that Casanova published after her return to Spain is undeniable; however, as critics have discovered, it is also problematic. As we have seen, although *Princesa* clearly addresses the social and political situation in Galicia, this aspect of the *novela* has proved difficult to assimilate into existing critical paradigms. Similarly, it may be, at least in part, that because the two works of fiction that are the focus of this chapter—*El pecado* and *El crimen de Beira-mar*—engage so directly with the unprecedented cultural and political developments then taking place in Galicia, they are among Casanova's least known. As I have argued elsewhere, the fragmented and partial nature of our understanding of both *fin de siglo* women's writing in Spain and *fin de século* Galician culture in general makes it doubly difficult to see these works in context (Hooper 2003, 2006a). Their focus on Galicia, together with Casanova's status as a woman and an émigrée, makes for an uneasy relationship with the mainstream of *fin de siglo* Spanish culture. At the same time, the fact that despite their subject matter they are written both in Spanish and by a woman provides no place for them in the Galician cultural narrative. The debate about which authors and works may be considered part of Galician culture has a long and difficult history, but since the 1950s the consensus has been in favor of the *criterio filolóxico*: the position that only works written in the Galician language can properly be considered Galician. Although the advantages of this criterion are obvious in the context of present-day Galicia, applying it retrospectively to a period such as the *fin de século* causes difficulties. As Kathleen McNerney and Cristina Enríquez de Salamanca observe in *Double Minorities of Spain*, few writers were monolingual in Galician; bilingualism (or even monolingualism in Castilian) was the norm (1994, 6). A consequence has been that cultural historians today see the *fin de século*, which was a period of rapid political and cultural change in Galicia, as a period of stagnation or decadence (Hooper 2006a). The need for retrospective legitimization of today's monolingual Galician cultural sphere makes it doubly difficult to assess writers such as Casanova in the context of the institutionalized cultural narrative. Nevertheless, as I suggest in this chapter, Casanova's work provides a valuable alternative perspective on Galician culture of the *fin de século*. It is just one example in a large and heterogeneous but almost entirely forgotten body of work that, I contend, must be taken into account if we are to understand the developments of that crucial period fully.

Like Casanova and her work, the BEG has proved difficult to place within the Galician cultural narrative, and for similar reasons. Its founding in 1910 was for José Antonio Durán one of the most important events in Galician cultural history (1974, 248); however, the BEG is not mentioned in canonical studies of the period (e.g., Carballo Calero 1975; Hermida 1995; and Tarrío Varela 1994). Based in Madrid, the BEG published fourteen texts, all in Spanish, between 1911 and 1913, at which time it came to a premature end following the death of cofounder Prudencio Canitrot. Durán sees the BEG as the model of the contemporary trend among the Galician community in Madrid toward "una especie de neo-regionalismo, cargada de política (básicamente agraria) y de literatura (neorromántica y modernista)" (1974, 248) [a sort of neoregionalism, loaded with politics (basically agrarian) and with literature (neo-Romantic and modernist)]. He describes its literary significance as "uneven," drawing attention to the presence of Ramón del Valle-Inclán and Manuel Murguía as the most important authors featured alongside "successful" Galician authors (such as Manuel Linares Rivas and Alberto Insúa) and young, untried authors (such as Wenceslao Fernández Flores and Manuel María Puga [alias Picadillo]). Although Casanova was the only woman featured in the collection, the fact that Durán does not mention her, since she was neither "important" (like Valle-Inclán and Murguía) nor a novice, implies that she was included as a "popular" author. According to Durán, the BEG's two young founders were characterized by their enthusiasm rather than by their sense. He observes, "La editorial pesa, desde el primer momento, de manera exagerada. . . . Uno

y otro [de los dos jóvenes editores] hacen prólogos y presentaciones abundantes" (1974, 248). [Right from the start, the publishing house suffered from an
overblown style. . . . Both young editors produced abundant prologues and
presentations.]

We see a prime example of these "abundant" editorial interventions in
Canitrot's prologue to *El pecado*, which reveals more explicitly than in any of
Casanova's previous works the limitations within which female authors had
to operate. Kathleen Glenn analyzes the prologue to *El pecado* as "an interesting verbal portrait of the Galician writer . . . [which] discloses far more about
its male author and late nineteenth-, early twentieth-century representations
of women than it does about Casanova herself" (1996, 47). It is certainly true
that Canitrot's highly rhetorical depictions of Casanova reflect the contemporary constructions of femininity that, as we have seen, she had long made it
her project to undermine:

> tan gentil dama . . . cuyo solo nombre, sonoro y armonioso, nombre de
> princesa, debe escribirse con pluma de cisne. (1911, 9)
>
> [such a noble lady . . . whose very name, sonorous and harmonious, a
> princess's name, should be written with a swan's feather].

> Es como una flor esplendente que luce en una eterna primavera y que a todos
> y a todo regala su lozanía y perfume. (9–10)
>
> [She is like a resplendent flower shining in an eternal spring who confers her
> verdancy and perfume on everybody and everything.]

> Sofía coloca por sobre todo su corazón propicio al sentimiento y sabe pasar
> por encima de las llamas del bien y del mal como una salamandra, sin
> quemarse. (11)
>
> [Sofía places her heart, inclined to sentiment, above all and has the ability to
> pass through the flames of good and evil like a salamander, without being
> burned.]

> Su nombre . . . hablábame no sé por qué, con insistencia llena de misterio, de
> un trozo de leyenda. (12)
>
> [Her name . . . spoke to me, I know not why, with an insistence laden with
> mystery, with a hint of legend.]

For a reader familiar with Casanova and her work, these descriptions ought, at least, to inspire a raised eyebrow. It is important to note, however, that Canitrot's description of Casanova does not stop where Glenn's critique does. He goes on to describe a meeting with the author where she kissed him in greeting: "Me sentí ungido . . . como Alejandro Sawa, a quien besó Víctor Hugo" (12). [I felt anointed . . . like Alejandro Sawa, who was kissed by Victor Hugo.] A strange comparison, if we are anticipating further icons of femininity, it suggests a (super)hyperbolic equation of Casanova with a writer who was considered by the Romantics to be the national bard of France. If Victor Hugo came to be considered the representative voice of nineteenth-century France, could Canitrot be suggesting that, through *El pecado*, Casanova— presented, despite the rhetoric of femininity, as a serious and accomplished writer—can help to establish a voice for Galicia? This may, indeed, have been Canitrot's intention (in fact, it was essentially the driving force behind the project as a whole); however, we can be fairly certain that although Casanova's work makes a clear contribution to Galician culture and identity at the *fin de século*, it is not precisely the contribution that her editors imagined.

The editorial description of *El pecado* as a "libro genuinamente regional" (Canitrot 1911, 15) [genuinely regional book] is hardly surprising in a collection based on local ties. The discrepancy between what Canitrot may have meant by this description and Casanova's interpretation of her brief is, however, considerably greater than editor, author, or even subsequent readers have acknowledged. Evidence of the long-term impact of the BEG's clever marketing strategy is the fact that although (like Casanova's other works) *El pecado* has received very little critical attention, the small number of critics who have looked at the collection have uncritically accepted Canitrot's definition of it as a regional, feminine text. For Ofelia Alayeto, the collection deals with "mostly . . . gallego themes" (1987, 42), whereas for Carolyn Galerstein and Kathleen McNerney, its central concern is "the fundamental incompatibility of man and woman in love and sympathy for life's victims" (1986, 71). For me, both of these descriptions are problematic. Most significant is the fact that even a cursory reading of *El pecado* will show the inaccuracy of Alayeto's observation—like Canitrot's claim that "todos los asuntos . . . son de la tierra" (1911, 15) [all the themes . . . are connected with the land]. Of the eleven stories, only two—"O campaneiriño" and "El ladrón"—come close to fulfilling this criterion. Only four others—"Más triste que el amor," "¡Qué tonta!" "El triunfo," and "Una acuarela"—make any reference to Galicia at all. Moreover, the collection is not as sentimental—in any sense of the word—as Galerstein and McNerney suggest. As a compilation of "greatest hits" from this part of Casanova's career, it picks up on a wide range of the issues that she wrote about in more detail elsewhere; I would argue that, if anything, the limited space available in the short story format highlights rather than conceals her critique. Under the circumstances, it is difficult to know what to make of both the conspiracy of silence that seems to have taken place between Casanova and her publishers with respect to the comparative lack of "regional" subject matter and the seeming willingness of so many readers to play along. I contend that the apparent disjunction between the marketing of *El pecado* and its actual message is deceptive and that, at least on Casanova's part, it reflects an extension of strategies that she had employed in her earlier fiction. In my opinion, her shift of focus onto the Galician dimension not only reveals the inadequacy of models of "Galician culture" both now and at the *fin de século*, as well as models of the Spanish *fin de siglo*, but also offers a powerful alternative approach to both.

It may seem, at least to those of us inclined toward cynicism, that the few stories in *El pecado* that live up to the promises made in the prologue are there simply as a smoke screen to divert attention from the radical and sometimes bitter critiques contained in many of the other stories. This may be the case in part: At the very least, they reveal Casanova's increasing skill at intuiting the level of respect for convention that she needed to provide in order to pursue her own objectives. At the same time, however, it is impossible to deny that these stories have a certain charm: They were certainly among Casanova's most popular. The most conventionally "Galician" of all, and probably the first to have been written, is "O campaneiriño," which enjoyed great success in both Poland and Galicia. Reprinted at least five times in the years that followed its first recorded publication in Polish in 1894 ("Janek Zakrystyan: Obrazek z Galicyi Hiszpańskiej"), "O campaneiriño" is a textbook example of the sort of regional writing that Richard Brodhead calls "cultural elegy" (1994, 120) and Donna Campbell describes as a celebration of continuity over disruption (1997, 8).[8] As such, it represents a genre that was enormously popular across the anglophone and hispanophone worlds in the early twentieth century but that—thanks, in part, to its perceived feminization—had until recently disappeared from the critical consciousness.

"O campaneiriño" is set in the village of San Julián de Veira, a fertile oasis nestled at the foot of some black mountains, surrounded by pine-scented meadows and loaded vines. It is the tale of Juan, the bell ringer of the title, who goes to war and returns—with his arms blown off—at the very moment that his sweetheart is marrying another man. It is the most consciously popular of the stories in *El pecado*, built on the familiarity of folk motifs such as Juan's promise that, no matter what, he will return to reclaim his love and the inevitability of the tragedy that ultimately overwhelms him. The Galicia of "O campaneiriño" is a rural idyll peopled by stock characters and evoked by means of linguistic Galicianisms (such as the title) and rather predictable allusions to "gaitas" [bagpipes], "aires gallegos" [Galician melodies], "poética tristeza" [poetic sadness], pine trees, and "campiñas de hermosura" [fields of beauty] (Casanova 1911, *El pecado*, 26–28). It is overshadowed by death, decline, and the war to which Juan and his contemporaries are called away, which—given the story's initial publication in 1894—is probably the Cuban War. The circular nature of the story, from the death of Juan's first love (his mother) to the symbolic death of his last, is represented by his ringing of the church bell on each occasion and by the decline of the village's manor house. The "viejo caserón que cuidaba de ocultar sus agrietados muros en las sombras de las acacias que lo circuían" (23) [old manor house struggling to conceal its cracked walls beneath the shadows of the acacia trees that surrounded it] becomes "las ruinas de una caserón, antes rodeado de acacias" (30) [the ruins of a manor house, formerly surrounded by acacia trees]. The decline of the manor house symbolizes, as it does for Casanova's compatriots and contemporaries Pardo Bazán and Valle-Inclán, the waning power of the old aristocracy, making the story an elegy for an inexorably vanishing way of life. It is the only sustained example in *El pecado* of this type of writing, but its position within the text—directly after the title story—suggests the desire (whether on the part of the author or the editor it is impossible to know) to give it prominence, perhaps to bolster the official marketing of the text as a parade of "paisajes y tipos" (Canitrot 1911, 15) [landscapes and characters].

In sharp contrast to "O campaneiriño" is "El ladrón," the only other story set in rural Galicia. Its setting is the village of "Merana" in the Bay of Coruña, a thinly veiled allusion to Mera, the village where Casanova and her family lived between 1896 and 1899. The author herself appears implicitly within the story as "una dama . . . de paso en la obscura aldehuela natal" (Casanova 1911, *El pecado*, 94) [a lady . . . passing through the obscure little village of her birth]. "El ladrón" is ostensibly the story of the capture and trial of Antón de Figueiro, the "thief" of the title, for the theft of some sacks of grain, which he has taken in order to finance his emigration to America. Casanova, following in the footsteps of her illustrious predecessors Rosalía de Castro and Concepción Arenal, offers a sensitive depiction of the conditions that underpin the two great Galician social problems of crime and emigration. The story contrasts reinvigorated versions of stock characters with examples of what Rachel DuPlessis calls the "communal protagonist" (1985, 5). "El ladrón" not only illustrates Sherrie Inness and Diana Royer's claim with respect to American writing of the same period that "portraits of rural life offered the chance for real social change since they often depicted the poor and disenfranchised"

(1997, 4) but also offers an example of the regional text as site for working out "conflicting narratives" of identity (McCullough 1999, 2). The story is woven from a network of tensions: between the individual and the group, between men and women, and between Galicia and Castile. When Pepucha (the tavern owner) discovers that her grain has been stolen, her cries attract a chorus of local women (Casanova 1911, *El pecado,* 89), and only Mari-Juana (the wife of Andrés, "el marinero") stands apart from the common call for vengeance. Later, the men join this group, and the village unites as a single, vengeful entity against Antonio: "¡Tírate al agua; tírate, animal, y acabas de una vez! ¡Tírate al agua!—repitió en formidable explosión el ansia popular" (93). ["Throw yourself in the water! Throw yourself in, animal, and end it once and for all! Throw yourself in the water!" cried the voice of common anguish in a fearsome outburst.]

The image of the baying crowd provides a springboard for a key element of the story and, implicitly, the collection: the voicing of a distinct Galician identity against the dominant version of Spanishness embodied in the Guardia Civil, whose arrival brings "la autoridad que se impone y hace curvar las cabezas en la obediencia . . . la justicia inquisidora que protege y castiga" (Casanova 1911, *El pecado,* 89) [the authority that imposes itself and causes heads to bow in obedience . . . the inquisitorial justice that protects and punishes]. Facing the *guardias,* the village undergoes a transformation, uniting against these representatives of oppression: "Sordamente, en las conciencias de los rústicos, bulló alucinante una protesta: la rebelión colectiva de la tribu libre" (89). [Silently, in the peasants' minds, a protest all at once boiled over: the collective rebellion of the free tribe.] That the Galicians are prepared to defend themselves—both physically and ideologically—is made clear in the description of the confrontation between the villagers and the *guardias:* "Los palos con que [los hombres] se ayudaban a sortear los baches del detestable caminejo eran, en sus manos batalladoras, cual armas en espera de combate" (90). [The sticks the men used to get around the potholes in the appalling little track were, in their battling hands, like weapons awaiting a fight.] "El ladrón" is an unusually explicit expression of Casanova's support for an increasingly self-confident Galicia—an issue that she would never address directly in her journalistic writings. The timely question of the relationship between a newly radicalized Galicia and the apparatus of the Spanish state and the related issue of communal culpability and communal responsibility are both only hinted at here. Casanova would return to explore them in greater depth three years later, as illustrated in the discussion of *El crimen de Beiramar* later in this chapter.

This critical redeployment of common features of the relatively unprestigious regional genre functions here as a subtle means by which Casanova can express a view of current events in Galicia. As a model for reading, it invites reconsideration of similarly forgotten texts by some of Casanova's Galician-language contemporaries—writers such as Heraclio Pérez Placer, Manuel Amor Meilán, and Francisca Herrera Garrido. Just as important, its useful-ness goes beyond the geographical peripheries to what we might term the so-cial peripheries, the groups that Galerstein and McNerney described as "life's victims." In fact, Casanova applies a similar strategy in another story in *El pecado*: "Luz en tinieblas" [Light in the Shadows], which is set exclusively in Madrid. As the opening words make clear, "Luz en tinieblas"—like "El ladrón"—is filtered through the narrator's position as part of the society that she describes: "Era Águeda, cuando yo la conocí, la más bonita muchacha del famoso barrio de Maravillas" (Casanova 1911, *El pecado*, 117). [Águeda, when I first met her, was the most beautiful girl in the famous Maravillas neighborhood.] Like the two Galician-centered stories, "Luz en tinieblas" is constructed from the colorful and evocative images characteristic of regional writing, but it uses them to very different effect. Like "O campaneiriño," it describes a society that is overshadowed by war—once again, the Cuban War, which keeps Águeda's beloved Juan away for four years. Unlike "O campanei-riño" however, the mood is not one of nostalgia; instead, it echoes *Lo eterno* in exploiting the symbolic possibilities of urban Madrid. Illustrating Michael Ugarte's observation that nineteenth- and early twentieth-century women writers often focus on pockets of a city rather than the city as a whole (1996, 20), "Luz en tinieblas" is very specifically located in the working-class Mara-villas neighborhood of Madrid. The two parts of the story both take place on July 15, four years apart. Both time and place are significant: July 15 is the eve of the feast day of Nuestra Señora del Carmen, which is also the birthday of the heroine, Águeda. Maravillas, the neighborhood around the Plaza Dos de Mayo (close to where Casanova herself grew up), was the heart of Spanish resistance to the French invasion of 1808. Resistance to the invasion was fa-mously led by the women of Maravillas, and this is the tradition within which Casanova places Águeda, with her "gracia picaresca heredada de aquellas manolas que con tanto patriotismo ayudaron a derrotar a los franceses" (Ca-sanova 1911, *El pecado*, 117) [picaresque grace inherited from those Madrid lasses who with such patriotism helped to defeat the French]. Against this background, the story of Águeda's struggle against neighborhood gossip, her mother's snobbery and ambition, and the cruel hand of fate that ultimately blinds her takes on a more universal meaning: Her fight for freedom from social and physical oppression is juxtaposed with that of the heroines who fought for Spain a century earlier. It is surely not insignificant that Águeda, as a working-class woman, is the only one of *El pecado*'s heroines who can move around freely in public spaces; even more significant is the fact that she is also the only one whose story ends in a happy marriage.

Águeda's story and her happy ending stand out because the majority of the female protagonists in the collection are from the part of society that Casanova knew best: the middle class. In consequence, their stories reflect the concerns that Casanova had been wrestling with ever since the publication of *Wolski* in 1894—chief among which, as we have seen, was the role of marriage. Of the eleven stories in the collection, five—"El pecado," "El triunfo," "Más triste que el amor," "¡Qué tonta!" and "En la casa de enfrente"—deal with the role of the Spanish middle-class woman that had been such an issue for Casanova throughout her career. Even more than the earlier works, *El pecado* focuses on the confinement of middle-class women within the private sphere and, more important, the consequences of violating that confinement. Unlike Águeda, the heroines of these stories are marked by their inability to move freely in public spaces: Their world is acutely limited. Leaving aside "El triunfo," which we have already examined under its original title, *Princesa del amor hermoso*, I turn now to the heroines of the remaining stories: Argentina ("El pecado"), Isabel ("¡Qué tonta!"), María ("En la casa de enfrente"), and the unnamed elderly woman of "Más triste que el amor," all of whose stories are driven by their struggle with the correlation between marital status and physical freedom.

The symbolic nature of space and place in the collection is nowhere clearer than in the opening (and title) story, in which Argentina Ordaz's violation of society's moral code is reflected by her banishment to the streets. Argentina has much in common with her predecessors in Casanova's works: Like Mara and Consuelo, she is orphaned. Like Mara, Consuelo, Laura, and María Cruz, she knows that she is expected to enter the world of romance and find a mate, yet she is reluctant. She tells her friend, "Ya tú sabes si tuve pretendientes. A ninguno quise nunca. . . . Inexplicable insensibilidad me aisló siempre" (Casanova 1911, *El pecado*, 18). [As you well know, I had suitors. I never loved any of them. . . . Some inexplicable insensibility always kept me apart.] She cannot explain this indifference, and her response is profound self-doubt and even self-hatred: "¿Qué enigma había en mi modo de ser? Lo ignoro, no lo entiendo. Ni yo misma me entiendo. . . . ¡Qué absurdo! ¡Qué abominable alma puso Dios en mí!" (18). [What enigma was there in my way of being? I do not know; I do not understand it. I don't even understand myself. . . . How absurd! What an abominable soul God gave me!"] Behind Argentina's confusion lie the conflicting images of femininity prevalent in *fin de siglo* discourse and—in yet another example of Casanova's dissatisfaction with female education—the lack of guidance available to women to make sense of them. For Argentina, as for the majority of Casanova's heroines, the life of the middle-class woman is "una paralela tendida en la llanura árida del bienestar vegetativo" (18) [a straight line stretching out across the arid plain of vegetative well-being], blighted by "la odiosa conciencia de una educación inhumana" (19) [the hateful consciousness of an inhumane education]. Argentina's inability to resolve the problem and her fear of the tedious life she will face if she submits are at the root of her inconsistent behavior.

Argentina's life changes when, after holding off her cousin and suitor, Rodrigo, for years because of her fears of domesticity, she sleeps with him on the night before he leaves for the war in Morocco. There he is killed on the first day of battle, and Argentina is left pregnant and alone. Shunned by her neighbors, in whom her "sin" inspires horror or, perhaps, fear for their own fragile respectability, she wanders the streets haunted by memories of Rodrigo. The church, which has loomed over the story ever since the opening scene on the steps of the parish church, authorizes society's response when a priest grants Argentina absolution on the condition that she repent and submit to the moral code that he and the church represent. Argentina refuses: "Yo no puedo, no quiero arrepentirme de haber dado la felicidad de mi amor al hombre que iba a morir por su patria. . . . Mi pecado fue hacerle sufrir, haberle amado tardíamente" (Casanova 1911, *El pecado,* 22). [I cannot, will not repent having given the joy of my love to a man who was going to die for his country. . . . My sin was to have made him suffer, to have loved him too late.] Her interpretation of sin does not correspond to that of the church or, by extension, that of society. She is concerned not with having broken social conventions but with having caused pain to another human being, but the church does not take such human considerations into account. The story ends with Argentina, completely isolated, excluded from society, and overwhelmed by nihilism, sobbing, "Todo es inútil en la execrable existencia humana, amar y no amar" (22). [Everything is useless in this execrable human existence, to love and not to love.] As her friend the narrator, sympathetic but powerless, embraces her, Casanova leaves us with a final tableau of female solidarity and compassion that resembles a deathbed scene (22).

Argentina's resistance to marriage, which sees her experience social death in the form of exclusion from the domestic spaces of respectable society, is founded on her inability to resolve the conflicting messages about marriage that she receives. "¡Qué tonta!" [How Silly!] explores these conflicting messages directly, through a conversation between three very different women, as the young, recently married Isabel dreams of joining her scientist husband in his laboratory, while the frivolous Laura and the pious elderly countess make every effort to discourage her. The story takes place against the background of a refined *salón*, where the women have gathered for afternoon tea: It is a typical domestic space, with only a window over the Atlantic to indicate the Galician setting. The disparaging rejection of Isabel's arguments by Laura and the countess and their adherence to stereotypical models of femininity—the loose woman and the beata—develop the thesis set out in the relationship between Mara and Doña María in *Wolski*: that female suffering is not entirely imposed by men and that women can often be one another's worst enemies.

According to Laura and the countess, the world is divided into separate masculine and feminine spheres: For them, man is the enemy and male-female relations are based on masculine desire. Men, according to the countess, are "carnívoros furiosos que necesitan carne fresca para saciar su apetito" (Casanova 1911, *El pecado,* 97) [crazed carnivores who need fresh meat to sate their appetite], and women like Isabel who try to transgress the boundaries, seeking more than simply physical union, are sick (99). Laura explains to Isabel that the division between the masculine and feminine spheres is not to be breached: "Desengáñate, los hombres tienen un camino, y las mujeres otro. En el de ellos todo a lo largo se ve repetida a lo infinito esta inscripción: 'Somos los dueños y hacemos lo que nos da la gana'" (100). [Don't fool yourself; men have one path, and women another. All along theirs, this inscription appears again and again, stretching off into the distance: "We are the masters, and we do what we like."] The countess continues the metaphor, invoking the influence of the church on women's lives: "Y en el camino de las mujeres . . . hay a cada paso una cruz en la que Dios ha escrito: 'Haz tu deber y no te metas en sicologiar'" (100). [And on women's path . . . there is a cross at every step, on which God has written: "Do your duty and don't start psychologizing."] Then Laura takes the joke, in the countess's opinion, one step too far, laughing, "Al pie de las cruces, el Diablo escribió a su vez en el suelo: 'Vivid lo mejor que podáis, pobrecitas mujeres, que también sois hijas de Dios'" (100). [At the foot of each cross, the devil, for his part, wrote on the ground: "Live as best you can, poor unfortunate women, for you too are God's children."]. The countess, horrified, tells Laura that she is as wrong as Isabel: "Tú has hecho del matrimonio una comedia divertida, y esta pobre un drama sombrío" (100). [You've made marriage into an amusing comedy, and this poor girl a serious drama.] Her choice of a dramatic metaphor underlines the artificiality of the institution and the "roles" that both parties, but particularly women, must play. For them, as for Águeda's mother in "Luz en tinieblas," marriage is a business transaction undertaken for various reasons, of which love is among the least important: "El matrimonio es la unión de dos seres que se gustan y se convienen: es la 'asotiation limited' [*sic*] de dos personas que tienen su esfera de acción fuera de sí mismos, en la sociedad, en la familia" (101). [Marriage is the union of two people who like one another and suit one another: It is the "limited association" of two people whose sphere of action lies beyond themselves, in society, in the family.] If this situation were to change, "se trastornaría todo en el mundo" (102) [everything in the world would go awry]. Isabel challenges her friends, arguing that if men and women have separate paths, "¿cómo han de poder ir unidos?" (101) [how are they to go on together?]. Laura answers, patronizingly: "¡Boba! Porque son caminos paralelos" [Silly girl! Because the paths are parallel], but Isabel is not satisfied: "Laura, dos seres que se unen para toda la vida, tienen que ir juntos por 'un solo' camino" (101). [Laura, two people who are joined for life have to go on together along "a single" path.] The conversation ends abruptly with Laura remarking dismissively, "¡Pero será tonta esta muchacha!" [But this girl must be silly!], to which the countess agrees, "tonta, tonta de remate" (102) [Silly, utterly silly].

What is the reader supposed to make of this story? Anyone familiar with Casanova's many nonfictional writings of the period would be only too aware that Isabel, like Mara in *Wolski*, is in part a mouthpiece for Casanova's own views. Like Mara, Isabel comes up against an older generation of women who actively oppose her desire to challenge the status quo, and the final image of her echoes our final glimpse of Mara as a behaloed angel: "[Isabel], cruzadas las manos en actitud dolorida, dijérase que simbolizaba en aquel salón de frívolas elegancias, al lado de la mesa que ofrecía deleites al paladar, lo más delicado y recóndito del espíritu femenino gallego nostálgico" (Casanova 1911, *El pecado*, 102). [(Isabel), hands folded in sorrow, seemed to symbolize, in that frivolously stylish salon, beside that table offering such delights to the palate, the subtlest depths of the nostalgic, feminine Galician spirit.] If Mara represents Polish womanhood, exploiting the margins of the nation to instigate social change, Isabel can fulfill the same role in Galicia. There is a certain paradox in Casanova's description of the feminine Galician spirit as "nostalgic," given that what Isabel is proposing is a radical reimagining of the institution of marriage: Just how radical is evident from her friends' belief that this reimagining will turn the whole world upside down. Like the ironic subtitle, "causerie," Casanova's recourse to a stereotypical image of Galician womanhood seeks to divert attention from the serious discussion at the heart of the story.

Casanova's point in "¡Qué tonta!" is, in my view, that those on the margins—whether of nation or gender—are in an ideal position to reimagine outdated and oppressive social conventions. It is quite another matter, of course, whether they will have the opportunity to do so, for, evidently, the potential

of this position cannot always be exploited in practice. Laura's placid suggestion that Isabel's dissatisfaction with her marriage could be attributed to her
husband's abusiveness highlights the rarely addressed question of domestic
violence, which Casanova explores in chilling detail in the story-in-dialogue
"En la casa de enfrente" [The House Opposite]. The story—centered on the
question of whether the protagonists will attend a grand ball that night—
dramatizes María's first tentative attempt to break away from her abusive husband, Luis, allegorizing the limited options available to women in a society
where they are entirely at the mercy of men. Looking beyond the "happy ending" of marriage, it asks what happens when conventions of masculinity and
femininity and male and female roles are taken to their logical conclusion.
Significantly, all of the action takes place in the boudoir, which is María's
private space: Luis's actions, his constant invasions and belligerence—culmi-
nating in the physical destruction of the furniture—consequently appear all
the more aggressive. Luis is sickly, and we increasingly realize that his sickness is both physical and moral: His vicious attacks on women in general, and
María in particular, are its most unpleasant symptom: "¡Eh! Pero ¿quién pide
lógica, cariño o sentido común a las mujeres? Hay que tratarlas como lo que
son; enseñándoles en una mano el látigo y en la otra un terroncito de azúcar.
Y como a los niños, hay que obligarles a obedecer" (Casanova 1911, *El pecado*,
106). "Ha! But who asks logic, affection, or common sense of women? You
have to treat them as what they are; showing them the whip in one hand and
a sugar cube in the other. And like children, you have to force them to obey.]
Luis's attitude toward women is paralleled by his attitude toward the group
of Moroccans who he has learned will be attending the ball, and his anxieties about both groups come together when he accuses María of getting ready
"para divertirte entre los salvajes marroquíes" (112) [to have a good time with
those Moroccan savages]. In other words, he provides yet another example
of the white, middle-class male response to the fin de siècle fears about the
breakdown of racial and gender boundaries that Casanova had already explored in *Wolski* and *Lo eterno*.

María's life represents the worst extreme of the life of the middle-class
woman that Argentina and Casanova's other heroines so fear. She is yet another victim of parents who consider marriage to be a financial transaction,
and she knows that her husband does not see her as a partner: "Me ha hecho
su criada, la enfermera de sus repugnantes males" (Casanova 1911, *El pecado*,
108). [He has made me his servant, a nurse for his revolting illnesses.] The
first hint of a rebellion—when she announces her desire to go to the ball that
Luis has suddenly decided he is too sick to attend (after forcing her o agree
to attend a few hours earlier)—provokes a reaction of extreme horror: "Tú

... tú quieres. ... ¡Pero, señor! ¿Qué ha pasado aquí? ¿Te has vuelto loca de repente, o es que naciste malvada? ¿Conque quieres ir a divertirte estando yo ... muriéndome? ¡Perversa! ¡Malvada!" (113). [You ... you want. ... My God! What's happened here? Have you suddenly gone mad, or were you just born wicked? So you want to go and have a good time while I'm ... dying? Perverse! Wicked!] Luis equates María's desire for independence with a pathological sickness that recalls the countess's reaction to Isabel in "¡Qué tonta!" but the stage directions describe it as "primera protesta de su carácter débil moldeado en las rutinas de una educación superficial" (113) [the first protest of a weak character shaped by the routines of a superficial education]. Nevertheless, the story ends where it began, as María, wrapped in a shawl, once again takes up her position gazing out of the window, confirming that, despite her rebellion, she is still trapped. Still, something has changed, and she is no longer alone:

> Siente pesado el corazón, la cabeza vacía, y en sus oídos zumba un murmullo singular, como de llantos de cientos de mujeres. ... Y atenta a las tenues modulaciones de aquel murmullo persistente, María esfuérzase en vano por descubrir si son ecos de maldiciones o de plegarias, los ecos que de no sabe dónde llegan hasta ella. (115)

> [Her heart feels heavy, her head empty, and in her ears there buzzes a curious murmur, like the weeping of hundreds of women. ... And alert to the faint modulations of that persistent murmur, María struggles in vain to discern whether the echoes that are coming to her from she knows not where are echoes of curses or of prayers.]

As in so many of Casanova's narratives, this ending is deliberately ambiguous: María's uncertainty about whether the voices are cursing her or supporting her suggests Casanova's ambivalence about whether open rebellion—for example, Spain's nascent feminist movement—can, in real terms, truly help women. In an unusual example of "writing beyond the ending," the story dramatizes Argentina's fear that rather than being the Holy Grail that the romance plot makes marriage out to be, it is merely another mechanism by which society keeps women in line. As María comments, "Pasé mi infancia en un convento lúgubre. ... Apenas salida de él entré en este caserón que es un hospital" (110). [I spent my childhood in a gloomy convent. ... I had barely left it when I entered this manor house, which is practically a hospital.] In other words, she has exchanged one prison for another. By giving María voice—and the dramatic form does this literally—and thus allowing her to vocalize her unhappiness, Casanova challenges the social and romantic conventions that have brought her to this position and that will attempt to keep her there, just as through the character of Luis she ridicules masculine fears of the breakdown of boundaries of race and gender. Most important, I believe, the combination of the story's title, "En la casa de enfrente," with the consciously contemporary Spanish setting is intended to "deliteraturize" the story: That is, Casanova is, in effect, telling the reader, "This could be happening in a house opposite yours." One of Casanova's most fascinating pieces, this story did not appear in the 1925 edition of *El pecado* and, as far I can ascertain, was never published again.

One possible future for María is established in another story, "Más triste que el amor" [Sadder Than Love]. As an old woman, this María also gazes out from the upstairs balcony of her crumbling Galician manor house and wonders whether her dissolute husband—also named Luis—would have abandoned her if she had been more willing to play the role of submissive female. Among the stories in this collection, "Más triste que el amor," with its nostalgia for a vanished past, is an unusual example of the sort of regional writing that Campbell calls a celebration of "the preservation, through writing, of the lives of humble, ordinary people in an environment threatened by time, change, and external disruption" (1997, 8). The story opens one February day, as the elderly woman and her brother return home from church to their "casona hidalga, más de dos [siglos] erguida en aquel ángulo provinciano de tierra gallega" (Casanova 1911, *El pecado,* 79) [noble manor house, standing for more than two (centuries) in that provincial corner of Galicia].[1] The background of fading splendor makes the pair's sad reminiscences on this thirtieth anniversary of their double wedding to another brother and sister all the more poignant, as the old woman suggests that their fault lay in failing to fulfill expected gender roles: "Si hubieras tenido más carácter con tu mujer . . ." [If you'd stood up to your wife more . . .], she tells her brother. "Debiste ser enérgico, inflexible. . . . Yo, por mi parte, fuí a veces tan severa con Luis, tan dura. . . . Si le hubiera tratado con más cariño, quizás . . ." (83). [You should have been vigorous, inflexible. . . . I, for my part, was sometimes too severe with Luis, too harsh. . . . If I'd treated him with more affection, then maybe . . .]

Like every other story in *El pecado* (with the exception of "Luz en tinieblas"), "Más triste que el amor" explores its protagonists' failure to resolve the romantic quest successfully. Like "El pecado," "El triunfo," and "Flores de acacia" in particular, it posits an alternative to the heterosexual romantic couple. As Rachel DuPlessis notes, a number of women authors have used the brother-sister bond as an alternative to romance to exemplify "the transgressive invention of narrative strategies . . . that express critical dissent from dominant narrative [and] take issue with the mainstays of the social and ideological organization of gender, as these appear in fiction" (1985, 5). Although Casanova's elderly brother and sister are drawn together in the realization that, in the words of the old woman, "somos los últimos de nuestra familia" (1911, *El pecado*, 83) [we are the last of our line], their responses are diametrically opposed. The old woman believes that their situation is "más triste aún que nuestro amor" (83) [sadder still than our love]: However negative her experience of marriage, it is still preferable to romantic failure. She laments, "¡Nada nos resta de nuestro pasado!" (84). [Nothing is left to us of our past!] In contrast, her brother has accepted the situation and has given up his idealistic vision of marriage in favor of the more prosaic realities of enjoying his food, caring for his pets, and reliving his memories:

> ¿Cómo que no? ¿y el recuerdo? El recuerdo es una evocación, y la evocación nos devuelve el pasado, nos "da" lo que "fué." . . . ¡Que no nos queda nada! En el alma, todo; fuera de nosotros. . . . Pero ¡si estamos rodeados de objetos que teníamos hace treinta años! Mi escritorio, tu cómoda, esos muebles. (84–85)

> [How so? What about memory? Memory is an invocation, and invocation brings the past back to us, "gives" us back what "was." . . . Nothing is left to us indeed! In our souls, there is everything; beyond ourselves. . . . After all, it so happens that we are surrounded by objects we owned thirty years ago! My writing desk, your dressing table, all that furniture.]

This response might be read as an affirmation of the power of the environment to resist external threats, illustrating Campbell's observation that "local color" writing is characterized by "a fascination with tracing the workings of heredity and a belief in the shaping power of the environment" (1997, 9). The thirty-year anniversary in the story is significant: "Más triste que el amor" was first published in 1898, thirty years after the revolution that ushered in six years of Republican rule. Perhaps the elderly siblings represent different responses to the destruction of the old Spain by a "brave new world"—can it be a coincidence that the brother's wife was called Aurora? The original version of the story ("Escena suelta") was set in Madrid, and (as with the 1926 edition of *Lo eterno*), the effect of removing the action from Madrid—with all its associations—is to de-emphasize the symbolic framework of the story. At the same time, however, the new version—like those of "¡Qué tonta!" and (as we will see) "Una acuarela"—serves to locate Galicia within universal debates whose implications reach far beyond the borders of Galicia, or even of Spain.

If this group of stories reveals a variety of the responses of middle-class women to the limitations placed on them by Spanish society and culture, two later stories, "Una acuarela" and "Flores de acacia," take a different perspective. Rather than address the social limitations embodied in love and marriage, they focus on the artistic and literary constructions of femininity that buttress these limitations. "Flores de acacia"—the only story in the collection that has no Galician or Spanish element—describes the unsettling experiences of a French painter (Moulin) at the hands of two Russian women who refuse to play the game of romance with him (see Chapter 5). Moulin does not learn from his experience; instead, he retreats into his art and into a defense of his apparently compromised masculinity. "Una acuarela"—one of Casanova's most overtly critical stories—has a very different outcome, however. In the first part of the story, the Galician watercolorist Perico Torres, recently returned from Italy, humiliates a young girl who has come to sit for him by forcing her to pose half-naked in front of his friends. In the second part, Torres's painting has won an award, but he cannot enjoy the accomplishment, because he knows that his treatment of the girl has caused her moral downfall. Set in different countries, the two stories show very different responses to the same issue: the gulf between real women and artistic images of femininity. What they have in common is the space where each unfolds: the artist's studio, a masculine space unlimited by the national boundaries that restrict so many of Casanova's heroines. Torres's studio is crammed with examples of flamboyance and inspiration: antique tapestries, ornamental chests, fine fabrics, and "envueltos en un torvellino [*sic*] de gasas de colores, vaciados del Parthenon, estatuillas de Pompeya, lucientes porcelanas de Lucca de la Robia" (Casanova 1911, *El pecado*, 74) [swathed in a whirlwind of colored gauzes, statues from the Parthenon, little figures from Pompeii, glimmering porcelain pieces by Lucca della Robia]. Similarly, Moulin, wearing a Chinese silk shirt, reclines on a cushion-covered Turkish divan that is "un capricho de sedas y oro" (141) [a caprice of silks and gold]. Like Enrique Wolski, he is presented as a representative of both his nation and his generation, the "síntesis de una generación y de una raza" (141) [synthesis of a generation and a race]. This generation and race, however, are without impetus or energy: "Aquel abandono del cuerpo en los blandos almohadones señalaba la pereza y el cansancio de una juventud no satisfecha" (141). [The body, reclining on the soft cushions, revealed the languor and fatigue of dissatisfied youth.]

Each studio exemplifies the exoticism and aestheticism of the decadent artist for whom it was a deliberately constructed space that promised artistic and sexual freedom: The paradigmatic artist's studio is that which was created by Duc Jean Floressas des Esseintes in Joris-Karl Huysman's *À rebours* (1883): a completely artificial and artistic environment, right down to the scent that pervades it. Huysman's vision was developed by Oscar Wilde in *The Picture of Dorian Gray* (1890), which opens in the studio of the artist Basil Hallward with Dorian's seduction and the creation of the picture that embodies the debates over aestheticism and the relationship between life and art. Both of these works explore the artist's studio as a means of escape from reality: des Esseintes constructs a physical environment that will protect him from the outside world, whereas Dorian's portrait protects him from the ravages of age, preserving the aesthetic at the expense of the moral. Yet if the studio promises the artist liberation from artistic and sexual mores, what does it mean for the women who are the subject of so many of his works? This is Casanova's question in "Una acuarela," which opens with Torres's declaration of his artistic manifesto, based on the mutual interdependence of love and art: "Creedme, mis queridos colegas, el arte necesita del amor, y el amor necesita para ahuyentar un tanto el hastío, riquezas, esplendores y libertad" (Casanova 1911, *El pecado,* 73). [Believe me, my dear colleagues, art needs love, and love, to ward off tedium, needs riches, splendors, and freedom.]

For Torres, love and art go hand in hand; however, although his art relies entirely on women, both for inspiration and finance, his treatment of them is arrogant, to say the least. He lures a poverty-stricken young girl into his studio with the promise of money: Full of sly insinuations, he tells her, "Te enseñaremos 'el oficio' y ganarás cuanto quieras, porque eres guapa" (Casanova 1911, *El pecado,* 74). [We'll teach you "the business," and you'll earn as much as you like, because you're pretty.] His violent reaction to her reluctance, as he rips her clothes from her body, leaving her naked, evokes not only the physical rape of an individual woman but also the symbolic rape of "woman" by art:

El pintor tiró violentamente de los nevados tules que la envolvían, y rasgándose, dejaron al [sic] niña, que se irguió rápidamente hasta quedar arrodillada; cruzó las manos en ademán suplicante, y sollozó con amargura y resignación indescriptibles estas palabras:

 ¡Madre mía! ¡madre mía! (75–76)

[The painter threw off the snow-white tulles that enveloped her, and ripping, they came away from the girl, who stood up so quickly that she fell to her knees; she crossed her hands in a gesture of supplication and sobbed with indescribable bitterness and resignation:

 "O Mother, Mother!"]

The words used to describe the girl's reaction are interesting—instead of feeling distress or fear or anger, she feels bitterness and resignation. The first section of the story ends with the consequences of her humiliation: We observe her leaving the house, tears still wet on her cheeks. Before she has gone very far, however, she undergoes a sudden change:

> Al perderse entre las obscuras callejas en busca de su miserable hogar, se detuvo un instante y sonrieron dulcemente sus labios. Recordó que la habían llamado hermosa muchas veces y acaso vió pasar ante sus ojos las primeras y deslumbrantes imágenes que ocultan los precipicios abiertos en el camino de las desheredadas. (76)

> [Disappearing into the gloomy alleyways in search of her miserable home, she stopped for a moment and a sweet smile played on her lips. She remembered all the times they had called her beautiful, and perhaps she caught a glimpse of the first dazzling images that conceal the open chasms on the path of the *desheredadas*.][2]

We learn in the second part of the story that Mariña's humiliation (only now is she named) has indeed been the catalyst for her moral downfall; the story ends with Torres's anguished rejection of the manifesto he set out on his return from Italy:

> ¡El arte! ¡El arte! Si en nombre de él o para él hemos de desflorar un alma, desposeyéndola de la castidad y el pudor: y si el cuerpo que copiamos en la fiebre santa de la inspiración, ha de ser codiciado en nuestras fiebres brutales de hombre, reniego del arte y de mí mismo y maldigo la idolatría de la forma! (Casanova 1911, *El pecado*, 77–78)

> [Art! Art! If in its name or on its behalf we must deflower a soul, stripping it of chastity and modesty: and if the body we copy in the sacred passion of inspiration must also be desired by our brutal, manly passions, then I renounce art and myself and I curse the idolatry of form!]

The link between art and love, which Torres initially saw as fruitful and productive, is here turned on its head, as art is seen as the tool of "brutal" masculine passion. The story becomes a critique of the objectification of woman in art, a symbolic rape that has as profound and traumatic an effect as the physical act itself. Where the artist's studio promised the (male) artist freedom from moral and artistic constraints, the implications for the few women allowed to enter were vastly different. Casanova was by no means the first woman to make this point: In the short poem "In an Artist's Studio" (1856), which evokes the relationship between Christina Rossetti's brother Dante Gabriel and his wife and muse, Lizzie Siddal, the poet equates the artist's relationship with his model with that of a vampire and his victim: "He feeds upon her face by day and night" (1990, 264). Like Mariña, the woman in Rossetti's poem is a shadow of her artistic image, which represents her "Not as she is, but was when hope shone bright / Not as she is, but as she fills his dream" (264). Torres's epiphany shows him not only that the image he has created, the one that is accepted as ideal in the discourse of art, bears no relationship to what he truly wants but also that it has, in fact, contributed to its destruction. "Una acuarela" is a brief but biting critique of the objectification and eroticization of woman by an inherently masculine artistic establishment. Moreover, by making Torres—the stereotypical decadent artist—Galician, Casanova locates Galicia firmly within the ambit of European fin de siècle culture, thus pushing the conventional bounds of both fin de siècle and *fin de século*.

If the artist's studio in "Flores de acacia" and "Una acuarela" represents a transnational space where images of femininity are constructed but real women have no place, the penultimate story in the collection, "Una ervingista," offers a tantalizing glimpse of a space where such inequities are challenged on a daily basis. "Una ervingista" stands out among the stories of *El pecado* for its explicitly autobiographical basis, its London setting, and its overt engagement with extratextual debates: It describes the narrator's encounter with the Russian Irvingite María Ivanowna Letrona in the library of the British Museum in London, "enriquecida con millares de libros y regida con un orden sólo en Inglaterra posible" (131) [endowed with thousands of books and ruled with an order possible only in England]. Seen against the fascination with space, and particularly the space afforded to middle-class women that we have seen to be a central element in *El pecado*, the library appears as a frontier zone, neither public nor private, where distinctions of class, race, and gender are minimal: "Había hombres de todos los países y mujeres de todas las clases sociales" (Casanova 1911, *El pecado,* 131). [There were men from every country and women from every social class.] Although most of the people the narrator observes are named and traceable, the first person mentioned is anonymous but introduces a framework of meaning that informs the entire story, that of the fallen civilization: "[el] egipcio de amarillenta tez que intenta conocer las verdades o las hipótesis de nuestra civilización para difundirlas entre aquella raza que hace cinco mil años amamantó con su ciencia al mundo entero" (131) [(the) sallow-faced Egyptian who tries to find the truths or hypotheses of our civilization in order to disseminate them among the race that five thousand years ago suckled the whole world with its knowledge]. He is surrounded by a wide range of contemporary intellectuals:

> El príncipe Krapotki, . . . con la agitación de un inspirado, escribe las incendiarias frases que, apenas llegadas a Rusia, los socialistas se repiten cautelosamente, más esperanzados en su fuerza y en su triunfo. . . . Aquella dama de correcto perfil que viste blusa de seda blanca con desenvoltura es mistress Coak, experta doctora en medicina. . . . El doctor Jauvier [es] defensor furibundo de su tierra de Haiti y entusiasta de su raza hasta el punto de afirmar, con su compatriota Fernusi, que la raza negra "es, físicamente, más hermosa que la blanca." . . . Müller Strübing [es] el célebre historiador de la literatura griega. (131–32)

> [Prince Kropotkin, . . . with the agitation of one inspired, writes the incendiary words that, once they reach Russia, the socialists repeat cautiously, more hopeful of their strength and their triumph. . . . That correctly attired lady in the shameless white silk blouse is Mistress Coak, expert doctor of medicine. . . . Doctor Janvier (is) ferocious defender of his Haitian homeland and passionate about his race to the point of claiming, with his compatriot Firmin,[3] that the black race "is, physically, more beautiful than the white." . . . Müller Strübing (is) the famous historian of Greek literature.][4]

These people work to extend boundaries of class, race, gender, or knowledge, and the narrator is thrilled to find that "la atmósfera cargada de ideas como lo está de electricidades el espacio durante la tempestad" (132) [the atmosphere, charged with ideas just as air is charged with electricity during a storm], allows her to ask questions that are impossible in the tightly controlled, closely monitored Spain of other stories:

> ¿Qué problemas van a resolverse?
> ¿Con qué nuevas formas va a surgir de la concepción la belleza?
> ¿Cuál de esos pensadores hará brotar de las cenizas que en el corazón lleva la escéptica juventud el fuego de un ideal que la fortalezca?
> ¿Cuál de esos seres es el elegido "inmortal de la gloria"? (132–33)

> [What problems are to be resolved?
> What new forms of beauty will arise from this thinking?

Which of those intellectuals will bring forth from the ashes that our skeptical youths carry in their hearts the fire of an ideal that will strengthen them?

Which of these people will be the chosen "glorious immortal"?]

The juxtaposition of these searching questions with the first introduction of Ivanowna suggests that she and her story may hold some of the answers. Against the background of the Egyptian Gallery, Ivanowna outlines for the narrator the basic tenets of Irvingite doctrine:

> Somos católicos: el Cristo que adora el Santo Padre es nuestro Cristo. Solamente que, en tanto que ustedes los apostólicos romanos no esperan verlo antes de morir, nosotros, los ervingistas, esperamos verlo en vida y pronto, porque el mundo no puede sostener tanta iniquidad. En la hora suprema del cataclismo que se acerca, Cristo vendrá de nuevo al mundo, y podremos oir su divina palabra y seguirle a la región del bien los que lo hayan merecido. (Casanova 1911, *El pecado*, 134)

> [We are Catholics: the Christ whom the Holy Father adores is our Christ. It's just that whereas you Roman Apostolics do not expect to see him before you die, we Irvingites expect to see him in life, and soon, for the world cannot long sustain such iniquity. At the supreme moment of the approaching cataclysm, Christ will return to the world, and we will hear his divine word, and those who have merited it will follow him to the dominion of good.]

Casanova devotes a considerable amount of space to the doctrines of the charismatic Irvingite movement, which was founded in the 1820s in London under the direction of Edward Irving (1792–1834), a pastor in the Church of Scotland. When Irving was expelled from the Church of Scotland in 1833, the sect was formalized and renamed the Catholic Apostolic Church. After his death from consumption in 1835, twelve apostles were appointed in London in anticipation of the coming Apocalypse. The apostles were not replaced as they died off, and by the time Casanova was writing, only one was still living. For many observers, the gradual disappearance of the apostles and the failure of the Apocalypse to appear discredited the Irvingites, but the approaching fin de siècle and the perceived breakdown of society gave them new hope. This hope is reflected in Ivanowna's response to the narrator's suggestion that the apostle may soon die:

No, no morirá antes que Cristo vuelva al mundo. Las revelaciones que
guarda nuestra Iglesia son terminantes: sabemos que la hora se acerca, se
acerca porque todo se desquicia en torno nuestro y el error se apodera de
las almas y la humanidad se envilece. Se acerca el "juicio final"; cuanto hay
de podredumbre en la tierra, quedará en la podredumbre abismado, y al
"mundo de Dios irán" los no Pecadores o los Pecadores que se arrepientan.
(134)

[No, he won't die before Christ returns to the world. The revelations
our Church holds are categorical: we know the hour is approaching, it is
approaching because everything is falling apart around us and wrongdoing
is taking hold of souls and humankind is becoming degraded. The "final
judgment" is approaching; all the corruption on earth will stay mired in its
own corruption, and the non-Sinners or the Sinners who repent "will go to
God's world."]

Irvingism is presented here as one more response to the end-of-century
sense of crisis that Casanova first explored in *Wolski*, which was probably written around the same time. The first part of "Una ervingista" is framed by references to the fallen Egyptian civilization—symbolizing contemporary fears
of social and cultural decline—and it takes place against the background of
"la galería grandiosa llena de rastros del destrozado Egipto" (Casanova 1911, *El
pecado*, 135) [the extravagant gallery bursting with relics of the fallen Egyptian
civilization]. As Ivanowna finishes her speech, Casanova's attention turns to
the inscriptions, the mummies, the sphinxes, and the statue of Horus, who,
she imagines, "abría hasta las diformes [*sic*] orejas sus labios negros, como
si a risa burlona le moviera nuestra conversación" (135) [stretched his black
lips back to his deformed ears, as if our conversation moved him to mocking
laughter]. The author herself does not comment on Ivanowna's beliefs; however, Horus's amusement suggests the indulgence of an older, wiser civilization. Like so many of the stories in *El pecado*, "Una ervingista" ends on a note
of ambiguity mixed with female solidarity:

¿María Yvanowna [*sic*] es una enferma? ¿es una insensata? Quizás ambas
cosas a la vez.
Yo, desde estas glaciales tierras de su país, la saludo con respeto, porque ha
sufrido y espera y ama. (139)

[Is María Yvanowna sick? Is she insane? Perhaps she is both.

I, from here on her frozen native soil, acknowledge her with respect, for she has suffered and hopes and loves.]

Ivanowna—who is, of course, not Spanish—is the only one of *El pecado*'s middle-class heroines who manages to break out of the limited spaces available to her (her marital home, her husband's studio, and her convent cell) to find her own space in London, locus of radical social change. The questions the narrator asks at the end of the story anticipate conventional judgments of such a rebellious woman as sick or insane—as indeed María is considered by Luis and Isabel is considered by Laura and the countess. However, the narrator's declaration of respect puts Ivanowna's battle on a par with that of the intellectuals described in the opening paragraphs. More than any other story, "Una ervingista" extends the range of the collection beyond purely national or regional concerns, by suggesting that solutions to Spain's problems will not be found in the confined spaces of Spain's compartmentalized society.

In *El pecado*, Casanova moves away from the central ground occupied in her earlier work to explore its peripheries as a locus for imagining social change. It is significant that there are virtually no representatives of the dominant group in these stories: Instead, they are peopled by the disenfranchised—women, the elderly, the disabled. The young men who, in the discourse of the time, were presented as the life force of the nation are here sick and afraid (like Luis), Bohemian and on the fringes of respectable society (like the artists Moulin and Torres), or dispatched to a war from which there is no guarantee that they will return whole (like Rodrigo and the two Juans). My reading of *El pecado* suggests a need to rethink existing critical approaches not only to *fin de siglo* Spanish literature but also to *fin de século* Galician writing, and raises questions that merit further research. For example, Casanova's active broadening of the remit of "regional" Galician literature pre-empts by more than a decade the well-known project of the Galician nationalist *Xeración Nós* to make Galician culture a microcosm of the universal, suggesting that some revision of the neglected, bilingual Galician culture of the *rexionalista* years (circa 1880–1916) might be productive. Casanova seems to exploit the concept of the *libro regional* in *El pecado* as a smoke screen for her presentation of controversial ideas about Spanish and Galician society and about the viability of the Spanish and Galician national projects. Her use of the frameworks of regional and women's writing and of the "paisajes y tipos" described in Canitrot's prologue reflects Roberto Dainotto's observation: "To put it bluntly," he writes, "regionalism is the figure of an otherness that is, essentially, otherness from, and against, history" (2000, 9). That is, the "otherness" that runs throughout the collection is a tool by which Casanova can critique the processes through which regional and gender stereotypes are constructed and perpetuated in art and literature and, in the process, challenge the limited spaces afforded to both *lo regional* and *lo femenino* in fin de siècle, *fin de siglo,* and *fin de século* culture.

Until recently, it seemed that *El pecado* was the final word on Casanova's critical intellectual project and that—together with the other two "greatest hits" compilations (*El cancionero de la dicha* and *Exóticas*) and her abortive excursion into theater (*La madeja*)—it brought the first prewar phase of Casanova's career to a rather retrospective end. In the summer of 1999, however, while I was working in the library of the Instituto da Lingua Galega in Santiago de Compostela, I came across Casanova's name linked with an unfamiliar title in the catalogue. Further investigation revealed that the work was a *novela corta*, published in 1914 and—if the title was any indication—based on a Galician theme. This text, *El crimen de Beira-mar*, was almost certainly Casanova's last published work before the outbreak of the World War I and her return to Poland in 1914. As far as I can ascertain, it was never reprinted after its initial publication as part of the series *El Libro Popular*, and it remains virtually unknown today. It has never been included in any of the published bibliographies of Casanova's work (e.g., Alayeto 1987, Couceiro 1954, and Martínez 1999), and Casanova's critics and biographers have never alluded to it. The novel is, however, a fascinating read not only on its own terms but also as an indication of the direction in which Casanova's work was beginning to move. It picks up on several of the key themes of *El pecado*: the relationship between Spain and Galicia, how we deal with "otherness," and the creation of regional and gender stereotypes. These themes, however, are set into a rather different framework, as Casanova shifts her focus not only to a purely Galician setting but also to ethical and epistemological questions: How is it, she asks in *El crimen de Beira-mar*, that such stereotypes and their related narratives come to be constructed? What are their real consequences for people's lives? And, perhaps most crucially, what responsibility does society have when the consequences of the narratives it tells prove to be nefarious rather than benign?

As with so many of Casanova's texts, the substantial questions that underpin the narrative are not necessarily evident on the first reading. On a superficial level, *El crimen de Beira-mar* is the melodramatic story of a crime of passion, the murder of the virtuous Rosa María (whose husband, Matías, is away in America) by her suitor, Antonio. It was published in the third and final year of *El Libro Popular*, the eighty-fifth title in the collection, and only the fourth by a woman, and it fits well into a collection whose earlier stories had carried titles such as *Infanticida* [Infanticide], *El Crimen en la calle de Tu-*

descos [The Tudescos Street Crime], *El asesinato de Sarah Bernhardt* [The Murder of Sarah Bernhardt], and *El amor, la codicia y la muerte* [Love, Avarice, and Death]. As in *Lo eterno* and several of the stories of *El pecado*, Casanova employs narrative techniques drawn from melodrama: The story opens as the villagers of Beira-mar [By-the-Sea] are leaving church after Mass. A group of men—the old philosopher Juan *de mi vida* [Dear Old Juan], Manuel *el Vinculeiro* [Manuel the Squire's Son], and Antolín Méndez—gossip as they watch their fellow villagers. In the process, they introduce the reader to a series of key issues, including emigration, the class struggle, and male-female relations. As they watch Antonio *el Castellano* [Antonio the Spaniard] head for Rosa María's house, Juan and Antolín have to restrain the furious, envious Manuel (chapter 1 of the novel). Antonio appears at Rosa María's house as she and her servant are preparing to put the baby to bed, and, overcome with passion, he tries to persuade her to elope with him. She refuses, however, reminding him that Matías is due to return in a few days (chapter 2). The next day, the village women wash their clothes in the river by the seashore and—echoing Castro—discuss not only the problems of emigration and the women left behind but also Rosa María's relationship with Antonio. When one of Rosa María's sons is swept away by the sea, Antonio arrives just in time to save him (chapter 3). That evening the men in the tavern discuss the rescue, and Manuel, in a jealous rage, pursues Antonio and demands that he leave the village (chapter 4). Ambushed, Antonio nevertheless refuses to leave; he and Manuel fight, two shots are fired, and they run off into the night (chapter 5). That night the steamer carrying Matías docks in Vigo, and the next morning the village gathers to discuss the previous night's events and the possible consequences upon Matías's return. As they watch Rosa María set off to board the launch that will take her to meet Matías, Antonio, enraged, shoots her in the chest at point blank range (chapter 6). The last part of the story describes the reaction of the village to the trial one year later. Manuel has used his influence on the court to prevent all the evidence from being heard, and many of the witnesses have lied under oath, all with the intention of preserving Rosa María's reputation. Antonio is sentenced to thirty years' imprisonment, and Matías returns to New York with his children (chapter 7).

Evidently, *El crimen de Beira-mar* has much in common with the earlier *Princesa del amor hermoso*/"El triunfo." Along with their common basis in the popular-melodramatic tradition, the two texts begin from the same essential premise: a love triangle in which a woman is caught between two men, one Galician and the other Castilian. *El crimen de Beira-mar*'s approach to its subject, however, differs greatly from that of the earlier text. Whereas *Princesa* is set among the upper classes and is constructed from a network of literary and classical allusions, *El crimen de Beira-mar* is set among the Galician peasantry (who appear only tangentially in *Princesa*) and is almost completely lacking in extratextual references, which makes it appear much closer to popular (rather than elite or literary) culture than its predecessor. Furthermore, the Galician dimension of the text is emphasized far more than in *Princesa*, as Casanova employs techniques drawn from the nineteenth-century *costumbrista* genre, such as textual footnoting (which she had used to great effect two decades earlier in *Wolski*). This is evident, for example, when she conveys atmosphere through domestic details and the use of Galician words: "Pepa canturreaba echando tojos en la *lareira*. Un pote ventrudo, familiar, colgado de la *gramalleira* eslabonada, despedía el vaho de las nabizas con restos de cerdo, delicia del *caldiño*" (Casanova 1914, *El crimen de Beira-mar*, 206, emphasis Casanova's). [Pepa hummed as she threw sprigs of gorse onto the *hearth*. A full-bellied, family-sized pot, hung from an *iron chain*, was steaming with the breath of the turnip leaves and pork trimmings, the best part of the *broth*.] By using such devices—and by drawing attention to them through her use of italic type—Casanova makes a nod to tradition that may draw the reader's attention away from the critique of contemporary society that underpins the narrative.

The Galician setting of *El crimen de Beira-mar* cements Casanova's narrative journey from the central, national locations of Spain and Poland (*Wolski, Lo eterno, Más que amor*), with their "paradoxical" alter egos of Africa and Lithuania, to the peripheral location of Galicia (*Princesa del amor hermoso, El pecado*), depicted not simply as a constituent part of Spain but rather as a national space with its own very real problems. Like the Poland of *Wolski* or the Spain of *Lo eterno*, the Galicia of *El crimen de Beira-mar* is a society divided along lines of ethnicity, class, and gender. These divisions, the text suggests, stem from the national and gender stereotypes that Casanova made it her project to critique throughout this part of her career. Like Carlos in *Más que amor* or Fernando in *Princesa del amor hermoso*, Antonio is depicted as the stereotypical Spanish male: black-haired, with flashing, long-lashed blue eyes full of passion and jealousy (Casanova 1914, *El crimen de Beira-mar*, 209). His nickname, "El castellano," makes his role in the drama clear. Like the *guardias* in "El ladrón," he is the (Spanish) outsider against whom all the (Galician) villagers unite. The village women describe him as "feo, negro y áspero en el hablar . . . sin gracia . . . un ladrón como todos" (213) [ugly, swarthy, and harsh-tongued . . . graceless . . . a thief like all of them], and the men conspire to run him out of the village. In contrast, Rosa María's Galician husband, Matías, away in New York and sending back money to support his family, is respected and beloved by all.

From the opening scenes, the narrative alternates between scenes of male and female community that allow Casanova to comment on customs that were not, perhaps, so foreign to her readers as the exoticized setting might suggest. While the men talk in the tavern or out on the roads, the women congregate at the seashore, an extension of the domestic space where they carry out their domestic duties and where freedom is possible only in men's absence: "Cuando nuestros maridos se van es como si nos enterraran en nuestras casiñas" (Casanova 1914, *El crimen de Beira-mar*, 212). [When our husbands leave, it's as if they'd buried us in our cottages.] Only Rosa María remains apart. She is seen first leaving the church in the company of her servant Pepa and then in her kitchen, reflecting the social requirement that "una mujer casada tiénese que encerrar en su casa y no dar oídas ni miradas a quien sea" (212) [a married woman should shut herself up at home and not see or speak to anyone]. The story of Rosa María, who is unique among Casanova's heroines as a married woman and a mother, is not the conventional tale of the difficult path toward marriage; it is, instead, an example of DuPlessis's "writing beyond the ending" in Casanova's exploration of the problems of a woman who has attained the so-called Holy Grail of marriage. Rosa María's situation highlights the difficulties of Galicia's rural women, whom Rosalía de Castro had commemorated in 1881 as the "viudas dos vivos" (1986, 167) [widows of the living], their husbands and fathers absent in the Americas. As the text shows, although the realities of life require women to take action and exert authority, they are nevertheless obliged to live according to a moral code that demands, at all costs, the protection of honor—"lo más grande del mundo" (Casanova 1914, *El crimen de Beira-mar*, 213) [the greatest thing in the world].

Perhaps because of this framework, Rosa María (unlike Casanova's previous heroines) remains one-dimensional. Casanova's focus in *El crimen de Beira-mar* is not the events of the story or the characters of Rosa María and Antonio or the symbolically absent Matías; it is the way the events and the reputations of the participants are seen, recounted, and ultimately shaped by society as a whole. As in *Princesa*, Casanova sets up her stereotypes only to move them to the side of the action. Every event is followed by a passage in which the villagers recall and reinterpret Rosa María's story, comments that are punctuated by reminders that nobody has actually witnessed any of the events under discussion. The most vocal of the village women, "la 'Raposa'" [The Vixen] refers to the "scandal" of Rosa María and Antonio, saying, "No miro más que para lo mío, ¿entiendes?, pero *viéronlo los demás*" (Casanova 1914, *El crimen de Beira-mar*, 213, emphasis Casanova's). [I mind my own business, you know? But *the others saw it all*.] Every event they comment on is adapted to fit their preconceptions. Antonio is a Castilian; therefore he must be a passionate, jealous seducer. Rosa María is a married woman who does not, apparently, follow the rules; therefore she is a "lagarta . . . mala madre . . . perra" (223) [slut . . . bad mother . . . bitch]. After Antonio shoots Rosa María, however, her reputation begins to change. As on every other occasion, the villagers take over the story, and, in the time leading up to the trial a year later, it recasts Rosa María as an innocent victim. Suddenly, the fact that nobody ever actually saw anything becomes a virtue. Everyone swears before the judge that Rosa María was killed because she would have nothing to do with Antonio, despite the fact that, as the village's elderly philosopher Juan *de mi vida* observes, "eso era mentir; porque vosotros *no lo sabíais*" (226, emphasis Casanova's) [that was a lie, because *none of you knew for sure*]. As a result, Antonio is sentenced to life imprisonment, but his conviction is suspect, as it is based on perjury committed by the entire village in "uno de esos desconcertantes movimientos de la psicología popular, que descubren en el espíritu humano las raíces del bien y del mal, enlazadas fatal e indisolublemente" (225) [one of those disconcerting shifts in the popular psychology that reveal in the human spirit the roots of good and evil, fatally and indissolubly entwined].

Like so many of Casanova's works, *El crimen de Beira-mar* ends on a note of despair. A year after Rosa María's death, Matías has returned with his children to New York, where (we are told) they can never be happy, because "sin madre, en todas partes, han de tener *morriña* de ella" (Casanova 1914, *El crimen de Beira-mar*, 227, emphasis Casanova's) [without a mother, wherever they go they will be *homesick* for her]. The villagers return home, one by one, grieving for Rosa María, who has now been fixed in the popular imagination as a virtuous, devoted wife, with no stain on her honor. Only old Juan *de mi vida* is uneasy, speaking the truth that underpins the entire story: "Todas las cosillas del mundo son así o de otra manera . . . [s]egún cómo se las mire, o se las tome" (226). [Everything in the world is like this or like that . . . (a)ccording to how you look at it or how you take it.] Similarly, *El crimen de Beira-mar* itself can be taken on two levels, embodied in the ambiguity of the "de" of the title. On one hand, it can be interpreted as a sentimental story, the melodramatic tale of a crime of passion *that took place in* Beira-mar. On the other hand, it is an indictment of the crime of a whole society that is prepared to disregard truth in order to preserve appearances: the crime *committed by* Beira-mar. In a move that recalls Enrique Wolski's pseudoscientific (but, in fact, simply prejudiced) view of his ethnically diverse patients, Antonio is destroyed because he is Castilian and because the villagers have preconceived notions of what that means. Meanwhile, Rosa María, initially vilified because she is perceived as having transgressed the unwritten social code of the "viudas dos vivos," is not liberated even by the posthumous rehabilitation of her reputation. Like Gelcha, Laura, Argentina, Mariña, and many of Casanova's other female protagonists, she is caught firmly within the bonds of femininity created and maintained by social and cultural expectation. As an exercise in "writing beyond the ending," Rosa María's story is profoundly pessimistic, for it reinforces Casanova's long-standing belief (born of personal experience) that marriage—so often portrayed as the ideal resolution to the female protagonist's quest—is not, in fact, the start of a new chapter but simply a prolonged conclusion to the existing one. In other words, she seems to be saying that as long as society remains wedded to the established gender roles, it does not matter how brave (or foolhardy) your actions are or how hard you try to improvise, for the action (with or without you) will always return to the preordained script.

The central role ascribed to social context and social pressure in *El crimen de Beira-mar* means that its Galician setting, like that of *El pecado*, has to be viewed as more than background decoration. In both cases, a geographical background that may initially seem purely ornamental in fact enables Casanova to insert herself surreptitiously into contemporary discussions about the forging of the new Galicia. Close readings of both texts reveal how she enters a debate dominated by masculine voices by means of her favorite strategy: manipulating her readers' expectations of conventionally "feminine" genres, in this case regional and sentimental writing. In *El pecado*, she achieves her aim by expanding the range of reference of "regional" Galician writing and inserting it into universal debates about the role of art and culture in the construction of identity. In *El crimen de Beira-mar*, this concern is developed further and reframed through Casanova's use of the familiar Galician themes of emigration and the "viudas dos vivos," by means of which she continues the social project (at that point, still largely unrecognized) of the woman she acknowledged as a foremother, Rosalía de Castro.

The project of both *El crimen de Beira-mar* and *El pecado* is to draw the specific concerns of early twentieth-century Galicia into a broader debate. Both texts are driven by a tension that stems not only from the rapidly changing relationship between a newly radicalized Galicia and the Spanish state but also from the universal issue of communal culpability and communal responsibility for the social and cultural impact of conventions on the realities of people's lives. Whereas in 1911 *El pecado* appears cautiously optimistic in proposing the margins of society as a locus for social change, however, *El crimen de Beira-mar* —published just three years later—sees no grounds for optimism. Mateo's departure at the end of the *novela* is symbolic: His decision to take the children to America signals that there can be no future for them in a Galicia where even their mother's death could not remove her from the tyranny of hearsay and expectation. Being located on the margins of the dominant culture, the text seems to be saying, is no guarantee of progressiveness: Even in Galicia, the pressure of social and cultural tradition and the unwillingness of society as a whole to acknowledge the consequences of its actions make social and political liberty a distant prospect, especially for women. This position would, of course, be vindicated throughout the twentieth century, as Casanova and other challenging and complicated women were progressively and decisively written out of Galician and Spanish cultural history—just as Rosa María and her story were forgotten in favor of a fictional and sanitized version, designed simply to reinforce the communal history of the perhaps not-so-fictional town of Beira-mar.

The denouement of *El crimen de Beira-mar* rejects both Galicia and Spain as potential locations for challenging social injustice, hinting tantalizingly at the possibilities of the new world. Unfortunately, however, we will always be left to wonder what this might have meant in terms of the development of Casanova's feminist intellectual and creative project, for at the outbreak of war in 1914, the year *El crimen de Beira-mar* was published, Casanova left Spain to be with her daughters and grandchildren in Poland. When she returned to writing fiction, five long and traumatic years later, her priorities had changed: Where before she had actively promoted a woman-centered vision of the present and future, she would now turn decisively toward an increasingly nostalgic and reactionary version of the past.

Conclusion

Sofía Casanova's decision to return to the front line of the war in Poland in 1914 rather than remain in the relative safety of Spain was primarily a personal one, but its effect on her professional life and on the career she had worked so hard to resuscitate over the previous five years was transformative. On one hand, it opened the door to an exciting new career as Eastern European correspondent for the newspaper *ABC*, a post she accepted in 1915 and would hold for the next twenty years. This position, in turn, led to her work as a commentator on social, cultural, and political events both in Eastern Europe and at home in Spain. On the other hand, Casanova's return to Poland brought to an abrupt end the critical, experimental, feminist trajectory that she had followed in the twenty years since *El doctor Wolski*. She would return to narrative after the war, with a series of *novelas cortas* (*Triunfo de amor, Episodio de guerra, Princesa rusa, Valor y miedo, Kola el bandido,* and *El dolor de reinar*) and (in 1930–1931) a pair of full-length novels (*Como en la vida* and *Las catacumbas de Rusia roja*), as well as several reeditions of *Wolski* and the revised (some might say neutered) versions of *Lo eterno* and *El pecado*. The tone and purpose of these novels and stories, however, is very different from those of the works examined in this study.

The revisions to *Lo eterno* that we saw in Chapter 3 herein give a flavor of the "new" Casanova: Her wartime experiences, together with the changing social and political climate across Europe and especially in Spain, made her far less willing to raise her head above the parapet, even with the protection of generic convention and reader expectation. Moreover, she was now into her sixties, a grandmother who had lived through the Russian Revolution and seen the consequences of extreme radicalism at first hand. In this light, it is hardly surprising that her worldview should change so significantly. Although the works of the 1920s have little of the subtlety of Casanova's prewar novels in terms of either content or style, they are not completely without interest. Novels such as *El dolor de reinar* and *Princesa rusa* develop Casanova's long-standing interest in questions of government, power, and authority, whereas *Kola el bandido, Valor y miedo,* and *Triunfo de amor* introduce a strong current of cultural essentialism and even orientalism in their focus on Russia and the East. From an initial reading, it rather appears that by the 1920s narrative for Casanova had become little more than a cipher through which to flesh out the ideas she was expressing much more directly in her role as a journalist and commentator (although the financial incentives undoubtedly played a part as well). A detailed critical and contextual study of Casanova's fictional and nonfictional works of the 1920s and 1930s would surely reveal much more, but that must remain a subject for another book.

In the present study, my concerns have been twofold: (1) I resolved to redress the obscurity into which Casanova and her works have fallen and to reveal, through systematic readings and analyses of her texts *on their own terms* and *in their own context*, the evidence of her participation in the social, cultural, and political debates of turn-of-the-twentieth-century Spain. (2) Recognizing that context is all, I set out to demonstrate that existing narratives of *fin de siglo* Spain and *fin de século* Galicia are inadequate for an appreciation of the vibrant, challenging diversity of this crucial period in the development of modern Iberian identities. Now, by means of conclusion, I draw attention to the key implications of the critical and theoretical model proposed herein. It is especially important that these implications be considered in terms of the vast and all but forgotten body of work by Casanova's sisters and foremothers that, in her Ateneo lecture, she so vividly likened to the utopian island of Atlantis, swallowed up by the sea (1910, *La mujer española en el extranjero,* 5).

Casanova and her novels prove beyond doubt that although histories of Spanish and Galician literature, including many of those dedicated to Spanish women's literature, present the years around the turn of the twentieth century as a "desert" for women writers, their absence from *fin de século/siglo* culture is a myth. The overwhelming dominance of traditional models for writing Galician and Spanish literary history—which depend on a representation of the Galician *fin de século* as a monolingual process of "virilization" (Carré Aldao 1911) or of the Spanish *fin de siglo* as Castile focused and, again, intrinsically masculine—has caused this myth to go largely uncontested. The effect, of course, is that the contribution of women and other minorities to the development of Iberia's national cultures during this pivotal period has become difficult to discern. What I set out to prove is that the myth of women's absence from *fin de século/siglo* culture and public life is entirely without foundation. Bio-bibliographical research, together with contemporary evidence from such writers as Sofía Casanova and Carmen de Burgos, indicates that well over 250 women wrote and published in the languages of Spain during the decades on either side of the turn of the twentieth century.[1] Sadly, most of their names remain forgotten, even by scholars of Hispanic women's writing, and their works remain largely unread and confined to (at most) one or two academic libraries. Access to these works would unquestionably prove transformative: Certainly, close readings of Casanova's works in their social and intellectual context, together with the few available studies of her contemporaries and their works, make untenable the widespread assumption that writing by women during this period is characterized by sentimentality and detachment from contemporary debate. In fact, as we have seen, Casanova— and she was not alone in this strategy—consciously used the conventions of sentimental fiction, along with those of other genres commonly dismissed as "feminine," to take part in such debates without attracting the adverse attention of her less-enlightened peers.

This reading of Casanova's works demonstrates that culture in Spain at the turn of the twentieth century was neither exclusively masculine nor focused on Castile. It is clear from recent research on better-known women writers of the period—such as Blanca de los Ríos (see González López 2001 and Hooper 2007), Emilia Pardo Bazán (see the innovative work of Joyce Tolliver [1998] and Maryellen Bieder [1990, 1992, and 1995]), and Carmen de Burgos (see Anja Louis's pioneering study of legal discourse and melodrama in Burgos's fiction [2005])—that these women were active participants in public debates about Spain's past, present, and future. They participated not only through journalism, lectures, and academic writings but also—less widely acknowledged—through fiction. More extensive (and accurate) bio-bibliographical research, together with textual analysis from a variety of critical perspectives, will undoubtedly show that, more than isolated exceptions, these women were representatives of a sizable community of female writers and intellectuals, who all addressed in different ways the same big questions as their canonical contemporaries.

Casanova and her contemporaries could not, of course, free themselves entirely from the traditional gender roles that society had educated them for and demanded that they assume. I maintain, however, that they were nevertheless conscious participants in the new "modern" world that—although later reconfigured and reinterpreted as the result of a masculine crisis of identity— was being created by both men and women. Women writers operated both inside and outside the mainstream: They recognized the "problem of Spain," but their configuration of it was different from that of their male peers, for whom the most pressing concern was "the problem of the (male) individual, his 'crisis of conscience' and *abulia* in a new world order" (Bieder 1992, 320). Literature played a vital role in both their reimagining of their social realities and their awareness of their inclusion in a vibrant and dynamic line of female intellectuals, a premise that reinforces Nancy Walker's observation that

> narratives are essential to our sense of place in a human continuum, and one of the strategies that women have employed to mark out their own places is to challenge the authority of existing narratives by telling them anew out of their own necessities. (1995, 11)

The difficulty, of course, for those of us who wish to read and study these authors and their works is that existing models of criticism and interpretation—having developed in response to a limited range of narrative modes and narrative voices from which women writers are, by default, excluded—are inadequate. Reading Casanova's prewar narrative in the light of Rachel DuPlessis's concept of "writing beyond the ending," Nancy Walker's concept of "disobedient writing," and Susan Lanser's work on "authoriality" shows that a broadly feminist, historicist, and text-based approach to the strategies that Casanova employs, the resources on which she draws, and the realities that she describes and contests can reveal previously unsuspected depths. I am conscious, of course, that there is—as there should be—more than one suitable approach: In fact, only by employing a wide variety of critical approaches—both theoretical and empirical—can we truly hope to begin to appreciate the multiple voices and visions of this unprecedented period of radical social and cultural change.

This study has undoubtedly raised many more issues than can be adequately addressed within the limitations of a single volume. One of the most important of these is the continuing need for the revision of existing models of criticism and cultural history writing—chief among them the generational model that continues to dog much scholarship on the *fin de século/siglo* today. Also vital is the question of the persistent focus that has been placed on canonical literary texts of the same period to the exclusion of both lesser-known texts and other cultural media. As a result, it has become fruitless to search out Galician and Spanish women of the *fin de século/siglo* in the canonical spaces of contemporary cultural and public life. Much of the published legacy of female intellectual life in Spain is found, instead, in such marginal areas as pedagogy, translation, conduct, and etiquette; in largely forgotten imprints, such as Madrid's Imprenta del Asilo de Huérfanos and Biblioteca Patria or Barcelona's Librería Católica; or in small local or specialist publishing houses.

The writers themselves were well aware that their culture was not limited to conventional canonical literature. When questioned about women in Spanish cultural life in the first decade of the twentieth century, Casanova and Burgos both included educators, singers, composers, and artists alongside novelists, poets, and journalists (Casanova 1910, *La mujer española en el extranjero*; Burgos 1906).

Even if we restrict ourselves—as I have done in this study—to fiction, these new objects of study and the theoretical and methodological revisions they inspire open up the fascinating possibility of juxtaposing the dominant version of Spanishness and the Spanish national narrative with newly recovered alternative narratives and perspectives on the transition to modernity. For example, studies of nineteenth-century social and cultural discourses by, among others, Alda Blanco, Cristina Enríquez de Salamanca, and Susan Kirkpatrick describe the gendering of national discourse and the construction of the doctrine of separate spheres—that is, of public or "masculine" space and private or "feminine" space. However, the gradual deconstruction of this rhetoric in works such as Casanova's *Lo eterno* (1907) and *El pecado* (1911), De los Ríos's *La niña de Sanabria* (1907), or Burgos's *La rampa* (2006) remains largely unstudied. What might we learn from a consideration of place and space or from the politics of urban representation in the growing number of female-authored *fin de siglo* texts that seek to portray settings other than the purely domestic—from Pardo Bazán's *Insolación* (2001 [first published in 1889]) through De los Ríos's *Madrid goyesco* (1908) and Casanova's *Lo eterno* (1907) to Burgos's *Los negociantes de la Puerta del Sol* (1989 [first published in 1919])? Questions of identity, and particularly of hybrid identities, also demand further attention. How are contemporary notions of race, class, gender, empire, nation, and region described and contested in works such as Carmen de Burgos's *Los inadaptados* (1990 [first published in 1909]), Blanca de los Ríos's *Sangre española* (1899) and *Melita Palma* (1901), Concha Espina's *La esfinge maragata* (1989 [first published in 1914]), Sofía Casanova's *De la guerra* (1916) or in the numerous collections of *cuentos regionales* to which so many *fin de siglo* women contributed? How might we trace the development of a public female voice—an idea rejected, of course, by Miguel de Unamuno in "A una aspirante a escritora" (1959–1964)—through prologues, lectures, journalistic and academic articles, and (in the light of recent work on feminist narratological theory) literary texts? How are contemporary images of masculinity and femininity described and contested or perpetuated in such widely differing works as Concha Espina's *La niña de Luzmela* (1909) and Gloria de la Prada's *El cantar de los amores* (1912), Emilia Pardo Bazán's *Una cristiana* (n.d. [first published in 1890]) and Concepción Gimeno's *Una Eva moderna* (1909), or Francisca Herrera Garrido's *Néveda* (1990 [first published in 1920]) and Blanca de los Ríos's *Las hijas de don Juan* (1989 [first published in 1907])?

Despite the advances since the last decade of the twentieth century, all of these questions and more remain to be answered. The recovery of these largely or wholly forgotten voices is a demanding but fascinating project to undertake: Close readings and contextualization have revealed Sofía Casanova—for so long remembered not as a writer but as "santa de saudade" [saint of longing], icon of Francoist femininity, and professional expatriate—to be an innovative and accomplished professional who enjoyed great critical and professional success in her lifetime. More important, as we are beginning to learn, she was far from unique in this category. As we uncover additional information about the society in which she and her colleagues moved, the debates in which they participated, and the strategies by which they negotiated between the demands of their personal and professional lives, we will learn (or perhaps relearn) to read their works on their own terms. Thus, we begin to discover an alternative to Casanova's nightmare vision of Spain's entire female culture submerged "cual Atlántida que devoró el mar," and we prove once and for all that she was very far from being, as she so poignantly feared in 1907, "extranjera en mi patria" [a stranger in my own land].

Complete Bibliography of Sofía Casanova's Published Works

Poetry

Collections

1885. *Poesías*. Madrid: A. J. Alaria.
1898. *Fugaces*. Biblioteca Gallega. A Coruña, Spain: Andrés
 Martínez, Tipográfico de la Casa de Misericordia.
1911. *El cancionero de la dicha*. Madrid: Regino Velasco Impresor.
1912. *El cancionero de la dicha*. 2nd ed. Madrid: Regino Velasco Impresor.
1941. *Poesías inéditas*. A Coruña, Spain: Real Academia Gallega.

In anthologies and works by other authors

1880. "Naufragan" and "Dolora." In *Escritoras españolas contemporáneas*.
 Madrid: Imprenta de la Biblioteca Universal, 88–90.
1884. "Gotas de agua," "Gradación," and "Cerrada la casa . . ."
 In *Álbum poético* [free with *La Ilustración Ibérica*].
 Barcelona: Editorial Ramón Molinas, 63, 161, 190.
1885. "Para el héroe," "Fantasía," "Íntima," "Arte y amor," and "El día en la
 mitad de su carrera." In *Álbum Poético* [free with *La Ilustración Ibérica*].
 Barcelona: Editorial Ramón Molinas, 52–54, 71, 87–88, 104.
1886. "Anhelo" and "En la tarde." In *Galicia y sus poetas (poesías escogidas de
 autores gallegos contemporáneos)*. Ed. Leandro Saralegui y Medina. El Ferrol,
 Spain: Establecimiento Tipográfico de Ricardo Pita, 182–83, 243–44.
1913. "Estás en la meseta lozana del camino" [dedicated to Javier Valcarce].
 In *Poemas de la prosa*. Ed. Javier Valcarce. Madrid: Perlado Paez, 7.
1914. "Prudencio Canitrot" [dedicated to the canitrot]. In
 *Prudencio Canitrot: La luz apagada. Cuentos. Crónicas. Prosas
 iluminadas*. Madrid: Imprenta de Antonio Narzo, 215.

1916.   "Los Caneiros." In *Betanzos en el Quinto Centenario del Voto a su glorioso patrono San Roque*. Betanzos, Spain: Imprenta de M. Villuendas, 23.

1927.   "El Dios que allí os escuchará clemente" [dedicated to Pepe Rubio]. In *Pepe Rubio: Mis memorias: Treinta y nueve años de actor y catorce de profesor numerario de declamación del Real Conservatorio de Madrid*. Ed. Sucesor de Rivadeneyra. Madrid: Francisco Beltrán.

1929.   "Vuelven." In *Antología [Los poetas* no. 35]. Madrid: Imprenta de Sordomudos, 12–14.

1929.   "Realidad"; "La noche." In *Antología de poetas gallegos [Los poetas* #41]. Madrid: Imprenta de Sordomudos, 50–51.

In journals and periodicals

1878.   "Mis recuerdos." *Semanario del Faro de Vigo*, no. 2755 (September 7).

1878.   "Un recuerdo." *Semanario del Faro de Vigo*, no. 2764 (September 28).

1878.   "¡Te bendigo!" *Semanario del Faro de Vigo*, no. 2768 (October 12).

1879.   "Los pesares de una virgen." *Semanario del Faro de Vigo*, no. 2877 (June 21).

1879.   "A mi inolvidable amiga la distinguida Señora Doña Basilisia Arias." *Semanario del Faro de Vigo*, no. 2968 (November 29).

1880.   "Seguidillas." *Semanario del Faro de Vigo*, no. 3009 (January 10).

1880.   "Cieno." *Semanario del Faro de Vigo*, no. 3093 (April 24).

1880.   "Un ideal." *Semanario del Faro de Vigo*, no. 3121 (May 29).

1880.   "A la Señorita Chirina Satorres en su natalicio." *Semanario del Faro de Vigo*, no. 3143 (June 26).

1880.   "Antítesis." *Semanario del Faro de Vigo*, no. 3188 (August 21).

1880.   "Ecos." *Semanario del Faro de Vigo*, no. 3217 (September 25).

1880.   "Un recuerdo a Toledo." *Semanario del Faro de Vigo*, no. 3229 (October 9).

1880.   "¿Te acuerdas?" *Semanario del Faro de Vigo*, no. 3264 (November 20).

1880.   "Yo." *Semanario del Faro de Vigo*, no. 3276 (December 4).

1880.   "Reflejos." *Revista de Galicia*, no. 1/14 (July 25): 211.

1881.   "Después del baile." *Potpurrí Literario, Folletín del Faro*, no. 3327 (February 8).

1881.   "¡Miserias!" *Potpurrí Literario, Folletín del Faro*, no. 3351 (March 9).

1881.   "Reflejos." *Potpurrí Literario, Folletín el Faro*, no. 3352 (March 10).

1881.   "Anhelo." *Los Domingos del Faro*, no. 287 (3586) (October 30).

1881.   "Miserio." *Los Domingos del Faro*, no. 289 (3600) (November 13).

1882.   "A A Coruña con motivo del naufragio ocurrido cerca de Camariñas." *El Telegrama* (A Coruña, Spain) (April 26).

1882.   "Confidencias." *Los Domingos del Faro*, no. 316 (3779) (June 11).

1882.   "Nubes." *Los Domingos del Faro*, no. 323 (3835) (August 6).

1882.   "La devoción del Cristo." *Los Domingos del Faro*, no. 340 (3927) (November 19).

1883.   "Un ideal." *Flores y Perlas* (March 8): 3.

1883. "Quemando flores." *Flores y Perlas* (April 22): 2–3.

1883. "Ida y vuelta." *Flores y Perlas* (April 12): 3.

1883. "Yo." *Flores y Perlas* (April 26): 2.

1883. "Yo." *Los Domingos del Faro,* no. 358 (4087) (April 29).

1884. "Contestación." *Semana Literaria* 25:6.

1884. "Los caracoles." *El Imparcial* (Madrid) (July 27).

1884. "Una mancha." *El Imparcial* (Madrid) (December 29).

1885. "El hombre de mar." *La Ilustración Ibérica* (Barcelona), no. 119 (April 11): 230–31.

1885. "Todo por nada." *La Ilustración Ibérica* (Barcelona), no. 145 (October 10): 647, 654.

1890. "El color de las penas." *Álbum Literario* (Ourense, Spain), no. 138 (September 21): 5.

1892. "El gineceo (ante un cuadro de Boulanger)." *La Ilustración Ibérica* (Barcelona), no. 491 (May 28): 339.

1893. "Invernales (a mi madre)." *Extracto de literatura: Semanario dosimétrico ilustrado* (Pontevedra, Spain) (September 16): 12.

1893. "Invernales (antes de ir a España)." *Extracto de literatura: Semanario dosimétrico ilustrado* (Pontevedra, Spain) (September 23): 11.

1894. "Óyeme." *La Ilustración Ibérica* (Barcelona), no. 620 (November 17): 726.

1895. "Suplica." *La Gran Vía* 88:148.

1895. "Al leer la noticia del naufragio del Reina Regente." *La Ilustración Ibérica* (Barcelona), no. 640 (April 6): 211–14.

1895. "Simbólica." *La Gran Vía* (May 5): 300.

1895. "Femeniles." *La Gran Vía* (May 25): 261.

1895. "Tempestad y calma." *La Gran Vía* (June 9): 379.

1896. "Arte y amor." *Revista Contemporánea* (Madrid), no. 490 (April 30): 127–28.

1896. "Arte y amor." *El Álbum Ibero-Americano* (May 7): 202.

1896. "Platónica." *Revista Contemporánea* (Madrid), no. 491 (May 15): 297.

1896. "María Rosa." *Revista Gallega* (A Coruña, Spain) (October 4): 3.

1896. "Invernales." *Revista Gallega* (A Coruña, Spain) (November 11): 4–5.

1897. "Sacrilegio." *Galicia Moderna* (Pontevedra, Spain), no. 18 (January 15).

1897. "Arte y amor." *Revista Gallega* (A Coruña, Spain) (February 14): 5.

1897. "Femeniles." *Revista Gallega* (A Coruña, Spain) (March 7): 5.

1897. "A mis amigos los marineros de Mera con motivo de la botadura de un bote." *Revista Gallega* (A Coruña, Spain) (July 11): 4.

1897. "A Rosalía Castro de Murguía." *Revista Gallega* (A Coruña, Spain) (August 22): 3.

1897. "A Rosalía Castro de Murguía." *El Eco de Santiago* (September 7).

1897. "Soneto." *Revista Gallega* (A Coruña, Spain) (September 12): 5.

1897. "Quejas." *El Álbum Ibero-Americano,* no. 15 (September 22): 418.

1897. "Miedo." *Galicia Moderna* (Pontevedra, Spain), no. 11 (October 1).

1897. "Canción." *Galicia Moderna* (Pontevedra, Spain), no. 12 (October 15).

1897. "Anhelo." *Revista Gallega* (A Coruña, Spain) (November 29): 4.

1897. "El color de las penas." *Follas Novas* (Havana), no. 1/18 (October 3): 2.

1897. "Ida y vuelta." *Follas Novas* (Havana), no. 1/23 (November 7): 2.

1898. "Tempestad de una tarde de verano." *Galicia Moderna* (Pontevedra, Spain), no. 19 (February 1).

1898. "Espejismos." *Galicia Moderna* (Pontevedra, Spain), no. 23 (April 1).

1899. "A la ciudad de Colonia con motivo de sus primeros juegos florales." *España Artística* (June 12): 4.

1899. "Arte y amor." *España Artística* (June 19).

1899. "Drozdowo." *Revista Gallega* (A Coruña, Spain) (August 6): 4–5.

1899. "Enigmática." *España Artística* (June 19).

1899. "Retratos: Laura y Luz." *Revista Gallega* (A Coruña, Spain) (August 7): 5.

1899. "Anhelo." *Follas Novas* (Havana), no. 3/120 (September 17): 2.

1900. "El gineceo." *España Artística* (May 21).

1900. "Canción." *España Artística* (August 20).

1900. "Soledad." *Miscelánea*, no. 57 (December 16): 631.

1900. "Confidencia." *Miscelánea*, no. 59 (December 30): 649.

1901. "Al volver." *Artes y Letras*, no. 45 (November 14): 792–93.

1902. "Enigmática." *El Álbum Ibero-Americano*, no. 20 (August 14): 358.

1903. "Invernales." *Revista Gallega* (A Coruña, Spain) (January 4): 5.

1903. "Tu memoria." *Revista Gallega* (A Coruña, Spain) (November 29): 5.

1905. "Gotas de agua." *Galicia* (Havana), 4/9 (February 26): 3.

1906. "Se marchitan las rosas." *Revista Gallega* (A Coruña, Spain) (October 21): 4.

1906. "En el camino." *Revista Gallega* (A Coruña, Spain) (November 4): 5.

1906. "Ideal." *Revista Gallega* (A Coruña, Spain) (November 11): 5.

1907. "Trova." *El Liberal* (Madrid) (January 7).

1907. "El Panteón." *Galicia* (Buenos Aires) (September 1): 3.

1907. "Dedicatoria." *El Liberal* (Madrid) (September 2).

1907. "Concepción Arenal." *Galicia* (Buenos Aires) (September 15): 6.

1907. "De la felicidad y sus misterios." *El Liberal* (Madrid) (October 1).

1908. "Fragmento." *Galicia* (Buenos Aires) (January 1): 9.

1908. "Alegoría." *El Liberal* (Madrid) (February 24).

1908. "Mayo florido." *Galicia* (Buenos Aires) (May 1): 163–64.

1908. "¡Galicia mía!" *Galicia* (Buenos Aires) (May 30): 47.

1909. "Vuelven." *Revista Crítica Hispano-Americana* (Madrid) (March 6): 100–102.

1909. "¡Galicia mía!" *Gaceta de Galicia* (Santiago) (March 16): 2.

1909. "Canciones: Pagana." *El Liberal* (Madrid) (June 16).

1909. "Dos caminos." *Prometeo* 10 (August): 65–66.

1909. "El buen regidor." *El Liberal* (Madrid) (November 27).

1910. "La tentación." *El Liberal* (Madrid) (May 20).

1910. "En la residencia real de la Lazienka." *El Liberal* (Madrid) (July 6).

1910. "La poesía del destierros." *El Liberal* (Madrid) (November 5).

1911. "La mujer y la patria." *El Liberal* (Madrid) (March 7).

1911. "Triste victoria." *Ilustración Gallega* (April 15): 2.

1911. "A Concepción Arenal." *Ilustración Gallega* (May 15): 25.

1911. "Amor." *El Imparcial* (Madrid) (May 29).

1911. "Carnavalesca." *El Imparcial* (Madrid) (November 4).

1911. "Cantos de amor y desdén." *El Liberal* (Madrid) (December 13).

1911. "Lucía y Asunción." *Ilustración Gallega* (December 15): 146.

1912. "De la vida y del arte." *La Tribuna* (February 9).

1912. "Napoleón en Chamartín." *La Tribuna* (February 18).

1912. "Napoleón en Chamartín." *El Imparcial* (Madrid) (February 18).

1912. "Naufragan." *Ilustración Gallega* (February 29): 194.

1912. "Mercedes de Velilla." *La Tribuna* (March 18).

1912. "Manuel Segura." *El Liberal* (Madrid) (June 2).

1912. "Saludo." *El Liberal* (Madrid) (June 2).

1912. "Dolorosa." *El Liberal* (Madrid) (July 9).

1912. "Canción." *Suevia* (Havana), no. 2/24 (July 28): 5.

1912. "Los Caneiros." *Nueva Era* (September 1).

1913. "La noche. Pleno día. Amanece." *El Liberal* (Madrid) (April 10).

1914. "Poesía de Sofía Casanova, leída en una gira al río Lérez." *Ilustración Gallega*, no. 44 (September 15): 8.

1921. "Miedo." *A Terra* (Córdoba, Argentina) 9:21.

1921. "Las flores de la reina." *ABC* (Madrid) (May 22): 6.

1921. "En el templo." *ABC* (Madrid) (June 5): 11.

1921. "Uno de ellos." *ABC* (Madrid) (November 15): 5.

1921. "Los novios (a Belita)." *ABC* (Madrid) (December 17): 9.

1921. "Ante el Cristo." *Blanco y Negro* (Madrid) (December 27).

1925. "Canción." *Blanco y Negro* (Madrid) (June 21).

1925. "Soedá." *El Compostelano* (September 17): 1.

1926. "Para el Almanaque Nuñez." *Revista Nuñez* (Betanzos, Spain).

1926. "Visión del crepúsculo." *Elite* (Caracas) 2 (66).

1926. "Visión del crepúsculo." *Blanco y Negro* (Madrid) (January 8).

1926. "Pensando en Barcía Caballero." *El Orzán* (A Coruña, Spain) (November 11): 4.

1927. "En la cumbre." *El Pueblo Gallego* (Vigo, Spain) (January 1): 3.

1927. "Hermanos sois de aquellos hombres que fueron antes astrólogos." *ABC* (Madrid) (May 29): 5.

1927. "Una tarde." *Blanco y Negro* (Madrid) (July 31).

1927. "Despedida." *Blanco y Negro* (Madrid) (August 14).

1927. "¿Infiel?" *Blanco y Negro* (Madrid) (October 2).

1927. "Zarina." *Blanco y Negro* (Madrid) (October 16).

1927. "La vida." *Blanco y Negro* (Madrid) (December 4).

1928. "Ni en sueños." *Blanco y Negro* (Madrid) (January 29).

1928. "La Dolorosa." *Blanco y Negro* (Madrid) (April 1).

1928. "Sonetos del triunfo." *Blanco y Negro* (Madrid) (September 2).

1928. "A noite." *Céltiga* (Buenos Aires), no. 92 (October 25): 1.

1929. "Los caneiros." *El Compostelano* (September 2): 4.

1933. "Ante el año que nace: Pensando en mi tierra." *La Voz de Galicia* (A Coruña, Spain) (December 31): 1.

1934. "Para la revista *SPES*." *Spes: Revista de Acción Católica* (Pontevedra, Spain) 5 (October).

1935. "Eu ben vin estar o moucho / cabo d'a fonte pequena. . . ." *Labor Gallega* (May 28).

1938. "Versos del dolor y de la gloria." *El Compostelano* (February 4): 4.

1938. "Versos sobre el Alzamiento Nacional." *La Voz de Galicia* (A Coruña, Spain) (February 10).

1938. "Versos del dolor y de la gloria." *El Compostelano* (February 18): 4.

1944. "La Dolorosa." *Finisterre* (Pontevedra, Spain) (April 8).

Narrative

Novels

El doctor Wolski: Páginas de Polonia y Rusia

1893. Extract from Chapter 15 published in *Extracto de literatura: Semanario dosimétrico ilustrado* (Pontevedra, Spain) (September 30): 3–6.

1894. Madrid: Imprenta del Sucesor de J. Cruzado a cargo de [on behalf of] Felipe Marqués

1896–1897. Serialized in *Revista Contemporánea* (Madrid), no. 493 (June 15): 547–52 to no. 512 (March 30): 101–106.

1907. As *Doktor Wolski (kartki z życia Polaków i Rosyan). Przekład z hiszpańskiego H.J.* Biblioteka dzieł wzborowych. Vols. 482, 483. Warsaw: Drukarnia Edytor Nicz i S-ka [Polish translation of *El doctor Wolski* by the well-known Polish translator H.J. (Hajota [Helena Pajzderska])].

1920. In *La Novela Corta* 255 (November 6). Madrid: Prensa Popular.

1925. In *Obras completas*. Vol. 2. Madrid: Librería y Editorial Madrid.

Lo eterno: Narración española

1907. [Librería de Escritores y Artistas.] Madrid: Librería Fernando Fe, Regino Velasco Impresor.

1920. In *La Novela Corta* 218 (March 6). Madrid: Prensa Popular.

Más que amor: Cartas

1908. Madrid: Regino Velasco Impresor.

1908.   As *Więcej niż miłość: Powieść wspólczesna*. [Polish translation of *Más que amor* by Casanova's daughters.] Kraków, Poland: Gebethner.

1931.   As *Idilio epistolar: Novela*. Madrid: M. Aguilar,

Como en la vida: Novela

1931.   Madrid: M. Aguilar, Impresor de J. Pueyo.

1947.   *Revista Literaria. Novelas y Cuentos. Publicación Semanal,* year 19, no. 351 (August 31). Madrid: Imprenta Diana.

Las catacumbas de Rusia roja: Novela

1933.   Madrid: Espasa-Calpe.

Novelas cortas

1909.   *Princesa del amor hermoso*. In *El Cuento Semanal* 156 (December 14). Madrid: Imprenta Artística Española.

1914.   *El crimen de Beira-mar*. In *El Libro Popular: Revista Literaria* 8 (February 24): 201–27. Madrid: Taller de Ediciones España.

1919.   *Triunfo de amor: Novela inédita de Sofía Casanova*. In *La Novela Corta,* year 4, no. 186 (July 26). Madrid: Prensa Popular.

1921.   *Episodio de guerra: Novela inédita*. In *La Novela Corta* 299 (September 3). Madrid: Prensa Popular.

1922.   *Princesa rusa*. In *La Novela Semanal,* year 2, no. 55 (July 29). Madrid: Publicaciones Prensa Gráfica.

1922.   *Valor y miedo: Novela inédita*. In *La Novela Corta,* year 7, no. 348 (August 5). Madrid: Prensa Popular.

1923.   *Kola el bandido*. In *La Novela Semanal,* year 3, no. 101 (June 16). Madrid: Publicaciones Prensa Gráfica.

1925.   *El dolor de reinar: Novela*. In *La Novela Semanal* 213 (August 8). Madrid: Publicaciones Prensa Gráfica.

1929.   *Valor y miedo*. In *Lecturas,* year 9, no. 100. Madrid: Sociedad General de Publicaciones.

1989.   *Princesa del amor hermoso*. In *Novelas breves de escritoras españolas (1898–1936)*. Ed. Ángela Ena Bordonada. Madrid: Castalia/Instituto de la Mujer, 151–94.

Collections of short fiction

1911.   *El pecado*. Biblioteca de Escritores Gallegos. Vol 10. Madrid: Imprenta de Alrededor del Mundo, Librería de los Sucesores de Hernando.

   Includes "El pecado," "El triunfo" (*Princesa del amor hermoso* under

a different title), "Una acuarela," Más triste que el amor" ("Escena
suelta" under a different title), "El ladrón," "¡Qué tonta!" "En la casa de
enfrente," "Luz en tinieblas," "Una ervingista," and "Flores de acacia."

1926. *El pecado: Novelas gallegas.* In *Obras completas.* Vol 3.
Madrid: Librería y Editorial Madrid.

Collection of short stories that differs from the 1911 edition.
Includes "De la aldea," "El pecado," "El triunfo," Más
triste que el amor," "El ladrón," and "Lo eterno."

1942. *El pecado.* In *Novelas y Cuentos* [núm. suelto/
separata]. Madrid: Editorial Dédalo.

1947. *El pecado.* In *Cartel* (Vigo, Spain) 9 (July 1).

1996. *Galicia la inefable.* Ed. Rosario Martínez Martínez. Cambados,
Spain: Xunta de Galicia/Secretaría Xeral da Presidencia.

Includes "De la aldca," "El ladrón," and "El peregrino penitente."

Short fiction published in journals and periodicals

"JANEK ZAKRYSTYAN: OBRAZEK Z GALICYI HISZPAŃSKIEJ"

1894. "Janek Zakrystyan: Obrazek z Galicyi Hiszpańskiej." In *Dwie
kuzyńki (Sprawa Leavenworth): Powieść z angielskiego przez
Katarzynę Green.* Warsaw: Drukiem Noskowskiego, 299–304.

Casanova is credited as Zofja Lutosławska in this supplement
to the journal *Słowo.* The main body is a Polish translation of
the novel *The Leavenworth Case* (1878), by the American author
Anna Katharine Green [Mrs. Charles Rohlfs] (1846–1935).

1896. As "El campanero de San Julián (Recuerdos de Galicia)."
["Janek Zakrystyan: Obrazek z Galicyi Hiszpańskiej."]
Revista Gallega (A Coruña, Spain) (August 23): 4–5.

1898. As "El campanero de San Julián." ["Janek Zakrystyan:
Obrazek z Galicyi Hiszpańskiej."] *Galicia Moderna*
(Pontevedra, Spain), no. 20 (February 15): 20–22.

1898. As "El campanero de San Julian." ["Janek Zakrystyan: Obrazek z Galicyi
Hiszpańskiej."] *Follas Novas* (Havana), no. 2/64 (August 21): 2.

1901. As "El campanero de San Julián (recuerdos de Galicia)."
["Janek Zakrystyan: Obrazek z Galicyi Hiszpańskiej."]
Revista Gallega (A Coruña, Spain) (February 24): 4–5.

1916. As "El campanero de San Julián (recuerdos de Galicia)." ["Janek
Zakrystyan: Obrazek z Galicyi Hiszpańskiej."] In *Narraciones
gallegas: Colección recogida de notables escritores regionales.*
Lugo, Spain: Imprenta de El Norte de Galicia, 178–85.

"ESCENA SUELTA"/"MÁS TRISTE QUE EL AMOR"

1899. *Revista Contemporánea* (Madrid), no. 561 (April 15): 101–6.

1899. *Álbum salón: Revista Ibero-americana de Literatura y Arte* (Barcelona), no. 17 (May 7): 196.

1899. *España Artística* (May 8).

1928. As "Smutniejsze niż miłość." ["Más triste que el amor."] *Bluszcz* (Warsaw).

MISCELLANEOUS

1897. "Una acuarela." *Revista Gallega* (A Coruña, Spain) (April 7): 5.

1898. "Una acuarela." *Follas Novas* (Havana), no. 2/54 (June 12): 2.

1899. "Cuento." *España Artística* (February 26): 3.

1909. "Mi pecado: Novela corta," *El Liberal* (Madrid) (October 31).

1927. "El ladrón," *Lecturas* (Madrid) (March): 229–34.

Additional Works

Published correspondence

1901. "De una ausente." [Letter from Sofía Casanova to Eugenio Carré.] *Revista Gallega* (A Coruña, Spain) (June 30): 3.

1903. [Letter from Sofía Casanova to Galo Salinas]. *Revista Gallega* (A Coruña, Spain) (November 29): 5.

Lyrics

1878. "Un consuelo: Recitado para piano. . ." Lyrics by Sofía P. de Casanova. Music by F. García Conde. Madrid: Nicolás Toledo.

Translations

1903. *Bartek el Vencedor.* Madrid: Librería Fernando Fe, Regino Velasco Impresor.

   Translation (from the Polish) of *Bartek Zwycięzca,* by Henryk Sienkiewicz (1846–1916).

1908. *Enrique Sienkiewicz: ¿Quo vadis? Primera versión española directa del polaco: La Novela de ahora.* 2 vols. Madrid: Saturnino Calleja.

   Translation (from the Polish) of *Quo vadis?* by Henryk Sienkiewicz (1846–1916). Illustrated by M. Picolo.

1909. *Zofja Kowalewska. Una nihilista. Novela rusa.* Madrid: Pérez Villavivencio Editor.

Translation (from the Russian) of *Nigilistka,* by Sofia Vasilevsna
Kovalevskaia (1850–1891). Dedicated to Alberto Insúa.

Lectures

1910. *La mujer española en el extranjero: Conferencia dada en el Ateneo de
Madrid el 9 de abril de 1910.* Madrid: Regino Velasco Impresor.

1919. *Impresiones de una mujer en el frente oriental de la Guerra Europea: Conferencia
leída el 25 de abril de 1919 en el Centro del Ejército y de la Armada de Madrid por
la Excma Señora Doña Sofía Casanova.* Madrid: Imprenta Gráfica Excelsior.

Theater

1913. *La madeja: Comedia frívola en tres actos y en prosa.*
Madrid: Regino Velasco Impresor.

1913. *La madeja: Comedia frívola en tres actos y en prosa. Los
Contemporáneos y los Maestros* 241 (August 8). Illustrated by
F. Mota. Madrid: Imprenta del Alrededor del Mundo.

Children's literature

1920. *Viajes y aventuras de una muñeca española en Rusia.* Biblioteca
Rodríguez. Burgos, Spain: Hijos de Santiago Rodríguez.

1927. *Podróże Karmeli.* [*Viajes y aventuras de una muñeca española en Rusia.*]
Biblioteka Książek Różowych. Vol. 19. Warsaw: Polska Zjednoczona.

Histories and memoirs

1924. *En la corte de los zares (del principio y del fin de un imperio).* In
Obras completas. Vol. 1. Madrid: Librería y Editorial Madrid.

> Dedication: "A mis paisanos, los gallegos, y en representación de ellos, a
> las señoras doña Alejandra Ulloa de Rubín y doña Dolores Morillo; a las
> cigarreras coruñesas y a los señores don Manuel Casás y don Fco. Catoyra."

1929. *En la corte de los zares (del principio y del fin de un imperio).*
In *Obras completas.* Vol. 1. 2nd ed. Biblioteca Rubén Darío.
Madrid: G. Hernández y Galo Saez Impresor.

1945. *El martirio de Polonia.* (With Miguel Branicki.) Madrid: Atlas.

1945. *El martirio de Polonia. Por Sofía Casanova y Miguel Brunicki*
[*sic*]. 2nd ed. *Un testimonio directo y documentado del
drama polaco.* Madrid: Ediciones Atlas, Aldus.

> First part: "Proemio," by "V" (Vicente Casanova?), pp. 5–17.

"Polvo de Escombros," by Sofía Casanova, pp. 21–88. Second part: "Estampas Polacas," by Miguel Branicki [*sic*], translated and adapted from the English by José del Río Sáinz, pp. 91–302.

1995. "La ocupación de Polonia en 1944: Relato inédito de Sofía Casanova." Ed. María del Carmen Simón Palmer. *Compás de Letras* 7:211–36.

2007. *En la corte de los zares: Del principio y del fin de un imperio.* Astorga: Editorial Akrón.

Prologues

1925. Introduction to *Zle kochana.* Biblioteka Laureatów Nobla. Vol. 36. Lwów-Poznan, Poland: Nakladem Wydawnictwa Polskiego.

Translation by Casanova's daughter Izabela Wolikowska (from the Spanish) of the play *La malquerida* by Jacinto Benavente (1866–1954). Casanova is credited as Zofia Lutosławska-Casanova.

Miscellaneous[1]

1899. "El día de difuntos." *Follas Novas* (Havana), no. 3/127 (November 5): 1.

1913. "Cantos de amor y de odio." *El Gran Bufón* 2:7.

1913. "Las dos barbaries." *Barbero Municipal* (Rianxo, Spain), no. 164 (August 30): 1.

1913. "El dolor." *Barbero Municipal* (Rianxo, Spain), no. 172 (October 25): 2.

Periodical Articles

Collections

Sobre el Volga helado: Narración de viajes
1903. Madrid: Regino Velasco Impresor,
1919. *La Novela Corta* (Madrid), year 4, no. 196 (October 4).

La revolución bolchevista (diario de un testigo)
1920. Biblioteca Nueva. Madrid: Artes Gráficas.

Dedication: "A los condes De Augallal [*sic*], mis queridiños, de los que estoy aunque lejos, muy cerca de ellos con el alma." Preface by "RC."

1989/1990. Biblioteca de Escritoras. Vol. 11. Madrid: Castalia/ Instituto de la Mujer, Unigraf.

Edited with an introduction and notes by María Victoria López Cordón.

2008. Astorga: Editorial Akrón.

Miscellaneous

1913. *Exóticas*. Madrid: Regino Velasco Impresor.

> Includes "La barbarie gris," "De la Europa asiática," "La ciudad del odio," "Las ejecuciones diarias," "La madre escuela," "La destrucción de España . . . en las calles de Varsovia," "Un crimen," "Sin derecho de asilo," "España en Polonia," "Extraordinaria historia de amor conyugal," "Un testamento, el Kaiser y Sienkiewicz," "El peregrino penitente," "Strindberg enamorado," "El amor de Wagner," "La edad peligrosa de la mujer," "Un nombre: Wispianski," and "Página familiar." Dedicated to Vicente Casanova.

1916. *De la guerra: Crónicas de Polonia y Rusia*. Madrid: Renacimiento, Regino Velasco Impresor.

> Dedicated to Casanova's mother. Prologue by N. Hernández Luquero.

1917. *De la revolución rusa en 1917*. Madrid: Renacimiento, Imprenta de Juan Pueyo.

1927. *De Rusia: Amores y confidencias*. In *Obras completas*. Vol. 4. Madrid: Librería y Editorial Madrid, Sucesores de Rivadeneyra.

> Collection of articles. Dedicated to Vicente Casanova. Includes "Camino de Tartaria" ("Sobre el Volga helado" under a different name), "Una ervingista rusa," "El intruso," "Flores de acacia," "Cosacos y censores," "Novela española castigada," "Como son," "Intelectualidad rusa," "Lo pintoresco," "Del amor y del desamor," "Hija de española," and "Misterios de realidad."

Articles in periodicals other than ABC

1899. "Fabulilla." *Revista Gallega* (A Coruña, Spain) (February 12): 4–5.

1909. "De la belleza, la filosofía y el amor." *El Liberal* (Madrid) (February 11).

1909. "Un nombre: El poeta Wispianski." *El Liberal* (Madrid) (March 4).

1909. "Cartas del norte: El testamento." *El Liberal* (Madrid) (July 26).

1910. "Las mujeres de un poeta." *El Liberal* (Madrid) (June 5).

1912. "Una carta a D. Juan Ponte Blanco." *La Nueva Era* (Madrid) (September 22).

1913. "Literatura femenina." *El Liberal* (Madrid) (January 4).

1915. "Una hermosa carta de Sofía Casanova desde el campo de la guerra." *Labor Gallega* (April 30).

1923. "Desde Polonia: El advenimiento del partido campesino." *La Voz de Galicia* (A Coruña, Spain) (June 28).

1925. "Don Juan Tenorio en Polonia." *Blanco y Negro* (Madrid) (January 25).

1925. "Palacios rusos." *Blanco y Negro* (Madrid) (May 3).

1925. "Galicia tierra mía." *Galicia* (Buenos Aires) (May 18): 9.

1925. "Europa y Galicia (I)." *El Eco de Santiago* (June 15): 1.

1925. "Europa y Galicia (I)." *El Eco de Santiago* (June 16).

1925. "Europa y Galicia (II)." *El Eco de Santiago* (June 17).

1925. "Europa y Galicia (II)." *El Eco de Santiago* (June 18).

1925. "Europa y Galicia (III)," *El Eco de Santiago* (June 19).

1925. "Europa y Galicia (III)." *El Eco de Santiago* (June 20).

1925. "Desde Polonia: Algo de Galicia aquí." *La Voz de Galicia* (A Coruña, Spain) (October 15): 1.

1925. "Cuento de verano: Amores por correspondencia." *Blanco y Negro* (Madrid) (November 25).

1927. "Crónicas." *Elite* (Caracas) 2, no. 85.

1927. "De otras tierras: ¿El arte ruso?" *Blanco y Negro* (Madrid) (January 16).

1927. "De tierras lejanas: Tipos rusos." *Blanco y Negro* (Madrid) (March 13).

1927. "Una tarde." *Blanco y Negro* (Madrid) (July 31).

1927. "Despedida." *Blanco y Negro* (Madrid) (August 14).

1927. "¿Infiel?" *Blanco y Negro* (Madrid) (October 2).

1927. "Zarina." *Blanco y Negro* (Madrid) (October 16).

1927. "La vida." *Blanco y Negro* (Madrid) (December 4).

1927. "Desde Polonia: El oro de la sangre." *Blanco y Negro* (Madrid) (December 11).

1927. "Mujeres rusas: Nihilistas y princesas." *Blanco y Negro* (Madrid) (December 25).

1928. "Desde Varsovia: Estrellas de la fé." *Blanco y Negro* (Madrid) (March 25).

1928. "Desde Polonia: Historia que parece mentira." *Blanco y Negro* (Madrid) (May 27).

1928. "Desde Polonia: Paisaje." *Blanco y Negro* (Madrid) (October 7).

1928. "La hermana de la zarina (Elisabeth Fiedorowna)." *Blanco y Negro* (Madrid) (December 9).

1929. "Artistas extranjeros: Un pintor batallista." *Blanco y Negro* (Madrid) (January 13).

1929. "Trasgos y meigas: Desde Rusia blanca." *Blanco y Negro* (Madrid) (February 17).

1929. "Episodio auténtico: La Muerte." *Blanco y Negro* (Madrid) (April 14).

1929. "Los gallegos por el mundo: Francisco." *Céltiga* (Buenos Aires), no. 105 (May 10).

1929. "Escena nocturna: Con su sombra." *Blanco y Negro* (Madrid) (May 26).

1929. "Página real: El ahorcado." *Blanco y Negro* (Madrid) (August 11).

1929. "Rutas pintorescas: En los montes Carpatos." *Blanco y Negro* (Madrid) (September 22).

1929. "Las hijas de los zares." *Blanco y Negro* (Madrid) (December 8).

1930. "Página infantil: Burrerías." *Blanco y Negro* (Madrid) (March 9).

1930. "Mujeres de la historia: Dos reinas polacas." *Blanco y Negro* (Madrid) (March 30).

1930. "Música polaca: Una nueva ópera." *Blanco y Negro* (Madrid) (May 4).

1930.   "Literatura moderna: El ingenio bolchevique."
        Blanco y Negro (Madrid) (June 29).

1930.   "Oración de una princesa." *Blanco y Negro* (Madrid) (July 20).

1930.   "Teatro ruso: Evreinoff." *Blanco y Negro* (Madrid) (July 30).

1933.   "Carta de Sofía Casanova a D. Cayetano Vaello." *Labor Gallega* (May 28).

1939.   "¡Aquella aldeana gallega!" *El Correo Gallego* (El Ferrol, Spain) (February 16).

1939.   "Aldeana de Galicia." *El Correo Gallego* (El Ferrol, Spain) (February 19).

1939.   "Recuerdo de Pío XI en Varsovia." *El Correo
        Gallego* (El Ferrol, Spain) (February 22).

1939.   "Novia gallega." *La Voz de Galicia* (A Coruña, Spain) (November 27).

Articles for ABC *newspaper*[2]

1915.   "La guerra en Rusia." (April 8): 7–8.

1915.   "Las batallas: Los hospitales. Los mártires." (April 13): 3–5.

1915.   "De la guerra en Rusia." (April 16): 7–8.

1915.   "Prisioneros y heridos: Las operaciones." (April 23): 9.

1915.   "¡Domingo de resurrección!" (April 29): 3–5.

1915.   "El espionaje." (May 5): 7–8.

1915.   "La batalla de los Carpatos." (May 14): 3–4.

1915.   "Las desdichas de Polonia." (May 24): 3, 4, 5, 7.

1915.   "Lo que piensan los rusos de los alemanes." (May 29): 3–5.

1915.   "Incertidumbre dolorosa." (June 7): 5, 7–8.

1915.   "Tren militar." (June 19): 4–6.

1915.   "Desde las posiciones del Naref." (June 24): 3–5.

1915.   "A orillas del Naref." (July 1): 3–6.

1915.   "Los gases asfixiantes: El espanto de las víctimas." (July 7): 3–5.

1915.   "La ciudad aterrada." (July 14): 4–6.

1915.   "La evacuación." (August 2): 3–6.

1915.   "Momento supremo." (September 17): 6–8.

1915.   "El avance alemán." (September 18): 3–4.

1915.   "En los caminos de la retirada (I) ." (October 13): 3–5, 7.

1915.   "En los caminos de la retirada (II) ." (October 15): 3–5, 7.

1915.   "La vida en Moscú. La situación política." (November 12): 5, 7–8.

1915.   "La destitución del gran duque: El cierre de la Duma." (November 13).

1915.   "Polonia, problema internacional." (December 2).

1915.   "Problema internacional." (December 5).

1915.   "La corte de los zares." (December 12).

1915.   "La opinión en San Petersburgo." (December 13).

1915.   "La paz en la guerra. La Princesa Urusof." (December 22).

1916.   "Esperando el despite." (January 10).

1916.   "El desastre servio." (January 13).

1916. "Las mujeres rusas." (January 20).

1916. "Los hospitales." (January 23).

1916. "Un año más." (February 3).

1916. "Fantasías sobre la paz (I)." (February 4).

1916. "Fantasías sobre la paz (II) ." (February 5).

1916. "La noche de Navidad." (February 20).

1916. "El sacrificio de los débiles." (February 28).

1916. "Digresión: Hombres y animales." (March 17).

1916. "Un jefe de gobierno relevado." (March 18).

1916. "Ansiedad." (March 22).

1916. "Negocios de la guerra." (March 23).

1916. "El desquive del gran duque." (April 1).

1916. "Los ecos de Verdún." (April 18).

1916. "De las regiones fabulosas." (April 20).

1916. "Días de ansiedad." (April 25).

1916. "La situación política." (April 26).

1916. "Niños y mujeres." (April 29).

1916. "Primavera de odios." (May 24).

1916. "Diario de viaje." (June 13).

1916. "Del pasado glorioso." (June 15).

1916. "Una nota subjetiva." (June 16).

1916. "Heroicidades inhumanas." (June 20).

1916. "En las posiciones." (June 22): 6.

1916. "Pascua florida." (June 29).

1916. "La vida en las posiciones." (July 4).

1916. "Actos heroicos." (July 5).

1916. "Nuevos infaustas." (July 6).

1916. "La derrota austríaca." (July 20).

1916. "La ofensiva rusa." (July 21).

1916. "La realidad de la ofensiva." (July 25).

1916. "La gran ofensiva de los aliados." (August 2).

1916. "El problema de Polonia." (August 4).

1916. "Política interior." (August 13).

1916. "La ofensiva rusa." (August 14).

1916. "El porvenir de Polonia." (August 25).

1916. "La neutralidad de España." (August 30).

1916. "La carestía de la vida." (September 11).

1916. "Renace el optimismo." (September 14).

1916. "Exaltación del sacrificio." (September 19).

1916. "Los niños." (September 27).

1916. "La ofensiva rusa." (September 29).

1916. "Divagaciones." (October 2).

1916. "Las amarguras de la lucha." (October 26).

1916. "Los horrores de la guerra." (October 27).

1916. "Más horrores bélicos." (October 29).

1916. "Notas tristes." (November 7).

1916. "Otro niño." (November 20).

1916. "Indigencia y miseria." (November 22).

1916. "Las crueldades de la historia." (November 25).

1916. "Agitación latente." (November 30).

1916. "El hombre del día." (December 2).

1916. "La desilusión de Polonia." (December 3).

1917. "Francisco José." (December 2).

1917. "Sienkiewicz." (January 23).

1917. "Las proposiciones de paz." (January 25).

1917. "Días de horror." (January 28).

1917. "Páginas de la historia contemporánea (I)." (January 30).

1917. "Páginas de la historia contemporánea (II)." (February 1).

1917. "In tenebras lux." (February 5).

1917. "Días luctuosas." (February 13).

1917. "Nochebuena." (February 16).

1917. "Documentos históricos." (February 19).

1917. "Balance horrible." (February 21).

1917. "De Rusia (I)." (March 27).

1917. "Aclaración (I)." (May 3).

1917. "Aclaración (II)." (May 6).

1917. "Malestar e inquietud." (May 10).

1917. "Incertidumbre." (May 11).

1917. "En plena lucha." (May 15).

1917. "El ejército y el pueblo." (May 17).

1917. "Los albores del nuevo régimen." (May 20).

1917. "Episodios de la revolución." (May 27).

1917. "La abdicación del zar." (May 29).

1917. "Entrevista histórica." (May 30).

1917. "Antes de la renunciación." (May 31).

1917. "La renunciación." (June 1).

1917. "La revolución se consolida." (June 9).

1917. "Rusia democrática." (June 10).

1917. "Las convulsiones revolucionarias." (June 11).

1917. "Las consecuencias de revolución." (June 12).

1917. "Detalles de la revolución (I)." (June 13).

1917. "Detalles de la revolución (II)." (June 14).

1917. "Triste ceremonia." (June 15).

1917. "Del drama tenebroso (I) (Rasputin)." (June 23).

1917. "Del drama tenebroso (II) (y de la actualidad)." (June 25).
1917. "Manifestaciones." (June 27).
1917. "Los hombres que vuelven." (June 29).
1917. "Confusión revolucionaria." (July 2).
1917. "Grandezas caídas." (July 7).
1917. "Los primeros disturbios de mayo (I)." (July 13).
1917. "Los primeros disturbios de mayo (II)." (July 14).
1917. "La venganza del engaño." (July 15).
1917. "La crisis del gobierno provisional." (July 16).
1917. "El pesimismo de los rusos (I)." (July 17).
1917. "El pesimismo de los rusos (II) (Andrejew y Gorki)." (July 18).
1917. "España en Rusia." (July 19).
1917. "Desorientación general." (July 20).
1917. "Mirando al fondo (I)." (July 26).
1917. "Mirando al fondo (II) (la voz del ejército)." (July 27).
1917. "Mirando al fondo (III) (la voz del ejército)." (July 29).
1917. "Descomposición general." (August 13).
1917. "Algunas cifras." (August 14).
1917. "En los frentes de batalla." (August 15).
1917. "Importancia de la revolución." (August 16).
1917. "De la lucha civil (I)." (August 17).
1917. "De la lucha civil (II)." (August 18).
1917. "El desastre de Galitzia (I)." (August 30).
1917. "El desastre de Galitzia (II)." (August 31).
1917. "De Rusia (I)." (September 1).
1917. "De Rusia (II)." (November 23).
1917. "El General Korniloff." (November 25).
1917. "Majestades caídas (I) (el destierro)." (November 26).
1917. "Majestades caídas (II)." (November 27).
1917. "La rendición de Riga (I)." (December 2).
1917. "La rendición de Riga (II)." (December 3).
1917. "La conferencia de Moscú (I)." (December 9).
1917. "La conferencia de Moscú (II)." (December 14).
1917. "La conferencia de Moscú (III)." (December 16).
1917. "La conspiración militar (I)." (December 20).
1917. "La gran asamblea democrática en San Petersburgo." (December 24).
1917. "La conspiración militar (II)." (December 31).
1918. "La república." (January 2).
1918. "De Rusia." (January 6).
1918. "El fin de la conferencia." (January 7).
1918. "Bárbaros y caballeros (I)." (January 9).
1918. "Bárbaros y caballeros (II)." (January 10).

1918. "Al terminar la desastre." (January 14).

1918. "La revolución maximalista (I)." (January 19).

1918. "La revolución maximalista (II)." (January 20).

1918. "La revolución maximalista (III)." (January 21).

1918. "La revolución maximalista (IV)." (January 22).

1918. "Las probabilidades (I)." (January 23).

1918. "Las probabilidades (II)." (January 24).

1918. "La derrota de Kerensky." (January 25).

1918. "En víspera del choque fatal." (January 27).

1918. "De Rusia." (February 4).

1918. "De Rusia." (February 9).

1918. "De Rusia." (February 12).

1918. "Armisticio." (February13).

1918. "Se conspira (I)." (February 18).

1918. "Se conspira (II)." (February 20).

1918. "De Rusia." (February 26).

1918. "Variaciones sobre el mismo tema." (February 27).

1918. "En el antro de las fieras (I)." (March 1).

1918. "En el antro de las fieras (II)." (March 2).

1918. "Del ciclo infernal (I)." (March 3).

1918. "Del ciclo infernal (II)." (March 4).

1918. "Del ciclo infernal (III)." (March 5).

1918. "Armisticio." (March 10).

1918. "Las grandes fraguas." (March 12).

1918. "De Rusia." (March 13).

1918. "Los chispazos de la gran fragua." (March 24).

1918. "Nieve y sangre." (April 18).

1918. "La única sesión de la constituyente (I) (Spiridowna)." (April 19).

1918. "La única sesión de la constituyente (II)." (April 20).

1918. "El congreso general de los Soviets (I) (habla Trotsky)." (April 21).

1918. "El congreso general de los Soviets (II) (habla Lenin)." (April 22).

1918. "La paz se firmará." (April 23).

1918. "La sombra de la derrota." (April 24).[†]

1918. "La hoguera." (May 10).

1918. "De Rusia." (May 11).

1918. "La magnánima diestra." (May 12).

1918. "El silencio de los imperios centrales." (May 13).

1918. "Habla el coloso de hierro y voluntad (el preludio)." (May 14).

1918. "Respuesta al coloso de hierro y de la voluntad." (May 15).

1918. "La capitulación." (May 17).

1918. "La proclamación del comisario." (May 18).

1918. "De Rusia." (May 21).[†]

1918. "De Rusia." (May 23).[†]
1918. "Firmada la paz: ¡Viva la guerra!" (May 24).[†]
1918. "La transformación comunal." (May 25).[†]
1918. "La paz y la derrota (I)." (May 26).[†]
1918. "La paz y la derrota (II)." (May 27).[†]
1918. "De Rusia." (May 29).
1918. "De Rusia." (May 30).[†]
1918. "Los crímenes de la revolución." (June 14).
1918. "Regias intimidades." (June 17).
1918. "Los intelectuales rusos (Gorky y Merezowsky)." (June 18).[*]
1918. "Los intelectuales rusos (Gorky y Merezowsky)." (June 20).[*]
1918. "De Rusia." (June 22).
1918. "Los embrollos de Rusia." (June 23).
1918. "La repatriación." (June 24).
1918. "La ciudad del hambre en fiesta." (June 25).[*]
1918. "Situación difícil." (July 19).
1918. "De Rusia." (July 20).
1918. "De Rusia." (July 21).
1918. "De Rusia." (July 22).
1918. "La familia imperial." (July 23).[*]
1918. "De Rusia." (July 24).
1918. "De Rusia." (July 26).
1918. "En plena revolución." (September 14).[†]
1918. "La vanguardia en el frente del Volga (I)." (September 26).
1918. "La vanguardia en el frente del Volga (II)." (September 29).
1918. "Las prisiones." (October 1).[*]
1918. "El movimiento bohemio." (October 2).
1918. "Los crímenes de la revolución." (November 4).[*]
1918. "La era del terror." (November 5).
1918. "La era del terror." (November 7).[†]
1918. "La era del terror." (November 8).[*]
1918. "El resurgir de Polonia." (December 13).
1918. "Efectos de la revolución (la situación en Polonia)." (December 14).
1918. "Los efectos de la revolución." (December 19).
1919. "La revolución en Polonia." (January 11).
1919. "Pilzuzki [*sic*], dictador." (January 14).
1919. "Más sobre Pilsudski." (January 15).
1919. "El triunfo muerto." (February 9).
1919. "Lo que se salva de la guerra." (February 11).
1919. "Las últimas batallas." (February 12).
1919. "De Polonia." (February 13).
1919. "De Polonia." (February 14).

1919. "De Polonia." (February 15).

1919. "Por la Europa del armisticio (I)." (April 9).

1919. "Por la Europa del armisticio (II)." (April 10).

1919. "Por la Europa del armisticio (III)." (April 11).

1919. "Por la Europa del armisticio (IV)." (April 24).

1919. "Por la Europa del armisticio (V)." (April 25).

1919. "Por la Europa del armisticio (VI)." (April 26).

1919. "Paréntesis de misericordia (para don Antonio Maura)." (April 30).

1919. "Por la Europa del armisticio (VII)." (May 7).

1919. "El secreto de Paderewski." (May 9).

1919. "Por la Europa del armisticio (VIII) (la cuestión judía)." (May 18).

1919. "Por la Europa del armisticio (IX) (la cuestión judía)." (May 22).

1919. "Por la Europa del armisticio (X) (la cuestión judía)." (May 27).

1919. "Por la Europa del armisticio (XI) (la cuestión judía)." (May 29).

1919. "Por la Europa del armisticio (XII) (la cuestión judía)." (May 31).

1919. "Por la Europa del armisticio (XIII) (la cuestión judía)." (June 15).

1919. "Por la Europa del armisticio (XIV) (la cuestión judía)." (June 17).

1919. "Dais alto testimonio de quienes sois, señores . . ." (June 17).

1919. "Después de la guerra (I) (noticias de Rusia)." (June 27).

1919. "Paz sin concordia." (July 10).

1919. "Después de la guerra (II) (noticias de Rusia)." (July 20).

1919. "Después de la guerra (III) (noticias de Rusia)." (July 25).

1919. "Por Galicia (I)." (August 18): 3–4.

1919. "Por Galicia (II)." (August 23): 3–5.

1919. "Por Galicia (III)." (August 26): 3–4.

1919. "Por Galicia (IV)." (September 10): 3–5.

1919. "Por Galicia (V)." (September 20): 3.

1919. "Por Galicia (VI)." (September 26): 3–5.

1919. "Por Galicia (VII)." (October 2): 3–5.

1919. "Por Galicia (VIII)." (October 10): 3.

1919. "De Rusia (I) (aniversario bolchevique)." (October 16): 3.

1919. "De Rusia (II) (aniversario bolchevique)." (October 23): 3.

1919. "De Rusia (III) (aniversario bolchevique)." (November 9): 3.

1920. "Por la Europa de la paz (I)." (January 1): 3.

1920. "Por la Europa de la paz (II)." (January 3): 3.

1920. "Por la Europa de la paz (III)." (January 9): 3.

1920. "Por la Europa de la paz (IV)." (January 13): 3.

1920. "Por la Europa de la paz (V)." (January 18): 3.

1920. "Por la Europa de la paz (VI)." (January 23): 3.

1920. "Por la Europa de la paz (VII)." (January 24): 3.

1920. "De Rusia (I)." (January 29): 3.

1920. "De Rusia (II)." (February 4): 3.

1920. "De Rusia (III)." (February 8): 3.

1920. "De Rusia (IV)." (February 13): 3.

1920. "De Rusia (V)." (February 26): 3.

1920. "La vida entre Alemania y Rusia (I)." (March 9): 3.

1920. "La vida entre Alemania y Rusia (II)." (March 11): 3.

1920. "La vida entre Alemania y Rusia (III)." (March 13): 3.

1920. "El fracaso de Europa (I)." (March 17): 3–4.

1920. "El fracaso de Europa (II)." (March 20): 3.

1920. "El fracaso de Europa (III)." (March 26):3.

1920. "El fracaso de Europa (IV)." (March 31): 3.

1920. "El fracaso de Europa (V)." (April 2): 7.

1920. "El fracaso de Europa (VI)." (April 6): 8.

1920. "Habla Merezewsky." (April 30): 3.

1920. "Los imperialistas vencidos (I) (Koltchak)." (May 5): 3.

1920. "Los imperialistas vencidos (II)." (May 7): 3.

1920. "El triunfo de Rusia." (May 10): 3.

1920. "España en Polonia (I)." (May 12): 3–5.

1920. "España en Polonia (II)." (May 13): 5–6.

1920. "La espera trágica." (May 30): 3–4.

1920. "Nada cambia." (June 8): 3.

1920. "¡Guerra! (la gran ofensiva polaca)." (June 10): 3–4.

1920. "Los nuevos hombres (I) (el jefe de estado polaco)." (June 15): 4–5.

1920. "Los nuevos hombres (II) (el jefe de estado polaco)." (June 18): 3.

1920. "Los nuevos hombres (III) (el jefe de estado polaco)." (June 21): 4–5.

1920. "Los nuevos hombres (IV) (el jefe de estado polaco)." (June 23): 3–4.

1920. "El desastre de la ofensiva (I)." (July 15): 5–6.

1920. "El desastre de la ofensiva (II)." (July 16): 3–4.

1920. "Los nuevos hombres (I) (el atamán ukrainiano, Peltura)." (July 17): 3.

1920. "Los nuevos hombres (II) (el atamán ukrainiano, Peltura)." (July 18): 4–5.

1920. "Los nuevos hombres (III) (el atamán ukrainiano, Peltura)." (July 20): 3.

1920. "Perfiles del caos (I)." (July 24): 3–4.

1920. "Perfiles del caos (II)." (July 27): 7–8.

1920. "Perfiles del caos (III)." (July 28): 3.

1920. "Páginas de la guerra (el exterminio de Polonia)." (August 12): 3.

1920. "Fe en la defensiva (I)." (August 14): 3.

1920. "Otra vez el peligro." (August 17): 3.

1920. "Los bolcheviques (I)." (August 18): 3.

1920. "Los bolcheviques (II)." (August 19): 3.

1920. "Ante el avance de los bolcheviques (II) [*sic*]." (August 24): 3–4.

1920. "Ante el avance de los bolcheviques (III)." (August 25): 3.

1920. "Ante el avance de los bolcheviques (IV) (August 27): 3–4.

1920. "Los bolcheviques (IV)." (September 14): 5.

1920. "Los bolcheviques (V)." (September 15): 3–4.

1920. "Los bolcheviques (VI)." (September 16): 3.

1920. "La batalla de Varsovia (VII)." (September 17): 3.

1920. "Los bolcheviques (VIII)." (September 22): 3.

1920. "Los bolcheviques (IX)." (September 24): 3–4.

1920. "Los bolcheviques (X)." (September 28): 3.

1920. "Los bolcheviques (XI)." (September 29): 3.

1920. "Los bolcheviques en Lomza (I)." (October 19): 3.

1920. "Los bolcheviques en Lomza (II)." (October 20): 3.

1920. "Los bolcheviques en Lomza (III)." (October 29): 3.

1920. "Los bolcheviques en Lomza (IV)." (October 30): 3–4.

1920. "Los bolcheviques en Lomza (V)." (November 6): 3.

1920. "Los bolcheviques en Lomza (VI)." (November 13): 3–4.

1920. "Los bolcheviques en Lomza (VII)." (November 14): 3–4.

1920. "Los bolcheviques en Lomza (VIII)." (November 25): 3.

1920. "Los bolcheviques en Lomza (IX)." (November 26): 3–4.

1920. "Intervalo de paz sin paz (I)." (December 10): 3.

1920. "Intervalo de paz sin paz (II)." (December 12): 3–4.

1920. "Intervalo de paz sin paz (III)." (December 20): 3–4.

1920. "Intervalo de paz sin paz (IV)." (December 23): 4–5.

1920. "Intervalo de paz sin paz (V)." (December 24): 3–4.

1920. "El poeta de Lituania (I)." (December 30): 3.

1921. "El plebiscito en Lituania y Silesia." (January 7): 4, 6.

1921. "El poeta de Lituania (II) ." (January 11): 3.

1921. "El plebiscito en Alta Silesia." (January 25): 3–4.

1921. "Latidos de fiebre." (February 3): 7.

1921. "Rusia ayer y hoy (I)." (February 17): 3–4.

1921. "Rusia ayer y hoy (II)." (February 23): 3–4.

1921. "Rusia ayer y hoy (III)." (February 24): 3–4.

1921. "Rusia ayer y hoy (IV)." (March 1): 3.

1921. "Rusia ayer y hoy (V)." (March 6): 3–4.

1921. "Triunfo y dudas." (March 16): 3–4.

1921. "Estancamiento." (March 18): 3–4.

1921. "Mirando a Rusia (I)." (March 26): 4–5.

1921. "Mirando a Rusia (II)." (March 31): 3–4.

1921. "La gran alianza." (April 2): 6–8.

1921. "Luz y tinieblas." (April 11): 3–4.

1921. "El feminismo triunfante (I)." (April 13): 3.

1921. "El feminismo triunfante (II)." (April 18): 3.

1921. "El feminismo triunfante (IV) [*sic*]." (May 5): 3–4.

1921. "El feminismo triunfante (III) [*sic*]." (May 7): 1, 2.

1921. "El feminismo triunfante (V)." (May 14): 4, 6.

1921. "Norteamérica y los niños hambrientos (I)." (May 24): 3–4.

1921. "Norteamérica y los niños hambrientos (II)." (May 31): 3–4.

1921. "Norteamérica y los niños hambrientos (III)." (June 1): 3–4.

1921. "Entran y hablan los bolcheviques (I)." (June 13): 3–4.

1921. "Entran y hablan los bolcheviques (II)." (June 18): 4.

1921. "Polonia y Napoleón (I)." (June 22): 3.

1921. "Polonia y Napoleón (II) (una mujer)." (June 26): 1–2.

1921. "La tragedia otra vez." (July 8): 3–4.

1921. "Alta Silesia." (July 9): 2–4.

1921. "Al día." (July 23): 6, 8.

1921. "Las contrariedades del escritor veraz." (July 30): 3, 5.

1921. "El alma fuerte." (August 13): 2, 4.

1921. "La intelectualidad rusa (I)." (August 24): 4–6.

1921. "La intelectualidad rusa (II)." (August 26): 4–6.

1921. "La intelectualidad rusa (III)." (August 27): 1–2.

1921. "El estado actual de Rusia (I)." (September 9): 3–5.

1921. "El estado actual de Rusia (II)." (September 12): 3–4.

1921. "De la invasión bolchevique (I)." (September 19): 3–4.

1921. "De la invasión bolchevique (II)." (September 23): 3–4.

1921. "De la invasión bolchevique (III)." (September 25): 2, 4.

1921. "La realidad." (October 4): 5.

1921. "Las emboscadas." (October 22): 2, 4.

1921. "Paisajes y hombres (I)." (October 26): 3–4.

1921. "Paisajes y hombres (II)." (October 29): 4.

1921. "Tregua de esperanza." (November 8): 3–4.

1921. "El tema candente." (November 11): 4–5.

1921. "Habla Korfanty (el epílogo)." (November 16): 4–5.

1921. "Los bolcheviques y Rusia (I)." (December 3): 3.

1921. "Los bolcheviques y Rusia (II)." (December 12): 6.

1921. "Los bolcheviques y Rusia." (December 14): 4–5.

1921. "Del amor y del desamor (I)." (December 30): 3–4.

1922. "Del amor y del desamor (II)." (January 7): 2–3.

1922. "Del amor y del desamor (III)." (January 14): 5–6.

1922. "Del amor y del desamor (IV)." (January 21): 1–2.

1922. "La estela del genio español (I)." (February 16): 3.

1922. "Al Santo Padre misericordioso." (February 18): 1–2.

1922. "La estela del genio español (II)." (February 25): 1–2.

1922. "Pío XII." (March 8): 5–6.

1922. "Leyendo la prensa rusa." (March 14): 3–4.

1922. "Entre Rusia y Alemania." (March 16): 4–5.

1922. "Complicaciones de la felicidad." (March 24): 3.

1922. "El teatro ruso." (March 28): 3.

1922. "Dominio espiritual en América." (April 10): 3.

1922. "Detalles de la catástrofe." (April 21): 3–4.

1922. "España y Rusia." (May 1): 3.

1922. "Los monárquicos rusos." (May 27): 1–2.

1922. "Moscú y Roma (I)." (June 7): 3.

1922. "Crisis de autoridad." (July 18): 3–5.

1922. "La pésima política." (August 16): 8.

1922. "El desenlace." (August 24): 3.

1922. "Los hijos de don Juan." (September 8): 3–4.

1922. "Dos culturas." (September 28): 3–4.

1922. "Errores del poder prusiano." (October 2): 3.

1922. "Huellas de Alemania." (October 28): 4–5.

1922. "Niños polacos y alemanes." (November 2): 3–4.

1922. "Las cárceles." (November 18): 1–2.

1922. "América y Mickiewicz." (November 21): 6.

1922. "Primeras lecciones." (November 24): 3.

1922. "La renuncia de Pilsudski." (December 19): 4–5.

1922. "Silueta de luz." (December 20): 5–6.

1922. "El 'comandante' " (December 23): 3.

1922. "El nuevo presidente." (December 29): 4–5.

1923. "A rey muerto . . ." (January 3): 3–4.

1923. "Lo dulce y lo práctico." (January 26): 5.

1923. "El asesinato del presidente." (February 2): 7–8.

1923. "Poesía y amores." (February 7): 3–4.

1923. "Con arma española." (February 8): 6.

1923. "Camino de España (I)." (February 16): 7.

1923. "Camino de España (II)." (February 19): 5.

1923. "Camino de España (III)." (March 2): 10–11.

1923. "La fiera y el hombre (I)." (March 14): 5–6.

1923. "La fiera y el hombre (II)." (March 15): 4–5.

1923. "Petición de clemencia." (March 20): 3.

1923. "El prendimiento o el beso de Judás." (March 24): 3.

1923. "Madrid (I)." (April 20): 4–5.

1923. "Madrid (II)." (April 26): 3–4.

1923. "Rusia (I)." (May 10): 6.

1923. "Rusia (II)." (May 14): 5–6.

1923. "El mariscal Foch en Polonia." (May 26): 21–22.

1923. "A través de Europa (I)." (June 14): 13–14.

1923. "A través de Europa (II)." (June 29): 27.

1923. "A través de Europa (III)." (July 2): 23, 25.

1923. "Otros hombres." (July 13): 12–13.

1923. "Cortejo de reyes (I)." (July 18): 13.

1923. "Cortejo de reyes (II)." (July 24): 15.

1923. "El patriarca ¿renegado?" (August 4): 22.

1923. "Conventos y juderías (I)." (August 18): 19–20.

1923. "Conventos y juderías (II)." (August 21): 11.

1923. "Se ve el incendio." (September 7): 11.

1923. "*ABC* en Polonia." (October 24): 7–8.

1923. "El príncipe y el aldeano (I)." (November 3): 23.

1923. "La gran batalla." (November 29): 15.

1923. "Se vive." (December 1): 26.

1923. "Ecos del triunfo." (December 13): 15.

1924. "Las víctimas sin culpa." (January 2): 13.

1924. "La renovación de lo idéntico." (January 24): 17–18.

1924. "Antes de la filípica." (February 6): 13.

1924. "Vladimiro Ulijanow Lenin." (February 8): 15–16.

1924. "Misterios de la realidad." (February 12): 15.

1924. "Libros de mujeres." (February 19): 17.

1924. "Una mañana . . ." (March 17): 17.

1924. "La contribución de lo bello." (March 28): 17.

1924. "El enigma del Oriente." (May 15): 13.

1924. "La virgen de Guadalupe y la de Koden." (June 19): 15–16.

1924. "Los diplomáticos (I)." (July 23): 15.

1924. "Los diplomáticos (III)." (July 28).

1924. "Los diplomáticos." (August 1): 19–20.

1924. "Zarpazos de la fiera." (August 19): 15.

1924. "Amante y asesina." (August 22): 19.

1924. "Ha ocurrido algo . . ." (September 12): 17.

1924. "Los alarmistas . . . alegres." (October 1): 16.

1924. "Los enemigos de España." (October 30): 19–20.

1924. "Teatro nacional." (November 3): 19–20.

1924. "Lo efímero y lo eterno." (December 6): 27–28.

1925. "Lo que cambia." (January 31): 27.

1925. "Impresiones de Rusia (I)." (February 19): 7–8.

1925. "Impresiones de Rusia (II)." (February 20): 8.

1925. "Impresiones de Rusia (III)." (February 27): 8.

1925. "El altar de la patria." (February 27): 10.

1925. "Impresiones de Rusia (IV)." (March 14): 15–16.

1925. "Impresiones de Rusia (V)." (March 27): 7.

1925. "Los niños rusos." (April 16): 4, 6.

1925. "Rusia pintoresca." (May 11): 3–4.

1925. "Europa y Galicia (I)." (June 12): 3–4.

1925. "Europa y Galicia (II)." (June 15): 5.

1925. "Europa y Galicia (III)." (June 16): 4–5.

1925.   "Las fronteras (I)." (July 20): 5–6.

1925.   "Las fronteras (II)." (July 21): 4–5.

1925.   "Las fronteras (III)." (July 30): 7.

1925.   "Desde Polonia (¡guerra!)." (August 20): 4–5.

1925.   "La ley agraria." (August 25): 3–5.

1925.   "Desde Polonia (los adoptantes)." (August 28): 3–5.

1925.   "Desde Polonia (hija de española)." (September 25): 3–4.

1925.   "Entran mis vecinos." (October 16): 20.

1925.   "La victoria para las españolas." (October 27): 4–5.

1925.   "De Rusia (I)." (December 15): 21–23.

1925.   "De Rusia (II)." (December 24): 21–22.

1925.   "De Rusia (III)." (December 27): 19–20.

1925.   "Expectación (II)." (January 27): 23.

1926.   "Empieza el año (I)." (January 21): 19.

1926.   "Con cllos y España." (February 20): 15 16.

1926.   "La amiga Rusia . . ." (February 27): 29.

1926.   "La joven aliada." (March 3): 20.

1926.   "Triunfo del teatro español." (April 2): 17–18.

1926.   "Tenemos que insistir." (April 24): 29–30.

1926.   "Las mujeres." (May 21): 7–8.

1926.   "La batalla." (June 2): 23.

1926.   "Algo de las causas." (July 13): 21.

1926.   "El dictador entre bastidores." (July 31): 22–23.

1926.   "La nueva etapa." (August 7): 16.

1926.   "Lo que dice Zinowiew." (August 17): 15.

1926.   "Visita de españoles." (September 10): 19–20.

1926.   "Alto en la subida." (September 22): 6–7.

1926.   "Secreto de los zares." (October 13): 8–11.

1926.   "Algo de Galicia aquí." (October 14): 7–8.

1926.   "Pedazos de epopeya." (October 21): 7, 9–10.

1926.   "Camino de España." (November 9): 7–8, 11.

1926.   "Del noviazgo." (November 17): 9–11.

1926.   "Chopin y la bandera." (December 14): 3.

1926.   "Coronas y destronados." (December 15): 3–4.

1926.   "Huella en la sombra." (December 20): 3–4.

1926.   "Realidad y misterio." (December 21): 3.

1927.   "España en el extranjero." (January 1): 48–49.

1927.   "Educación y poesía (I)." (January 13): 6–7.

1927.   "La educación y la poesía (II)." (January 19): 3–4, 6.

1927.   "Como nos ven en el extranjero." (January 24): 4, 6.

1927.   "Polonia lucha." (January 25): 3.

1927.   "Del país de los Soviets (I) (cosas de Rusia)." (February 16): 4.

1927. "Del país de los Soviets (II) (cosas de Rusia)." (February 18): 3.

1927. "Del país de los Soviets (III) (cosas de Rusia)." (February 21): 7.

1927. "Del país de los Soviets (IV) (cosas de Rusia)." (February 23): 3.

1927. "La fiesta de la Planta (I)." (March 16): 6.

1927. "La fiesta de la Planta (II)." (March 18): 6.

1927. "Rusos y chinos (el jefe de los nordistas)." (March 21): 6.

1927. "Los niños de España y Rusia." (March 22): 3–4.

1927. "Demanda de perdón." (April 2): 3, 6.

1927. "Lo viejo y lo nuevo (I)." (April 6): 3.

1927. "Lo viejo y lo nuevo (II)." (April 7): 3–4.

1927. "Un asesino arrepentido (la expiación)." (April 12): 3–5

1927. "Detalles del conjunto babilónico." (May 5): 3.

1927. "Camino adelante." (May 11): 3–4.

1927. "Mujeres (I)." (May 20): 3–4.

1927. "Viendo la vida." (May 24): 6.

1927. "Mujeres (II)." (June 9): 3, 5–6.

1927. "La perversa política." (June 13): 6.

1927. "Mujeres (III)." (June 15): 4–5.

1927. "Íntimamente." (June 21): 3–4.

1927. "Un asesinato político." (June 23): 3, 5.

1927. "Las negras rutas." (July 8): 7, 9.

1927. "Un congreso católico." (July 19): 6.

1927. "Un poeta." (July 20): 7, 10.

1927. "Fantasmas imperiales." (August 10): 3.

1927. "Novelas de la realidad (I)." (August 11): 4–5.

1927. "Novelas de la realidad (II)." (August 15): 3.

1927. "Males que exijen remedio." (August 19): 6–7.

1927. "Otros mares (I)." (September 8): 3–4.

1927. "Otros mares (II)." (September 13): 3, 6.

1927. "La pesca (del Báltico al Cantábrico)." (September 16): 3–4.

1927. "La ruta de Dantzig." (September 23): 3–4.

1927. "La última sesión del 'Seim.' " (October 4).

1927. "Viejas ciudades." (October 11): 3–4.

1927. "La danza de los siglos." (October 13): 5–6.

1927. "Las sombras de los días." (October 19): 6.

1927. "Mar adentro (III)." (October 21): 3, 5–6.

1927. "El aniversario bolchevique." (November 7): 3–4.

1927. "El eterno desconocimiento de España." (November 11): 3–4, 6.

1927. "La muerte del diablo (I)." (November 23): 7.

1927. "La muerte del diablo (II)." (November 30): 6.

1927. "La muerte del diablo (III)." (December 5): 3–4.

1927. "La guerra bolchevique (I)." (December 19): 6.

1927. "La guerra bolchevique (II)." (December 21):6–7.

1927. "La guerra bolchevique (III)." (December 23): 3–4.

1928. "La guerra bolchevique (IV)." (January 6): 3–4.

1928. "Cara a Rusia: Los hombres." (January 10): 3–4, 7.

1928. "De cara a Rusia (II) (los hombres)." (January 23): 6.

1928. "De cara a Rusia (III) (los hombres)." (January 25): 7.

1928. "La tragedia bolchevique." (February 3): 3–4.

1928. "La farsa y el drama." (February 22): 6–7.

1928. "La luz del camino." (February 27): 6–7.

1928. "Las elecciones." (March 2): 6.

1928. "Todavía Carnaval." (March 7): 3–4.

1928. "De los misterios rusos." (March 17): 3–4, 6.

1928. "Información." (March 26): 3–4.

1928. "La añoranza de Rusia." (March 28): 3–4.

1928. "El divorcio y la literatura (I)." (April 11): 6–7.

1928. "El divorcio y la literatura (II)." (April 16): 6.

1928. "El divorcio y la literatura (III)." (April 17): 3.

1928. "El divorcio y la literatura (IV)." (April 20): 3–4.

1928. "¡Paso a un rey exótico!" (May 8): 3.

1928. "Algo de España." (May 18): 3–4.

1928. "Como se lucha." (May 24): 3–4, 6.

1928. "La amenidad que se aleja." (May 29): 3, 6.

1928. "La musa de Galicia." (June 12): 3–4, 6.

1928. "Literatura feminina (I)." (June 21): 6–7.

1928. "Literatura feminina (II)." (June 25): 7.

1928. "Literatura feminina (III)." (June 27): 3–4.

1928. "Literatura feminina (IV)." (July 11): 3.

1928. "Literatura feminina (V)." (July 16): 3.

1928. "La venganza de las nieves." (July 18): 6.

1928. "Paréntesis de pacifismo." (July 19): 4–6.

1928. "En el regio homenaje." (August 15): 7.

1928. "Literatura feminina (VI)." (August 17): 3–4.

1928. "Literatura feminina (VII)." (August 21): 3–4.

1928. "Desde la costa báltica." (August 24): 3.

1928. "El mar triste." (September 11): 3.

1928. "El avance práctico." (September 13):3, 6.

1928. "El gran libro abierto." (September 19): 3.

1928. "Las impresiones del camino." (September 26): 3–4.

1928. "La luctuosa noticia." (October 4): 3.

1928. "Comentarios de estos días." (October 15): 6.

1928. "Contornos sociales." (October 16): 6.

1928. "Ciudades Europeas (breve descripción de lo más notable de Varsovia: la capital polaca)." (October 21): 3–6.

1928. "Lo desconocido." (October 23): 7.

1928. "La última zarina." (November 12): 3–4, 6.

1928. "Insisto." (November 15): 3, 6.

1928. "Inverosímil." (November 23): 3–4.

1928. "La dulzura de elogiar." (November 30): 3–4.

1928. "Otra vez Rasputin (I)." (December 11): 3, 5–6.

1928. "Otra vez Rasputin (II)." (December 14): 3.

1928. "Otra vez Rasputin (III)." (December 20): 3, 5–6.

1928. "Otra vez Rasputin (IV)." (December 25): 3–4.

1928. "El gran duque Nicolas." (January 17): 7.

1929. "El teatro judío (representación de una leyenda hebraica)." (January 10): 11–12.

1929. "España y Polonia." (January 24): 3–4.

1929. "Francisco." (January 29): 6–7.

1929. "La caza (I)." (February 18): 7.

1929. "La caza (II)." (February 20): 3–4.

1929. "La caza (III)." (February 22): 3–4.

1929. "Jubiloso después." (March 1): 7.

1929. "Ciudades europeas (la polaca Wilno de admirable historia y territorio pintoresco)." (March 3): 3–4.

1929. "La paz." (March 8): 8.

1929. "Episodios de guerra (I)." (March 14): 3, 5–6.

1929. "Episodios de guerra (II)." (March 18): 6–7.

1929. "Episodios de guerra (III)." (March 20).

1929. "Horas de Andalusia (I)." (April 6): 3.

1929. "Horas de Andalusia (II)." (April 10): 6–7.

1929. "Horas de Andalusia (III)." (April 17): 9–10.

1929. "Horas de Andalusia (IV)." (April 20): 7–9.

1929. "De los claros días." (May 30): 7.

1929. "¿Qué hacen las agencias?" (June 17): 7.

1929. "Mirando lejos." (June 26): 3–4, 6.

1929. "Eva belicosa." (June 27): 11.

1929. "Un viaje." (July 15): 7.

1929. "Las espinas de triunfo." (July 22): 4, 6.

1929. "El teatro en Varsovia (la nueva comedia de Bernard Shaw)." (July 25): 11–13.

1929. "Del teatro ruso (el poder de las tinieblas)." (August 1): 11.

1929. "Se miran las esfinges (I)." (August 16): 7.

1929. "Se miran las esfinges (II)." (August 22): 3–4.

1929. "Noticias." (August 30): 6–7.

1929. "Pinceladas." (September 18):4, 6.

1929. "De uno a otro extremo." (September 26): 6–7.

1929. "En el río Dunajec." (October 4): 5–6.
1929. "Fiesta militar." (October 24): 3, 5–6.
1929. "Prócer español (I)." (October 29): 7.
1929. "Prócer español (II)." (November 4): 6–7.
1929. "Parlamentarios (I)." (November 19): 6–7.
1929. "Parlamentarios (II)." (November 22): 6–7.
1929. "Los animales." (November 29): 7, 9.
1929. "Epílogo y prólogo (I)." (December 18): 3.
1929. "Epílogo y prólogo (II)." (December 26): 3, 6.
1929. "Los bolcheviques." (December 31): 3, 6.
1930. "Lo que ocurre en Rusia (I)." (January 14): 6–7.
1930. "Lo que pasa en Rusia (II)." (January 22): 6–7.
1930. "Lo que pasa en Rusia (III)." (January 28): 3.
1930. "En una iglesia." (February 18): 3.
1930. "Lo que se dice." (February 24): 7.
1930. "De una vida (I)." (March 27): 3.
1930. "De una vida (II)." (April 4): 4, 6.
1930. "De una vida (III)." (April 9): 3–6.
1930. "Pánico y retirada." (April 22): 4–6.
1930. "Se oyen los clarines." (May 21): 3.
1930. "¡Qué bonito y qué nuevo!" (May 28): 6.
1930. "La dulce paz campestre." (June 18): 4, 6.
1930. "Del fondo femenino rural." (June 25): 3.
1930. "Sobre el polvo la luz." (July 17): 3, 6.
1930. "Voces amigas." (July 24): 3.
1930. "Charla al 'Rom.' " (July 29): 6.
1930. "Stalin." (August 12): 3–4.
1930. "Rusia." (August 19): 3.
1930. "La esperanza." (August 22): 3–4, 6.
1930. "Literatura bolchevique (I)." (September 11): 3.
1930. "Literatura bolchevique (II)." (September 16): 3, 5–6.
1930. "Nada nuevo al norte." (October 17): 6.
1930. "Camino de trincheras." (November 11): 5–6.
1930. "Sin embargo . . ." (November 19): 3.
1930. "Predicar." (December 4): 3.
1931. "Del incendio bolchevique." (January 6): 6.
1931. "La paz de Moscú." (January 13): 10.
1931. "El aviso trágico." (January 15): 8–9.
1931. "Las alegres comadres." (January 22): 10.
1931. "Como en la vida." (February 18): 3.
1931. "Perspectiva." (February 22): 12.
1931. "Habla el alma." (March 1): 4–5, 6.

1931. "Un sabio." (March 9): 3–4.

1931. "Matrimonios." (March 16): 3–4.

1931. "Tanto de culpa." (March 26): 10.

1931. "El tema candente." (April 1): 4–5.

1931. "Lo eterno." (April 20): 3.

1931. "Voz de mujer." (May 5): 3.

1931. "El silencio." (June 26): 16.

1931. "Aviso leal." (June 27): 24.

1931. "*ABC* en las fronteras eslavas (Stalin retrocede)." (July 20): 24.

1931. "*ABC* en las fronteras eslavas (el hombre del día)." (July 22): 4.

1931. "Condicionalmente." (August 3): 8.

1931. "Esperemos." (August 25): 16.

1931. "Sigue la retirada." (August 31): 3.

1931. "*ABC* en las fronteras eslavas (I) (protesta)." (September 16): 3.

1931. "*ABC* en las fronteras eslavas (II) (intolerable)." (September 21): 3.

1931. "Desde Varsovia (dos repúblicas)." (October 2): 12.

1931. "También nosotras." (November 4): 4.

1931. "La gloria del bien." (December 7): 4–5.

1931. "¿Y ahora: Qué?" (December 9): 4.

1931. "Efemérides." (December 14): 3–4.

1932. "Emocionante." (January 23): 24.

1932. "*ABC* en las fronteras eslavas." (January 26): 3.

1932. "*ABC* en tierras rusas (I)." (February 1): 3–4.

1932. "*ABC* en tierras rusas (II)." (February 13): 24.

1932. "Divorcios." (February 24): 5.

1932. "*ABC* en Rusia (I)." (March 14): 5.

1932. "*ABC* en Rusia (II)." (March 22): 3.

1932. "Del teatro." (April 14): 14.

1932. "Ex oriente lux (un zarpazo al dragón moscovito cerca de Mukden)." (April 18): 3.

1932. "El huésped blanco." (June 29): 5.

1932. "Un libro." (July 2): 20.

1932. "Tierras y mares." (July 9): 24.

1932. "Como en Caldea y Babilonia." (August 4): 7.

1933. "*ABC* en fronteras eslavas." (January 13): 3.

1933. "Optimismo." (January 17): 4.

1933. "Insistiendo." (February 11): 16.

1933. "El derecho de Adán." (February 24): 3.

1933. "*ABC* en Dantzig." (March 16): 3.

1933. "Al lado de la revolución." (March 25): 20.

1933. "Arrecia el fuego." (April 12): 3.

1933. "El más triste proletariado." (April 20): 3.

1933.   "Poema contra el amor." (May 20): 20.

1933.   "*ABC* en Polonia." (May 27): 20.

1933.   "De Rusia." (June 12): 3–5.

1933.   "*ABC* en Polonia." (July 5): 15.

1933.   "*ABC* en Dantzig." (July 20): 3.

1933.   "*ABC* en Polonia: La escuela." (August 7): 16.

1933.   "*ABC* en Polonia." (August 15): 3.

1933.   "*ABC* en los Carpatos." (September 9): 19–20.

1933.   "Los sabios y la guerra: Einstein y Freud." (September 13): 3.

1933.   "*ABC* en Varsovia." (October 14): 20.

1933.   "Camino de España." (October 26): 3.

1933.   "España." (November 15): 3.

1933.   "Ejemplo." (December 2): 20.

1934.   "En la hora definitiva." (January 4): 3.

1934.   "Reivindicación espiritual." (January 15): 3–4.

1934.   "El mejor sistema." (January 20): 21.

1934.   "Unas palabras." (February 19): 3.

1934.   "Sin ellas." (March 4).

1934.   "El ideal y los aranceles." (March 29): 3.

1934.   "Amigo de España." (April 6): 5.

1934.   "Camino de ruinas." (May 5): 16.

1934.   "La visita de Barthou." (May 9): 3.

1934.   "Siempre igual." (May 19): 16.

1934.   "Por la justicia." (June 9): 16.

1934.   "El triunfo de España." (June 27): 5.

1934.   "Judíos y cristianos." (July 7): 17.

1934.   "El vértigo." (July 18): 6–7.

1934.   "Junto al volcán." (July 23): 16.

1934.   "El agua enemiga." (August 9): 6–7.

1934.   "*ABC* en Varsovia (oyendo las campanas)." (August 20): 3–4.

1934.   "Página rural." (September 8): 16.

1934.   "En los aires." (September 14): 8–9.

1934.   "El modernismo amoral." (September 27): 15.

1934.   "Triste comparación." (October 24): 15–16.

1934.   "¡Viva España!" (November 1): 4–5.

1934.   "De lejos y cerca." (November 5): 16.

1934.   "La horrible perspectiva." (November 29): 4.

1934.   "*ABC* en Varsovia." (December 18): 3.

1935.   "El oso herido." (January 31): 4.

1935.   "Naranjas españolas." (February 16): 16.

1935.   "Mirando a Rusia." (February 25): 5.

1935. "*ABC* en Varsovia." (March 19): 3.
1935. "*ABC* en Varsovia." (March 20): 3.
1935. "La sonrisa del Lord." (April 15): 4–5.
1935. "Los días sin calma." (May 13): 5.
1935. "Los amigos de ocasión." (June 3): 5.
1935. "El mariscal de Pilsudski ha muerto." (June 5): 10.
1935. "El hombre." (June 13): 4.
1935. "Sombra y luz." (July 8): 4–5.
1935. "Mirando en torno." (July 31):–5.
1935. "Camino abierto." (August 5): 3–4.
1935. "De cara al Báltico." (August 30): 4–5.
1935. "No sólo en Abisinia." (September 2): 4–5.
1935. "¡Guerra, Guerra!" (September 10): 3.
1935. "Esperando." (October 9): 16.
1935. "Realidades." (October 19): 23.
1935. "*ABC* en Polonia: Recordando." (November 13).
1935. "El gran escándalo." (November 15): 17.
1935. "La sensibilidad." (December 20): 17.
1936. "*ABC* en Varsovia." (January 10): 4.
1936. "Comentarios." (January 17): 16.
1936. "Hay que mirar al fondo (E.T.)." (February 17): 3.
1936. "La lógica de lo ilógico." (March 18): 3.
1936. "Después de la batalla." (March 19): 16.
1936. "*ABC* en Varsovia." (April 2): 4.
1936. "Un tema nuevo." (April 9): 18.
1936. "La política." (April 10): 3.
1936. "Al día." (June 11): 4.
1936. "Lo nuevo en lo eterno." (June 22): 16.
1936. "Un recuerdo." (July 8): 3–4.
1936. "Los vencedores." (July 13): 3.
1936. "Mirando a Rusia." (July 15): 3.
1939. "La espera trágica." (August 25).
1939. "Mi cuarta guerra." (December 16): 9.
1940. "En guerra." (February 14): 3.
1944. "Lejos y cerca." (June 6).

Unverified articles

1921. "Triunfo del Mariscal." (December 16).
1922. "Comentarios al tratado de Rapallo." (May 14).
1922. "De lo que no se habla." (May 22).
1922. "Moscú y Roma (II)." (June 11).

1922. "El metropolitano de Lwow." (June 14).

1922. "Las viudas." (July 5).

1922. "Historia y aclaraciones (I)." (July 23).

1922. "Historia y aclaraciones (II)." (July 25).

1922. "Los ladrones." (November 10).

1922. "Amor del romancero." (December 17).

1923. "Vida en las juderías (I)." (September 15): 23–24.

1923. "Vida en las juderías (II)." (September 23).

1923. "Esperando." (October 19).

1923. "El príncipe y el aldeano (II)." (November 3).

1924. "La hora de la mujer." (April 16).

1924. "Fin de un suplicio." (May 8).

1924. "Ráfaga de luz." (June 7).

1924. "¿El fin justifica los medios?" (July 1).

1924. "Los diplomáticos (II)." (July 26).

1925. "No cambian mis vecinos." (September 23).

1925. "El comisario Chicherin." (October 24).

1926. "Triunfo del teatro español." (March 28):3–34.

1926. "El feminismo de una diplomática." (April 9).

1926. "De Rusia misteriosa." (April 29).

1926. "Pensando en un rey (I)." (May 5).

1926. "Pensando en un rey (II)." (May 16).

1926. "La política y la dictadura." (May 26).

1926. "Los motivos y la situación." (June 10): 25–26.

1926. "Que Dios perdone." (June 16).

1926. "Diplomáticos y 'ministras' hispanófilos." (August 20).

1926. "La obra de Dzierzynski." (September 3).

1927. "Las impresiones del camino." (May 6).

1927. "Mujeres (III)." (June 20).

1929. "Del teatro." (April 23): 11.

1929. "Lejos de España (las grandes rutas europeas)." (April 25): 6–7.

1930. "¡Veinticinco años!" (June 18): 44.

1932. "Lo eterno." (April 18).

1932. "La verdad." (May 14).

1932. "Intervalo lírico." (May 21).

1934. "*ABC* en Varsovia." (June 13).

1935. "Los crímenes de Petersburgo y Moscú." (January 5).

APPENDIX II

Más que amor (1908)

Index of Letters

I	190[?]. María to Halina. December 1. Kalinowo, Poland, 7–8.
II	190[?]. María to Sor María de la Paz. June 6. Warsaw, 8–9.
III	[n.d.]. María to Daniel Olivar. February 10. Warsaw, 9–12.
IV	María to Rafael Solares. March 2. Warsaw, 12–22.
V	María to Rafael Solares. April 2. Warsaw, 23–26.
VI	María to Madame Gabrielle Capistou. May 15. Warsaw, 26–29.
VII	María to Carlos de Vargas. May 20. Warsaw, 29–31.
VIII	María to Carlos. June 19. 31–33.
IX	María to Carlos. July 3. 33–35.
X	María to Carlos. July 31. 35.
XI	Carlos de Vargas to María. August 10. Madrid, 36–37.
XII	María to Carlos. August 16. Kalinowo [Poland], 36–40.
XIII	11 noche. 41 [addendum to previous letter].
XIV	Carlos to María. August 24. Madrid, 42–44.
XV	María to Carlos. September 10. Kalinowo, 44–47.
XVI	Carlos to María. October 6. Madrid, 47.
XVII	María to Carlos. October 12. 47–48.
XVIII	Carlos to María. October 20. 49–52.
XIX	María to Carlos. October 30. 53–56.
XX	Carlos to María. November 5. 57–59.
XXI	María to Carlos. November 14. 60–65.
XXII	María to Carlos. November 24. 65–68.
XXIII	María to Carlos. November 30. 68–72.
XXIV	Carlos to María. December 7. 72–74.
XXV	Carlos to María. December 8. 74–76.
XXVI	Carlos to María. December 9. 76–77.
XXVII	Carlos to María. December 11. 78–81.
XXVIII	María to Carlos. December 18. 81–83.

XXIX   María to Carlos. December 20. 83–86.

XXX   María to Carlos. December 22. 86–87.

XXXI   Carlos to María. Telegram. December 22. 88.

XXXII   Carlos to María. Telegram. December 23. 88.

XXXIII   Carlos to María. Telegram. December 24. 88.

XXXIV   Carlos to María. December 24. 89.

XXXV   Carlos to María. December 25. 90–92.

XXXVI   María to Carlos. December 25. 92–93.

XXXVII   María to Carlos. December 26. 93–94.

XXXVIII   María to Carlos. December 28. 95–97.

XXXIX   María to Carlos. December 31. 98–101.

XL   Carlos to María. December 31. 101–3.

XLI   190[?]. María to Carlos. January 1. 103–7.

XLII   María to Carlos. January 3. 107–11.

XLIII   Carlos to María. January 2. 111–14.

XLIV   María to Carlos. January 6. 114–15.

XLV   January 7. 115–21 [addendum to previous letter].

XLVI   María to Carlos. January 8. 122–31.

XLVII   Carlos to María. January 8. 131–38 [censored].

XLVIII   María to Carlos. January 10. 138–40.

XLIX   Carlos to María. January 10. 140–43.

L   María to Carlos. January 12. 143–49.

LI   María to Carlos. January 13. 149–55.

LII   Carlos to María. January 13. 155–57.

LIII   Carlos to María. Telegram. January 17. 157.

LIV   Carlos to María. January 18. 157–60.

LV   Carlos to María. January 21. 160–61.

LVI   María to Carlos. January 21. 162–64.

LVII   María to Carlos. January 24. 165–66.

LVIII   Carlos to María. January 25. 167–69.

LIX   Carlos to María. January 26. 170–72.

LX   María to Carlos. January 29. 172–75.

LXI   Carlos to María. February 2. 175–78.

LXII   Carlos to María. February 3. 178–79.

LXIII   María to Carlos. February 6. 179–81.

LXIV   Carlos to María. Telegram. February 9. 181.

LXV   María to Carlos. Telegram. February 11. 182.

LXVI   Carlos to María. February 13. 182–85.

LXVII   Carlos to María. February 16. 185–86.

LXVIII   María to Carlos. Telegram. February 16. 186.

LXIX   Carlos to María. February 17. 186–87.

LXX   María to Halina. February 25. 187–90.

LXXI   María to Halina. March 1. 190–93.

LXXII   Carlos to María. March 8. 193–94.

LXXIII   María to Carlos. Telegram. March 12. 194.

LXXIV   Carlos to María. Telegram. March 14. 195.

LXXV   Carlos to María. March 14. 195–96.

LXXVI   María to Carlos. March 19. 197–98.

LXXVII   March 26. 199–200 [addendum to previous letter].

LXXVIII   Carlos to María. April 7. 200–201.

LXXIX   Carlos to María. Telegram. April 8. 201.

LXXX   María to Carlos. Telegram. April 8. Fuenterrabia [Spain], 201.

LXXXI   María to Halina. April 12. Aranjuez [Spain], 202–8.

LXXXII   María to Halina. April 15. Aranjuez [Spain], 208–15.

LXXXIII   María to Halina. April 17. Aranjuez [Spain], 216–24.

LXXXIV   María to Halina. April 21. Aranjuez [Spain], 224–27.

LXXXV   María to Halina. April 28. Aranjuez [Spain], 227–33.

LXXXVI   María to Halina. April 28. Aranjuez [Spain], 233–42.

LXXXVII   María to Halina. April 28. Aranjuez [Spain], 242–45.

LXXXVIII   Carlos to María. April 28 (night). Madrid, 246–47.

LXXXIX   María to Halina. April 30. Aranjuez [Spain], 248–55.

XC   María to Halina. May 7. Aranjuez [Spain], 255–58.

XCI   María to Halina. May 8 Aranjuez [Spain], 258–61.

XCII   Carlos to María. Telegram. May 11. Barcelona, 261.

XCIII   Carlos to María. May 12. Madrid, 262–63.

XCIV   Carlos to María. September 12. Madrid, 263–64.

XCV   Carlos to María. October 13. Madrid, 264–68.

Notes

1. Casanova's works are listed apart from the general Works Cited (see Appendix I).

2. Unless otherwise noted, all translations into English are mine.

3. In addition, Casanova consulted such intellectuals as the Italian writers Mario Pilo and Ginebra Speraz; the Italian historian Guglielmo Ferrero and his wife, the scientist Gina Lombroso; the British Hispanist James Fitzmaurice-Kelly; the French Hispanist Alfred Morel Fatío; the French poet and dramatist Edmond Rostand; the French dramatist Edouard Schuré; the Russian freethinker Maria Naumowa; the Portuguese historian Joaquim Pedro de Oliveira Martins; the Scandinavian feminist Ellen Key; the Tartar Prince Chamilow; the Polish intellectual Julian Baltazar Marchlewski; and the Polish writer Henryk Sienkiewicz. She also cited a number of contemporary texts, not all of which were widely known in Spain—such as Schuré's *Femmes inspiratrices et poétes annonciateurs* (1900), the anonymous *España hace cincuenta años a los ojos de un diplomático extranjero*, Compte Paul Vasili's *La societé de Madrid*, Pierre Louÿs's *La femme et le pantin* (1898), Maurice Barrès's *Du sang, de la volupté et de la mort* (1894)—and made more oblique references to the American Hispanist Kenneth Mackenzie, the Italian writer and patriot Gabriele D'Annunzio, and the British writers Martin Hume and L. Higgin. Casanova's remarks about those whose opinions she does not agree with are scathing. For example, Hume apparently believes that "el nombre de *Emelia* Pardo Bazán es un pseudónimo" [the name of (*Emilia*) Pardo Bazán is a pseudonym], to which Casanova acidly comments that the author is clearly "poseedor de un secreto que ni sospechamos" (Casanova 1910, *La mujer española en el extranjero*, 27, emphasis Casanova's) [privy to a secret of which we have no notion at all].

4. The published offprint of the lecture is accompanied by a collection of press cuttings from various Madrid newspapers, all of which give a positive review of

Casanova's lecture but many of which appear to have largely missed the point (see Casanova 1910, *La mujer española en el extranjero,* 41–56).

5. For more detailed information about her life, refer to the two principal published biographies of Casanova: Alayeto 1992 and Martínez Martínez 1999.

6. In a brief memoir dated 1942, Casanova remembered, "En cuanto mis versos empezaron a sonar y Sofitina era la poetisa celebrada en círculo reducido, empecé a firmarme 'Sofía Casanova,' pensando con el corazón en que no desapareciera el apellido de mi abuelo. Si soy alguien algún día—me dije a los 18 años—por ese apellido me conocerán. Fue esa decisión un fiel cariño y gratitud a mi abuelo. Mi hermano Vicente tomó mi ejemplo" (quoted in Simón Palmer 1996, 193). [As soon as my verses began to be heard and Sofitina was a poet(ess) celebrated among a limited circle, I began to sign as 'Sofía Casanova,' hoping in my heart to prevent my grandfather's surname from dying out. If one day I am somebody—I said to myself at the age of 18—that is the surname people will know me by. That decision was a show of faithful affection and gratitude to my grandfather. My brother Vicente followed my example.]

7. The play ran for one night at Madrid's Teatro Español. For more information, see Simón Palmer 1989.

8. The fluid nature of Spanish naming practices further complicates bio-bibliographical research into women writers. Spaniards conventionally use two surnames, the first from their father, the second from their mother, but either can be dropped for personal or social reasons or simply for reasons of euphony or length (some individual surnames can have two, three, or even four elements). It is uncommon for Spanish women to drop their birth name on marriage, but some adopt their husband's name as an addition: This is why Casanova is sometimes credited as Sofía Casanova *de Lutosławski.* In the previous paragraph, I have given the most commonly found name for each writer as standard, with additional elements in square brackets. In short, to search a catalogue for a single writer, one might have to look under two, three, or even four different names.

9. See, for example, Ribbans 1999. The concept of the Generation of 1898 has itself been subject to scrutiny ever since Ricardo Gullón's "La invención del 98" (1968). For responses to this scrutiny, see John Butt's revisionist essay "The Generation of 1898: A Critical Fallacy?" (1980) and María Dolores Dobón's (belated) rebuttal, "Sociólogos contra estetas: Prehistoria del conflicto entre modernismo y 98" (1996).

10. Modernism is a particularly pertinent example, because as Felski suggests, its precepts have been used throughout the twentieth century to justify the exclusion of women from intellectual and public life. In *The Gender of Modernity,* Felski counters the assumptions that underpin even feminist work on the period, as she argues that we cannot continue to see modernism as the standard from which women's work is simply a deviation, because "if women's interests cannot be unproblematically aligned with the dominant conceptions of the

modern, neither can they simply be placed outside of them" (1995, 16). In other words, what is necessary is a rethinking of the categories of both modernism and femininity as historically and geographically contingent, given increasing evidence that "the intersection of femininity and modernity plays itself out *differentially* across the specifics of sociohistorical context" (9). Although based largely on French- and English-language sources, Felski's distinction between modernism as a literary movement and modernity as a historical period provides a model for explaining why it is so difficult to study women's writing and their participation in the forging of the modern nation within the existing models of Spanish literary history.

11.   This is equally true of modernisms beyond Spain. As Suzanne Clark argues in *Sentimental Modernism* (her defense of American women's participation in 1920s cultural circles), "From the point of view of literary modernism, sentimentality was both a past to be outgrown and a present tendency to be despised" (1991, 3).

12.   Roberta Johnson has already shown convincingly that *fin de siglo* women writers who increasingly recognized that "bourgeois respectability is not the glue that holds the nation together" (1996, 172) were prepared in their works to challenge the bourgeois conventions and institutions that they perceived as oppressive or limiting to women. Their criticisms form a direct contrast to the works of their male peers, about whom Johnson notes, "If the men of the '98 . . . were, or at least considered themselves, radical in their programs for the public aspects of the nation and in their approach to artistic forms, they were exceptionally conservative in the domestic agenda they portrayed in their fiction" (1999, 249). In her most recent study *Gender and Nation in the Spanish Modernist Novel*, Johnson theorizes this contrast as a distinction—broadly along gender lines— between "aesthetic" (i.e., canonical) modernism and the "social" modernism of women writers, where "form may be more traditional (realist, melodramatic, sentimental), but the message, especially about the social roles of women, is radically new" (2003, 5).

CHAPTER 2

1.   First published in book form in 1894, *El doctor Wolski* achieved great critical acclaim and commercial success. It was serialized in *Revista Contemporánea* in 1896–1897, published in Polish—in a version by the well-known translator HJ (Helena Pajzderska, also known as Hajota)—as *Doktor Wolski (kartki z życia Polaków i Rosyan)* in 1907, reprinted in the weekly *La Novela Corta* in 1920, and finally issued as the second volume of Casanova's *Obras completas* in 1925.

2.   [Enrique is a superior man. His life has a noble mission to fulfill. Will I be able to help him? Won't I find myself inferior to him?]

3.   Interestingly, however, the name of the protagonist seems to be a nod to a long history of Polish-Spanish relations. Piotr Dunin Wolski (1531–1590), bishop of

the Polish city of Płock, was a diplomat at the court of the Spanish king Philip II; his personal library of more than three hundred Spanish books laid the foundation for the Spanish collections of Kraków's Jagiellonian Library.

4. This journey is described in the travelogue *Sobre el Volga helado*, first published in book form in 1903.

5. Adam Mickiewicz (1798–1855) was the greatest Polish poet of the nineteenth century and a central figure in the Polish Romantic movement. He spent much of his life in exile in Russia and Western Europe. His most famous works include *Pan Tadeusz, Konrad Wallenrod,* and *Dziady.*

6. The "Great Improvisation" of part 3 of *Dziady* marks the transition of Polish Romanticism from acceptance of the gulf between the Romantic hero and his society that is characteristic of Western Romanticism to the belief that the shared mission of the hero and his society is to free that society from the oppression of the partitions. The hero, Konrad, imprisoned for his nationalist beliefs, cries out, "Nazywam się Milijon—bo za milijony / Kocham i cierpię katusze" [My name is Million—because for millions / I love and suffer agonies" (Mickiewicz 1998, pt. 3:2). The poem, which envisions a future in which the nation's sufferings are equated with Christ's Passion, prophesies that a future saviour of Poland will be born of a foreign mother and that his name will be "44."

7. Jan Matejko (1838–1893) was a prolific creator of paintings that narrated emblematic events from Poland's past (such as *Bitwa pod Grunwaldem* [The Battle of Grunwald] and *Kazanie skargi* [The Kazan Sermons]) or that portrayed historical figures (such as *Stańczyk,* a sixteenth-century court jester).

8. Henryk Siemiradzki (1843–1902) was a creator of historical paintings set mainly in the ancient world. His most famous canvas was *Pochodnie Nerona* [Nero's Torches], which depicted the torture of Christians by Emperor Nero. The great influence of his work on Sienkiewicz, his contemporary, is particularly evident in Sienkiewicz's novel *Quo vadis?* (1895).

9. It is significant, as we will see later, that the Virgin of Ostrobrama is Lithuanian (Poland's national icon is the Virgin of Częstochowa). The chapel of Our Lady of Ostrobrama is in the parish of St. Teresa in Vilnius, Lithuania, where it is the object of pilgrimages from all over Lithuania. Both Catholic and Orthodox Christians venerate the chapel. Many Polish churches today remain dedicated to Our Lady of Ostrobrama.

10. Jan Sobieski (1624–1696), elected King Jan III of Poland (1674–1696), defended Christian Europe against the Ottoman Empire, raising the Siege of Vienna in 1683. Although the empire was not partitioned until 1772, his death saw the effective end of Polish independence.

11. Tadeusz Kościuszko (1752–1817) served George Washington in the American Revolutionary War. In 1789, back in Poland, he fought for Stanisław Poniatowski against the Russians. He led the doomed 1794 uprising, was captured by the

Russians and imprisoned for two years, and eventually retired first to France and later to Switzerland.

12. The Chuvash Republic, which borders Tatarstan and was part of the Russian Empire after the sixteenth century, became an autonomous republic in 1920. The Chuvash people are descended from the Bulgars; their language is among the Turkic group believed to include the last remaining descendants of the Old Bulgaric language.

13. Cheremiss was the former name for the Mari people who were incorporated into Russia in 1552. The Mari Republic, which was constituted in 1936, borders the Chuvash Republic, but the two are not related. Chuvash is a Turkic language, and Mari is a Finno-Ugric language.

14. The *starowiare* [old believers] are the descendants of dissident Christians who split from the Russian Orthodox Church in the seventeenth century. They preserve medieval traditions, including fasting, wearing peasant garb, and observing at least forty religious holidays.

15. The spelling of the Polish popular name for this disease is actually "kołtun." The *Oxford English Dictionary* gives the formal alternative "plica polonica," defined as "[a] matted filthy condition of the hair due to disease; Polish plait."

16. See particularly *Księgi narodu polskiego i pielgrzymstwa polskiego* [Books of the Polish Nation and of the Polish Pilgrimage], which compare the union of Poland and Lithuania to the union of husband and wife, two souls in one body.

CHAPTER 3

1. *Lo eterno*, which first appeared in 1907, is a short work of only 118 pages—that is, less than half the length of *El doctor Wolski*. It was reprinted in a slightly modified version by *La Novela Corta* in 1920 and last appeared in 1926, much revised, as one of five novels and short stories in volume 3 of Sofía Casanova's *Obras completas*.

2. The most likely publication is *El Cuento Semanal*, founded in 1907, the first of the *novela corta* collections that proliferated in the first decades of the twentieth century. The founder and editor of *El Cuento Semanal* was Eduardo Zamacois. Two years later Casanova would publish her novel *Princesa del amor hermoso* in the collection. A slightly altered version of *Lo Eterno* would, of course, be published by *La Novela Corta* in 1920.

3. Silvestre Moreno, the Moroccan-identified Franciscan friar in Pardo Bazán's *Una cristiana*, is presented as a positive character. In contrast with other literary priests, he is unequivocally masculine, utterly engaging, and very much part of the real world; in his connection with Morocco, it seems that he is designed to interrogate the different values that lie beyond the homogenizing idea of *moro,* drawing a distinction between the cultural identity of Moorishness and the

Islamic faith. A closer reading suggests, however, that he is a willing agent of the church and a soldier at the service of Spain's colonial project—quite the opposite of Juan (see Hooper 2006b, 176–80). In contrast, Nazarín is ambiguous in terms of not only race but also gender. Benito Pérez Galdós's novel, which is more interested in the attempts of other characters to pin down Nazarín, to define and describe him, can be seen as a meditation on the desirability—or even the possibility—of applying the discourses of Anglo-European orientalism to the Spanish situation (see Hooper 2006b, 181–86).

4.   In the 1926 edition, this outing becomes a trip to the *campo* outside the unnamed city (Casanova 1926, *Lo eterno,* 187).

5.   In the 1926 edition, several pages of detailed urban description are replaced by the line "Fuése en derechura al domicilio de Álvarez" (Casanova 1926, *Lo eterno,* 207). [He went straight to Álvarez's house.]

6.   Almost this entire chapter is removed in the 1926 edition, which situates Juan's moment of revelation simply amid "la quietud de la blanca capital gallega" (Casanova 1926, *Lo eterno,* 209) [the tranquility of the white Galician city].

7.   Interestingly (given the close friendship between Blanca de los Ríos and Casanova), *La niña de Sanabria* is set in the same year (1898) as and the Sanabria palace occupies the same street (El Pretil de los Consejos) as the Villabrizo palace in *Lo eterno.*

8.   It is an association far removed from that expressed in Miguel de Unamuno's poem "El Cristo de Velázquez," begun in 1913 but not published until 1920, which meditates on the painting as the image of a truly Spanish Christ.

9.   As Carmen Martín Gaite convincingly demonstrates in *Desde la ventana* (1987), such criticisms of the tedious lifestyle of the Spanish woman and the often frustrated desire for self-expression had been commonplace in Spanish women's writing since the sixteenth century. Casanova, like many of her contemporaries, argued passionately for Spanish women to have a more active role in the life of the nation. In her lecture *La mujer española en el extranjero,* for example, she challenged the men in her audience to "encauzar el espléndido manantial de la actividad femenina, que hoy se pierde . . . en las murmuraciones de la holganza, o la devoción sin caridad de los conventos" (1910, 37) [to undam the splendid torrent of female activity, which today is being lost . . . in idle gossip or the uncharitable devotion of the convent].

CHAPTER 4

1.   *Más que amor* was first published in Madrid in 1908. The Polish translation, by Casanova's daughters María and Izabela, was first serialized in the daily newspaper *Gazeta Codzienna* and, also in 1908, was then published in book form by Gebethner in Kraków.

2. Given that the novel was published in Polish in 1908 and was widely available, the family's purported ignorance seems unlikely. Perhaps the reaction that Alayeto encountered can be attributed to the fact that in Poland the novel was not received as a romance.

3. Ela Balicka (born Gabriela Iwanowska) held a doctorate in biology from the University of Geneva and also served as a politician. With her husband, the sociologist Zygmunt Balicki, she was a leading member of the right-wing nationalist party Narodowa Demokracja [National Democracy], of which Casanova's close friend Roman Dmowski served as leader and in which Casanova's daughters also held membership

4. The introductory poem in *Más que amor,* "A la bella y grande Ela Balicka," appears to collude in the "masking" to which Lanser refers. The poem replaces the normal framework of an epistolary novel, whereby the narrative somehow tells the story of its own publication.

5. In *The Madwoman in the Attic*, Sandra Gilbert and Susan Gubar argue that "by projecting their rebellious impulses not into their heroines but into mad or monstrous women (who are suitably punished in the course of the novel or poem), female authors dramatize their own self-division, their desire both to accept the strictures of patriarchal authority and to reject them. What this means, however, is that the madwoman in literature by women is not merely, as she might be in male literature, an antagonist or foil to the heroine. Rather, she is usually in some sense the *author's* double, an image of her own anxiety and rage. Indeed, much of the poetry and fiction written by women conjures up this mad creature so that female authors can come to terms with their own uniquely female feelings of fragmentation, their own keen sense of the discrepancies between what they are and what they are supposed to be. . . . In projecting their anger and dis-ease into dreadful figures, creating dark doubles for themselves and their heroines, women writers are both identifying with and revising the self-definitions patriarchal culture has imposed upon them" (1978, 78–79).

6. It is the date of *Popioły* that enables us to situate the action of *Más que amor* between December 1904 and October 1907, despite the fact that the timeframe is given in the original only as 190–.

7. There are several towns and villages by this name in Poland: one is less than five miles from the Lutosławski family estates at Drozdowo.

8. For an overview of Żeromski's work, see the entry on Żeromski in Czerwiński 1994 (459).

9. According to Plato, Ananke was the mother of the Moirae, or Fates, and the personification of the force of destiny. She was also the mother of Adrasteia (daughter of Jupiter and distributor of rewards and punishments) and the goddess of unalterable necessity. "Ananke" is also the title of a poem by Casanova's friend Tadeusz Miciński (included in the 1902 collection *W mroku*

gwiazd [In the Darkness of the Stars]), which was heavily influenced by Miciński's visit to Casanova in Galicia in 1898–1899.

10. The numbering of letters is mine. For a full list, with dates, places, and correspondents, see Appendix II herein.

11. Although Casanova does not discuss the text itself in the article (which describes how she took her grievance to the Russian governor of Warsaw), it is unique as an example of the author discussing her writing. The letter appears in the Spanish edition of the novel, with the following footnote: "Esta carta fue la castigada como 'atentatoria al Estado' por el Gobierno militar de Varsovia con 500 rublos. En la edición hecha en Cracovia (Austria) la autora ha tenido que suprimir algunos conceptos, para que el libro circule y no sea confiscado en Rusia" (1908, *Más que amor,* 131). [This letter was the one fined 500 rubles as "an attack on the State" by the Warsaw military Government. In the edition published in Kraków (Austria) the author has had to suppress some ideas, so that the book could circulate without being confiscated in Russia.]

12. Ploszowski is the hero and (through his journal) the narrator of Sienkiewicz's 1890 novel *Bez dogmatu* [Without Dogma]. Through his perpetual indecision, he prevents his own happiness, sacrifices that of others, and finally succumbs to intellectual neurasthenia.

13. This is a reference to another of Sienkiewicz's novels, *Rodzina Polanieckich* [The Polaniecki Family] (1894/1895), which shows his ideology growing closer to that of the National Democrats, in particular their vision of Poland's capitalist prosperity under the protection of czarist Russia.

14. This detail dates the action to 1906, when—unable to build viable support—the Moret government and the three equally short-lived liberal administrations that followed it tried to unite the various factions of the party behind an anticlerical program.

CHAPTER 5

1. "Generación del 07" was a term coined in a special 1920 issue of *La Novela Corta* (25.3) written by the *colaboradores* themselves. Although no women took part, Emilia Pardo Bazán, Carmen de Burgos, and Concha Espina were discussed in the chapter "La mujer y la novela."

2. I do not include here texts by Gregorio Martínez Sierra (María Lejárraga), because their true authorship was not a matter of public knowledge at the time.

3. After 1914, Burgos dominates the publication lists, on a par with the most prolific male authors, such as Antonio de Hoyos y Vinent, Felipe Trigo, Joaquín Dicenta, and Rafael López de Haro. The only "new" names are Adela Carbone and, in the 1920s and 1930s, Margarita Nelken, Magda Donato, Sara Insúa, and Pilar Millán Astray. Works by Fernán Caballero and Carolina Coronado also

appeared posthumously, and a translation of a work by the Italian writer Grazia Deledda appeared in 1924.

4. The cover of *Fémina* (1910), which features a portrait of Barco, states that the *novela* was "recomendado en el concurso" [commended in the competition]. After its publication, Barco seems to have disappeared from public—or at least from literary—life.

5. Casanova's use of the archaic *can* [dog] instead of the common Spanish equivalent *perro* seems to me a deliberate invocation of Castro's image of the lover as "canciño de cego" [a blind man's dog] (*can* is the common word for dog in Galician).

6. According to Beramendi and Núñez Seixas, more than four hundred of these societies were founded between 1907 and 1910 (1995, 65).

7. There is no pagination in the original; the numbering is mine.

8. "O campaneiriño" [The Little Bell Ringer], the title the story is given in the 1911 edition of *El pecado*, is in Galician rather than Spanish. This is the only time the Galician title appears; elsewhere the story is published as "El campanero de San Julián" [The Bell Ringer of San Julián].

CHAPTER 6

1. The 1911 edition of *El pecado* reads "más de dos años," but this may well have been a typo, as it clearly makes no sense in the context; "siglos" is my best guess for what was intended.

2. This is clearly a reference to the end of Benito Pérez Galdós's novel *La desheredada* [The Disinherited Lady], in which Isidora Rufete, abandoning her son, disappears into the streets of Madrid in a graphic description of social death: "Salió, efectivamente, veloz, resuelta, con paso de suicida; y como éste cae furioso, aturdido, demente en el abismo que le ha solicitado con atracción invencible, así cayó ella despeñada en el voraginoso laberinto de las calles. La presa fue devorada, y poco después, en la superficie social, todo estaba tranquilo" (1997, 480). [She left, then, quick and resolute, with a suicide victim's step; and just as a suicide victim falls furiously, headlong, demented into the abyss that has called him or her with invincible attraction, so she plummeted into the whirling labyrinth of the streets. The prisoner was devoured, and before long, on the surface of society, all was calm.]

3. Louis-Joseph Janvier, author of *L'égalité des races* (1884), and Anténor Firmin, author of *De l'égalité des races humaines* (1885), were Haitian intellectuals who were at the center of British debates on race in the 1880s and 1890s. As is often found in Casanova's works, the transcription of names is inaccurate.

4. Herman Müller Strübing (1812–1893) was a German scholar noted for his work on Aristophanes and Friedrich von Schiller.

CONCLUSION

1.   For more information, see the electronic database "Spain's Women Intellectuals, 1890–1920," hosted by the University of Liverpool: *http://pcwww.liv. ac.uk/~chomik/2home.html.*

APPENDIX I

1.   Although I have bibliographical information for these references, I have not seen the works themselves; therefore, I am unable to categorize them.

2.   Articles published between April 8, 1915, and January 23, 1916, are collected in *De la guerra.* Articles published between May 3, 1917, and December 3, 1917, are collected in *De la revolución rusa.* Articles published between January 19, 1918, and April 22, 1918, are collected in *La revolución bolchevista.* Articles marked * appear in full in *La revolución bolchevista.* Articles marked † appear in partial or revised form.

Works Cited

Alayeto, Ofelia. 1987. "Sofía Casanova: An Annotated Bibliography." *Bulletin of Bibliography* 44:44–51.

———. 1992. *Sofía Casanova (1861–1958): Spanish Poet, Journalist, and Author*. Potomac, Md.: Scripta Humanistica.

Altman, Janet. 1982. *Epistolarity: Approaches to a Form*. Columbus: Ohio University Press.

———. 1995. "Women's letters in the Public Sphere." In Goldsmith and Goodman, *Going Public*, 99–115.

Azaña, Manuel. 1913. *Memoria leída en el Ateneo de Madrid el día 11 de noviembre de 1913, con motivo de la inauguración del curso académico*. Madrid: Imprenta de los Sucesores de M. Minuesa de los Ríos. Available at *www.ateneodemadrid.com/biblioteca_digital/folletos/Memoria-1913.txt*.

Azorín [José Martínez Ruíz]. 1959–1963. *Obras completas*. Madrid: Águilar.

Balfour, Sebastian. 1997. *The End of the Spanish Empire, 1898–1923*. Oxford, England: Clarendon.

———. 2002. *Deadly Embrace: Morocco and the Road to the Spanish Civil War*. Oxford, England: Oxford University Press.

Barco, Ángela. 1910. *Fémina*. In *El Cuento Semanal* 171. Madrid: Imprenta Artística Española.

Bates, John. 2001. "Poland." In Jones, *Censorship*.

Beramendi, Xusto, and Xosé Manoel Núñez Seixas. 1995. *O nacionalismo galego*. Vigo, Spain: A Nosa Terra.

Bieder, Maryellen. 1990. "Between Genre and Gender: Emilia Pardo Bazán and *Los pazos de Ulloa*." In Valis and Maier, *In the Feminine Mode*, 131–45.

———. 1992. "Woman and the Twentieth-Century Spanish Literary Canon: The Lady Vanishes." *Anales de la Literatura Española Contemporánea* 17:301–24.

———. 1995. "Gender and Language: The Womanly Woman and Manly Writing." In Charnon-Deutsch and Labanyi, *Culture and Gender in Nineteenth-Century Spain*, 98–119.

Blanco, Alda. 1989. Introduction to *Una mujer por caminos de España*, by María Martínez Sierra. Madrid: Castalia, 7–42.

————. 1993. "But Are They Any Good?" *Revista de Estudios Hispánicos* 27.3: 463–70.

————. 1995. "Gender and National Identity: The Novel in Nineteenth-Century Spanish Literary History." In Charnon-Deutsch and Labanyi, *Culture and Gender,* 120–36.

Blanco Asenjo, Ricardo. 1885. Prologue to *Poesías,* by Sofía Casanova. Madrid: A. J. Alaria, 7–16.

Blanco García, Padre Francisco. 1891. *La literatura española en el s. XIX.* Madrid: Saenz de Jubera Hermanos.

Bordonada, Ángela Ena, ed. 1989. *Novelas breves de escritoras españolas, 1900–1936.* Madrid: Castalia/Instituto de la Mujer.

Bretz, Mary Lee. 2001. *Encounters across Borders: The Changing Visions of Spanish Modernism, 1890–1930.* Lewisburg, Pa.: Bucknell University Press/London, Associated University Presses.

Brewer, E. Cobham. 1898. *Dictionary of Phrase and Fable.* Philadelphia: Henry Altemus. Available at *www.bartleby.com/81/3879.html.*

Brodhead, Richard H. 1994. *Cultures of Letters: Scenes of Reading and Writing in Nineteenth-Century America.* Chicago: University of Chicago Press.

Brownlow, J. P., and J. W. Kronik, eds. 1998. *Intertextual Pursuits: Literary Mediations in Modern Spanish Narrative.* Lewisburg, Pa.: Bucknell University Press/London: Associated University Presses.

Buffery, Helena, Stuart Davis, and Kirsty Hooper, eds. 2007. *Reading Iberia: Theory, History, Identity.* Oxford, England: Peter Lang.

Bugallal y Marchesi, José Luis. 1958a. "Sofía Casanova, la santa que murió de saudade." *ABC* (February 18).

————. 1958b. "Sofía Casanova: Un siglo de glorias y de dolores." *Boletín de la Real Academia Gallega* 28:141–72.

Burgos, Carmen de. 1906. *La mujer en España: Conferencia pronunciada en la Asociación de la Prensa en Roma el 28 de abril de 1906 por Carmen de Burgos Seguí.* Valencia, Spain: Sempere.

————. 1911. *Giacomo Leopardi: Su vida y sus obras.* Valencia, Spain: Sempere.

————. 1989. *Los negociantes de la Puerta del Sol.* In Bordonada, *Novelas breves de escritoras españolas,* 197–259. [First published in 1919.]

————. 1990. *Los inadaptados.* Granada, Spain: Caja General de Ahorros y Monte de Piedad de Granada. [First published in 1909.]

————. 2006. *La rampa.* Ed. Susan Larson. Buenos Aires: Stockcero. [First published in 1917.]

Butt, John. 1980. "The Generation of 1898: A Critical Fallacy?" *Forum for Modern Language Studies* 16:136–53.

Campbell, Donna M. 1997. *Resisting Regionalism: Gender and Naturalism in American Fiction, 1885–1915.* Athens: Ohio University Press.

Canitrot, Prudencio. 1911. Prologue to *El pecado,* by Sofía Casanova. Biblioteca de Escritores Gallegos Vol. 10. Madrid: Imprenta de Alrededor del Mundo, Librería de los Sucesores de Hernando.

Cansinos-Asséns, Rafael. 1982. *La novela de un literato: Hombres, ideas, efemérides, anécdotas.* Madrid: Alianza Editorial.

Carballo [Carvalho] Calero, Ricardo. 1975. *Historia de la literatura galega contemporánea.* Vigo, Spain: Galaxia.

Carré Aldao, Uxío [Eugenio]. 1911. *Literatura gallega. Con extensos apéndices bibliográficos y una gran antología de 300 trabajos escogidos en prosa y verso de la mayor parte de los escritores regionales. Segunda edición puesta al día y notablemente aumentada en el texto y apéndices.* Barcelona: Casa Editorial Maucci.

Carroll, Berenice, ed. 1976. *Liberating Women's History.* Urbana: University of Illinois Press.

Castro, Rosalía de. 1986. *Follas Novas.* Vigo, Spain: Galaxia. [First published 1881.]

———. 1990. *Cantares gallegos.* Vigo, Spain: Galaxia. [First published in 1863.]

Charnon-Deutsch, Lou. 2003. "Gender and Beyond: Nineteenth-Century Spanish Women Writers." In Turner and López de Martínez, *Cambridge Companion to the Spanish Novel,* 122–37.

Charnon-Deutsch, Lou, and Jo Labanyi, eds. 1995. *Culture and Gender in Nineteenth-Century Spain.* Oxford, England: Oxford University Press.

Clark, Suzanne. 1991. *Sentimental Modernism: Women Writers and the Revolution of the Word.* Bloomington: University of Indiana Press.

Colmeiro, José, Christina Dupláa, Patricia Greene, and Juana Sabadell, eds. 1995. *Spain Today: Essays on Literature, Culture, Society.* Hanover, N.H.: Dartmouth College, Department of Spanish and Portuguese.

Couceiro Freijomil, Antonio. 1954. "Pérez de Eguía Casanova, Sofía." In *Diccionario bio-bibliográfico de escritores* III. Santiago de Compostela, Spain: Bibliófilos Gallegos, 82–83.

Czerwiński, E. J. 1994. *A Dictionary of Polish Literature.* Westport Conn.: Greenwood.

Dainotto, Roberto. 2000. *Place in Literature: Regions, Cultures, Communities.* Ithaca, N.Y.: Cornell University Press.

Davies, Ann. 2001. "Don Juan and Foucauldian Sexual Discourse: Changing Attitudes to Female Sexuality." *European Studies: A Journal of European Culture, History and Politics* 17:159–70.

De la Prada Navarro, Gloria. 1912. *El cantar de los amores.* Madrid: Los Contemporáneos 168.

De los Ríos Nostench, Blanca. 1899. "Sangre española." *Revista Contemporánea* (Madrid) 113 (March 15): 449–83.

———. 1901. *Melita Palma: Novela.* Biblioteca Mignon. Vol. 17. Madrid: Rodríguez Serra.

———. 1907. "La niña de Sanabria." In *Obras completas.* Vol. 2. Madrid: Establecimiento Tipográfico de Idamor Moreno.

———. 1908. "Madrid goyesco." In *El Cuento Semanal* 68. Madrid: Imprenta Artística Española.

———. 1989. "Las hijas de don Juan." In Bordonada, *Novelas breves de escritoras españolas,* 67–125. [First published in 1907.]

Dijkstra, Bram. 1986. *Idols of Perversity: Fantasies of Feminine Evil in Fin-de-Siècle Culture.* New York: Oxford University Press.

Dobón, María Dolores. 1996. "Sociólogos contra estetas: Prehistoria del conflicto entre modernismo y 98." *Hispanic Review* 64/1:57–72.

DuPlessis, Rachel Blau. 1985. *Writing beyond the Ending: Narrative Strategies of Twentieth-Century Women Writers*. Bloomington: Indiana University Press.

Durán, José Antonio. 1974. "Biblioteca de Escritores Gallegos." In *Gran Enciclopedia Gallega*. Vol. 3. Ed. Ramón Otero Pedrayo. Santiago de Compostela, Spain: Silverio Cañada.

Eile, Stanisław. 2000. *Literature and Nationalism in Partitioned Poland, 1795–1918*. New York: St. Martin's Press in association with University of London, School of Slavonic and East European Studies.

Espina, Concha. 1909. *La niña de Luzmela*. Madrid: Ricardo Fé.

———. 1989. *La esfinge maragata*. Ed. Carmen Díaz Castañón. Madrid: Castalia/Instituto de la Mujer. [First published in 1914.]

Felski, Rita. 1995. *The Gender of Modernity*. Cambridge, Mass.: Harvard University Press.

Gabriele, John P, ed. 1999. *Nuevas perspectivas sobre el 98*. Frankfurt Am Main, Germany: Anthropos.

Gage, John. 1993. *Colour and Culture: Practice and Meaning from Antiquity to Abstraction*. London: Thames and Hudson.

Galerstein, Carolyn L., and Kathleen McNerney, eds. 1986. *Women Writers of Spain: An Annotated Bio-bibliographical Guide*. New York: Greenwood.

García Martí, Victoriano. 1957. "Sofía Casanova de Lutoscowky" [*sic*]. *ABC* (June 1): 12.

Gilbert, Sandra M. 2001. "Widow." *Critical Inquiry* 27/4:559–79.

Gilbert, Sandra M., and Susan Gubar. 1978. *The Madwoman in the Attic: The Woman Writer and the Nineteenth-Century Literary Imagination*. New Haven, Conn.: Yale University Press.

Gilroy, Amanda, and W. M. Verhoeven, eds. 2000. *Epistolary Histories: Letters, Fiction, Culture*. Charlottesville: University of Virginia Press.

Gimeno de Flaquer, Concepción. 1909. *Una Eva moderna*. In *El Cuento Semanal*, year 3, no. 152 (November 26). Madrid: Imprenta Artística Española.

Glenn, Cheryl. 1994. "Sex, Lies, and Manuscript [*sic*]: Refiguring Aspasia in the History of Rhetoric." *College Composition and Communication* 45:180–99.

Glenn, Kathleen M. 1996. "Epistolary transgressions in Sofía Casanova's *Más que amor*." *Hispanófila* 116:47–55.

Goldsmith, Elizabeth C., and Dena Goodman, eds. 1995. *Going Public: Women and Publishing in Early Modern France*. Ithaca, N.Y.: Cornell University Press.

Gómez Aparicio, Pedro. 1974. *Historia del periodismo español: De las guerras coloniales a la dictadura*. Madrid: Editora Nacional.

Gómez de Baquero, Eduardo. 1911. "El cancionero de la dicha." *El Imparcial* (June 26): 3.

González López, María Antonieta. 2001. *Aproximación a la obra literaria y periodística de Blanca de los Ríos*. Madrid: Fundación Universitaria Española.

Gordon, Ann D., Mari Jo Buhle, and Nancy Shrom Dye. 1976. "The Problem of Women's History." In Carroll, *Liberating Women's History*, 75–92.

Granjel, Luis. 1968. "La novela corta en España (1907–1936)." *Cuadernos Hispanoamericanos* 222:477–508.

Greenaway, Kate. 1884. *The Language of Flowers*. London: E. Evans.

Greenslade, William. 1994. *Degeneration, Culture, and the Novel, 1880–1940*. Cambridge, England: Cambridge University Press.

Gullón, Ricardo. 1968. "La invención del 98." *Cuadernos Hispanoamericanos* 76:150–59.

Hermida, Modesto. 1995. *Narrativa galega: Tempo do rexurdimento*. Vigo, Spain: Xerais.

Herrera Garrido, Francisca. 1990. *Néveda: Historia dunha dobre seducción*. Ed. María Camiño Noia. Vigo, Spain: Xerais. [First published in 1920.]

Herzberger, David. 1998. "Splitting the Reference: Postmodern Fiction and the Idea of History in Francoist Spain." In Brownlow and Kronik, *Intertextual Pursuits*, 126–42.

Hooper, Kirsty. 2003. "Girl, Interrupted: The Distinctive History of Galician Women's Narrative." *Romance Studies* 21/2:101–14.

———. 2006a. "Novas cartografías nos estudos galegos: Nacionalismo literario, literatura nacional, lecturas posnacionais." *Anuario de Estudos Literarios Galegos 2005*, 64–73. [English translation: 2007. "New Cartographies in Galician Studies: From Literary Nationalism to Postnational Readings." In Buffery, Davis, and Hooper, *Reading Iberia*, 125–42.]

———. 2006b. "Reading Spain's African Vocation: The Figure of the Moorish Priest in Three Novels of the *Fin de Siglo* (1891–1907)." *Revista de Estudios Hispánicos* 40.1:175–99.

———. 2007. "Death and the Maiden: Gender, Nation and the Imperial Compromise in Blanca de los Ríos's *Sangre española* (1899)." *Revista Hispánica Moderna* 60.2:171–85.

Howard, June. 1999. "What Is Sentimentality?" *American Literary History* 11.1: 63–81.

Hurtado, Ámparo. 1998. "Biografía de una generación: Las escritoras del noventa y ocho." In Zavala, *Breve historia feminista de la literatura española*, 139–54.

Imboden, Rita Caterina. 2001. *Carmen de Burgos "Columbine" y la novela corta*. Bern, Switzerland: Peter Lang.

Inness, Sherrie, and Diana Royer, eds. 1997. *Breaking Boundaries: New Perspectives on Women's Regional Writing*. Iowa City: University of Iowa Press.

Johnson, Roberta. 1993. *Crossfire: Philosophy and the Novel in Spain, 1900–1934*. Lexington, University of Kentucky Press.

———. 1996. "Gender and Nation in Spanish Fiction between the Wars (1898–1936)." *Revista Canadiense de Estudios Hispánicos* 21/1:167–79.

———. 1998. "The Domestication of Don Juan in Women Novelists of Modernist Spain." In Brownlow and Kronik, *Intertextual Pursuits*, 222–38.

———. 1999. "The Domestic Agenda of the Generation of '98." In Gabriele, *Nuevas perspectivas sobre el 98*, 239–50.

———. 2003. *Gender and Nation in the Spanish Modernist Novel*. Nashville: Vanderbilt University Press.

Jones, Derek, ed. 2001. *Censorship: A World Encyclopaedia*. London: Fitzroy Dearborn.

Kirkpatrick, Susan. 1995. "Gender Difference in *Fin de Siglo* Literary Discourse." In Colmeiro, Dupláa, Greene, and Sabadell, *Spain Today*, 95–102.

————. 2003. *Mujer, modernismo y vanguardia en España (1898–1931)*. Madrid: Cátedra.

Krauel, Ricardo. 2001. *Voces desde el silencio: Heterologías sexuales en la narrativa española moderna, 1875–1975*. Madrid: Ediciones Libertarias.

Krzyżanowski, Julian. 1978. *A History of Polish Literature*. Warsaw: PWN.

Lanser, Susan. 1992. *Fictions of Authority: Women Writers and Narrative Voice*. Ithaca, N.Y.: Cornell University Press.

Ledger, Sally, and Roger Luckhurst. 2000. *The Fin de Siècle: A Reader in Cultural History, c. 1880–1900*. Oxford, England: Oxford University Press.

López Aydillo, Eugenio. 1907. *Galicia ante la solidaridad*. Madrid: Imprenta Gutenberg-Castro.

López Cordón, María Victoria. 1989. Introduction to *La revolución bolchevista*, by Sofía Casanova. Madrid: Castalia/Instituto de la Mujer, 7–72.

Lorde, Audre. 1983. "The Master's Tools Will Never Dismantle the Master's House." In Moraga and Anzaldúa, *This Bridge Called My Back*, 94–101.

Louis, Anja. 2005. *Women and the Law: Carmen de Burgos, an Early Feminist*. Woodbridge, England: Tamesis.

Martínez Martínez, Rosario. 1999. *Sofía Casanova: Mito y literatura*. Santiago de Compostela, Spain: Xunta de Galicia.

McCullough, Kate. 1999. *Regions of Identity: The Construction of America in Women's Fiction, 1885–1914*. Stanford, Calif.: Stanford University Press.

McNerney, Kathleen, and Cristina Enríquez de Salamanca, eds. 1994. *Double Minorities of Spain: A Bio-bibliographic Guide to Women Writers of the Catalan, Galician, and Basque Countries*. New York: Modern Language Association.

Mickiewicz, Adam. 1998. *Dziady* [Forefathers' Eve]. Warsaw: Instytut Badań Literackich. [First published in 1832.]

Modleski, Tania. 1982. *Loving with a Vengeance: Mass-Produced Fantasies for Women*. New York: Methuen.

Molina, César Antonio. 1990. *Medio siglo de prensa literaria española (1900–1950)*. Madrid: Endymion.

Moraga, Cherríe, and Gloria Anzaldúa, eds. 1983. *This Bridge Called My Back: Writings by Radical Women of Color*. NewYork: Kitchen Table Press.

Nerín, Gustau. 1997. "Mito franquista y realidad de la colonización de la Guinea española." *Estudios de Asia y África* 32.1:9–30.

Osorio, Olga. 1997. *Sofía Casanova*. Santiago de Compostela, Spain: Xunta de Galicia.

Pardo Bazán, Emilia. 2001. *Insolación*. Madrid: Cátedra. [First published in 1889.]

————. 2003. *La quimera*. In *Obras completas*. Vol. 5. Ed. and prologue by Antonio Carreño. Madrid: Fundación José Antonio de Castro, 1–400. [First published in 1905.]

————. N.d. *Una cristiana*. In *Obras completas*. Vol. 18. Madrid: Renacimiento. [First published in 1890.]

Paredes Méndez, María Francisca. 2003. "La regeneración nacional y el discurso de género en la ficción española de 1900 a 1931." Ph.D. diss., University of Kansas.

Pedraz Marcos, Azucena. 2000. *Quimeras de Africa: La sociedad española de africanistas y colonialistas.* Madrid: Polifemo.

Pérez, Janet. 1988. *Contemporary Women Writers of Spain.* Boston: Twayne.

Pérez Galdós, Benito. 1997. *La desheredada.* Madrid: Alianza Editorial. [First published in 1881.]

Pitollet, Camille. 1958. "Unas notas sobre Sofía Casanova." *Boletín de la Biblioteca de Menéndez Pelayo* 34:133–52.

Porębowicz, Edward. 1894. "Powieść Hiszpańska na temat polski" [A Spanish Novel on a Polish Theme]. *Świat* 7:498–99.

Porter, Brian. 2000. *When Nationalism Began to Hate: Imagining Modern Politics in Nineteenth-Century Poland.* New York: Oxford University Press.

Radway, Janice. 1984. *Reading the Romance: Women, Patriarchy and Popular Fiction.* Chapel Hill: University of North Carolina Press.

"RC" [José Ruíz Castillo Basala]. 1989. "Sofía Casanova." In Casanova, *La revolución bolchevique.* Madrid: Castalia. [First published in 1920.]

Ribbans, Geoffrey. 1999. " 'No lloréis, reíd, cantad': Some Alternative Views on the Generation of 98/*Modernismo* Debate." In Gabriele, *Nuevas perspectivas sobre el 98,* 131–59.

Riley, Denise. 1988. *Am I That Name? Feminism and the Category of "Women" in History.* London: Macmillan.

Rose, Gillian. 1993. "The Politics of Paradoxical Space." In *Feminism and Geography: The Limits of Geographical Knowledge.* Minneapolis: University of Minnesota Press, chap. 7.

Rossetti, Christina. 1990. "In an Artist's Studio." In *The Complete Poems of Christina Rossetti.* Vol. 3. Ed. R. W. Crump. Baton Rouge: Louisiana University Press, 264.

Scott, Joan Wallach. 1997. Introduction to *Feminism and History.* Ed. Joan Wallach Scott. Oxford, England: Oxford University Press, 1–13.

Showalter, Elaine. 1991. *Sexual Anarchy.* London: Bloomsbury.

Simón Palmer, María del Carmen. 1989. "Sofía Casanova, autora de *La madeja.*" *Actas del Tercer Congreso de Estudios Galdosianos* 2:531–36.

———. 1991. *Escritoras españolas del s. XIX: Manual bio-bibliográfico.* Madrid: Castalia, Nueva Biblioteca de Erudición y Crítica.

———. 1996. "Infancia y juventud de Sofía Casanova: Autógrafo inédito." *Revista Literaria* 58/115:179–93.

Sizemore, Christine. 1989. *A Female Vision of the City: London in the Novels of Five Spanish Women.* Knoxville: University of Tennessee Press.

Tarrío Varela, Anxo. 1994. *Literatura galega: Aportacións a unha historia crítica.* Vigo, Spain: Edicións Xerais de Galicia.

Tofiño Quesada, Ignacio. 2003. "Spanish Orientalism: Uses of the past in Spain's colonization in Africa." *Comparative Studies of South Asia, Africa, and the Middle East* 23.1–2:141–48.

Tolliver, Joyce. 1998. *Cigar Smoke and Violet Water: Gendered Discourse in the Stories of Emilia Pardo Bazán.* Lewisburg Pa.: Bucknell University Press.

Turner, Harriet, and Adelaida López de Martínez, eds. 2003. *The Cambridge Companion to the Spanish Novel from 1600 to the Present*. Cambridge, England: Cambridge University Press.

Ugarte, Michael. 1994. "The Generational Fallacy and Spanish Women Writing at the Turn of the Century." *Siglo XX/20th Century* 12/1–2:261–76.

———. 1996. *Madrid 1900: The Capital as Cradle of Literature and Culture*. University Park: Pennsylvania State University Press.

Unamuno, Miguel de. 1959–1964. "A una aspirante a escritora." In *Obras completas*. Vol. 4. Madrid: Aguado, 711–19. [First published in 1907.]

———. 2000. *En torno al casticismo*. Madrid: Alianza Editorial. [First published in 1895.]

Urioste, Carmen de. 1994. "Marginalidad y novela corta (España 1907–1938)." *Romance Languages Annual* 6:593–98.

Valera, Juan. 1956. *Correspondencia de don Juan Valera (1859–1905): Cartas inéditas*. Ed. and with an introduction by Cyrus C. DeCoster. Madrid: Castalia.

Valis, Noel, and Carol Maier, eds. 1990. *In the Feminine Mode: Essays on Hispanic Women Writers*. Lewisburg, Pa.: Bucknell University Press.

Valle-Inclán, Ramón del. 1994. *Sonata de otoño. Sonata de invierno. Memorias del Marqués de Bradomín*. Ed. Leda Schiavo. Madrid: Espasa Calpe.

Venclova, Tomas. 1998. "Native Realm Revisited: Mickiewicz's Lithuania and Mickiewicz in Lithuania." Wiktor Weintraub Memorial Lecture, Harvard University, April 2. Reprinted in *Krasnogruda* 8. Available at *www.pogranicze.sejny.pl/archiwum/krasnogruda/pismo/8/forum/vencl.htm*. Accessed May 28, 2007.

Walicki, Andrzej. 1994. *Poland between East and West: The Controversies over Self-Definition and Modernization in Partitioned Poland*. Cambridge, Mass.: Harvard University, Ukrainian Research Institute.

Walker, Nancy K. 1995. *The Disobedient Writer: Women and Narrative Tradition*. Austin: University of Texas Press.

Warhol, Robyn. 1989. *Gendered Interventions: Narrative Discourse in the Victorian Novel*. New Brunswick, N.J.: Rutgers University Press.

Weber, Robert. 1968. "Unidad y figuras en la *Sonata de otoño* de Valle-Inclán." *Cuadernos Hispanoamericanos* 75:179–97.

Wolikowska, Izabela. 1961. *Roman Dmowski: Czlowiek, polak, przyjaciel* [Roman Dmowski: Man, Pole, Friend]. Chicago: Komitet Wydawniczego.

Yuval-Davis, Nira. 1997. *Gender and Nation*. London: Sage.

Zavala, Iris, ed. 1998. *Breve historia feminista de la literatura española (en lengua castellana)*. Vol. 5. *La literatura escrita por mujer (del s. XIX a la actualidad)*. Barcelona: Anthropos.

Żeromski, Stefan. 1904. *Popioły* [Ashes]. Warsaw: Gebethner and Wolff.

Index

ABC, 6–8, 105, 169, 179, 188–208
Acuña, Rosario de, 10
Africa, 53–54, 56–57, 75–77, 81, 103, 164. *See also* Morocco
Alas, Leopoldo, 12, 42, 54
Álvarez Poll, Consuelo, 10
Álvarez Tubau de Palencia, María, 10
angel, 48, 149
    domestic angel, 70
    of the hearth, 44
Arenal, Concepción, 10, 125, 143
Ateneo de Madrid. *See* Madrid: ateneo
authorship, 19, 25–26, 28, 50, 70–71, 77, 99, 104
    authoriality, 172
    and gender, 109
    private voice, 19, 25, 80–82
    public voice, 68, 71, 74
    See also Lanser, Susan
autobiographical writing
    in *El doctor Wolski* (Sofía Casanova), 23–25
    in *El pecado* (Sofía Casanova), 157
    as a genre, 10
    in *Más que amor* (Sofía Casanova), 79–80
Azorín, 61, 87, 110–11, 120–21, 135

Balicka, Ela, 81, 219n3
Barco, Ángela, 112, 127, 221n4

Biblioteca de Escritores Gallegos, 137–41
Biedma, Patrocinio de, 10
Blanco Asenjo, Ricardo, 5
Blanco García, Padre Francisco, 17
Blanco y Trigueros, Carmen, 10
Bugallal y Marchesi, José Luis, 3
Burgos, Carmen de, 11, 14, 114, 129, 171, 220n1, 220n3
    El veneno del arte, 60
    Giacomo Leopardi, 119
    La flor de la playa, 19
    La mujer en España, 10, 173
    La rampa, 60, 173
    Los inadaptados, 26
    Los negociantes de la Puerta del Sol, 60, 173
    and the *novela corta*, 111–12

Campoamor, Ramón de, 5, 25
Canitrot, Prudencio, 136, 138–41, 143, 161, 175
Cansinos-Asséns, Rafael, 14–15
Casanova, Sofía
    "Cien leguas sobre el Volga helado," 5
    Como en la vida, 8, 14, 169
    De la guerra, 7, 173
    De la revolución rusa, 7
    De Rusia: Amores y confidencias, 8
    El cancionero de la dicha, 14, 138, 162
    En la corte de los zares, 8, 78, 95–96

Casanova, Sofía *(cont.)*
 Exóticas, 6, 138, 162
 Fugaces, 5, 51
 La madeja, 6, 112, 138, 162
 La mujer española en el extranjero, 1–3,
  10, 19, 74, 105, 170, 173, 213n3,
  213n4, 218n9
 La revolución bolchevista, 7, 14
 Las catacumbas de Rusia roja, 8, 169
 Poesías, 5
 Polvo de escombros, 8
 Sobre el Volga helado, 4–6, 21, 51,
  216n4
 *Viajes y aventuras de una muñeca
  española en Rusia*, 7
Casanova, Vicente, 6, 105
Castelao, 106
Castro, Rosalía de, 10–11, 106, 122–23, 125,
  135, 143, 163, 165, 167, 177, 221n5
 Cantares gallegos, 119–22, 125
 Flavio, 42
 Follas novas, 8, 125
Catholic Church
 in Galicia, 124
 influence on women, 49, 58, 72–73,
  77, 147–48
 in Poland, 32
 and Spanish colonialism, 55–57,
  61–62, 77
 See also Irvingism; Virgin Mary
censorship
 of *Más que amor*, 79, 97
 in Poland, 30–31, 33
Chacel, Rosa, 60
city
 and degeneration, 36, 38–39
 and modernity, 48–49
 in women's writing, 59–60, 145, 173
colonialism
 in *El doctor Wolski*, 37
 Spanish, in Morocco, 56–57, 76–77
 See also Catholic Church: and
  Spanish colonialism

Contemporáneos, Los, 112
Contreras de Rodríguez, María del Pilar,
 10
Coronado, Carolina, 10, 220n3
Cuba, 5, 56, 116
 war in, 66–67, 143, 145
Cuento Semanal, El, 109, 111, 217n2
Curie, Marie, 2
Częstochowa. *See* Virgin Mary: Virgin of
 Częstochowa

Darwinism, 35–37, 39, 64–65
Dato Muruais, Filomena, 11
degeneration. *See* city: and degeneration
De la Prada, Gloria, 11, 112
 El cantar de los amores, 113–14, 126–27,
  173
De la Riva [y Callol de] Muñoz, María
 Luisa, 10
Del Olmet, Luis Anton, 138
De los Ríos, Blanca, 10, 26, 171
 La niña de Sanabria, 60, 173, 218n7
 Las hijas de Don Juan, 60, 114–15, 174
 Madrid goyesco, 60, 173
 Melita Palma, 173
 and the *novela corta*, 111–12
 Sangre española, 173
Dmowski, Roman, 97, 219n3
domestic angel. *See* angel: of the hearth
domestic sphere
 in literature, 17, 20, 26, 68, 112, 173
 and women's role, 2, 60, 85, 107, 147,
  165
domestic violence, 150–52
Don Juan, 74, 101, 186, 198
 in *Princesa del amor hermoso*, 18, 108,
  114–15, 121–22
 See also De los Ríos, Blanca: *Las hijas
  de Don Juan*
DuPlessis, Rachel Blau, 54–55, 143, 152, 165
 "writing beyond the ending," 18,
  75–76, 90, 103, 165, 172

Echegaray, José de, 5
education, female, 25, 42–45, 47, 49, 112–13, 126, 147, 151, 171
Eguílaz [y Renart de Parada], Rosa, 10
emigration
    in *El crimen de Beira-mar*, 162–63, 165, 167
    in "El ladrón," 143
Espina, Concha, 11, 111–12, 114, 220n1
    La esfinge maragata, 173
    La niña de Luzmela, 68, 173
eugenics, 23, 35–36

Fernández Shaw, Carlos, 105
Ferrari, Emilio, 80
flowers, language of, 130–32
Fuentes, Magdalena, 10

Galicia
    intellectuals, 51, 105–6, 137
    nationalism, 106, 120, 161
    regionalism. *See* rexionalismo
    Solidaridad gallega, 125
    women's writing, 8–11, 114, 138–39, 170, 172
García, María [Malibrán], 10
García Martí, Victoriano, 3
Generation of 1898, 63, 109–11, 120, 214n9
Generation of 1907, 110
Gimeno de Flaquer, Concepción, 10, 111–12, 114
    Una Eva moderna, 19–20, 60, 112–13, 126, 174
Gómez de Baquero, Eduardo, 14
Guerrero, María, 10

Herrera Garrido, Francisca, 8, 11, 145, 174
Herrero y Ayora de Vidal, Melchora, 11
Hoyos y Vinent, Antonio, 110, 220n3

Irvingism, 159–60

Kościuszko, Tadeusz, 34–35, 41, 216n11

Lamadrid, Teodora, 10
language of flowers, 130–32
Lanser, Susan, 19, 26, 76, 81, 172, 219n4
Leopardi, Giacomo, 118–20
Libro Popular, El, 112, 138, 162
Lithuania, 18, 27–29, 33, 46–50, 76–77, 81, 103, 164, 216n9, 217n16
Lugrís Freire, Manuel, 51, 123–24, 137
Lutosławska, Halina, 5, 51, 105, 136–37
Lutosławska, Izabela [Wolikowska], 28, 97, 105, 185, 218
Lutosławska, Jadwiga, 5, 28, 51
Lutosławska, María, 28, 105, 218
Lutosławski, Wincenty, 5–6, 28, 51, 105, 136
    messianist philosophy, 29
    as model for *Wolski*, 23–24

madness. *See* mental illness
Madrid
    ateneo, 2–4, 10, 60, 105–6, 120–21, 170
    Casanova in, 5–7, 51–52, 105–6, 136–38
    as original setting for "Más triste que el amor," 153
    as setting for *Lo eterno*, 58–59, 62, 65–66, 74, 77
    as setting for "Luz en las tinieblas," 145
    as setting for *Más que amor*, 100–101
    See also city
Malibrán, María. *See* García, María
marriage
    discussion of, 147–48
    female writers' rejection of, 18–19, 90, 103, 107, 126, 147, 150–51, 167
    as plot resolution, 55, 71, 74–75, 79, 117, 146. *See also* sentimentality
Martínez Sierra, María, 60, 220n2
Matejko, Jan, 32, 216n7
mental illness, 81–82, 99
    female desire for independence seen as, 84–85, 131, 148, 150–51, 161
    as national condition, 83, 103–4